SEATTLE, PAST TO PRESENT

SEATTLE

PAST TO PRESENT

By Roger Sale

UNIVERSITY OF WASHINGTON PRESS
SEATTLE AND LONDON

Copyright © 1976 by the University of Washington Press
First printing, October 1976
Second printing, November 1976
Paperback edition, with corrections, 1978
Printed in the United States of America

11 10 09 08 07 06 05   9 8 7 6 5

University of Washington Press
PO Box 50096
Seattle, WA 98145-5096, U.S.A.
www.washington.edu/uwpress

Library of Congress Cataloging-in-Publication Data

Sale, Roger.
    Seattle, past to present.
    Bibliography: p.
    Includes index.
    1. Seattle—History. I. Title.
F899.S457S24   979.7'77   76-7798
ISBN 0-295-95615-1 pbk.

The paper used in this publication meets the minimum requirements of American
National Standard for Information Sciences—Permanence of Paper for Printed
Library Materials, ANSI Z39.48-1984. ⊗

For Jack Brenner

Preface

THIS is a book about Seattle's history, a series of essays that offers one person's sense of how the city began, took shape, and came to be as it is. It is not a work of social science in the usual sense, in that it does not restrict its data or its themes—I have liked to think I might use almost any evidence to illustrate a point—and it does not employ a single method. It is not, like a formal history, crammed as full of facts and details as can be made room for. My aim has been to describe and discuss what for me are the most important and most characteristic truths about each of the city's various major periods. By not attempting a central narrative, and by not using a single method, I hope I have left myself free and flexible enough to use the best of a variety of methods. There is straight narrative history here, as well as economics, geography, sociology, demography, and political science, but rather than isolate these branches of study one from another I have used them in concert, emphasizing each when it seemed most important to do so.

In the last generation, and especially in the last decade, interest in the history of cities and regions has markedly increased. Among professionals, urban studies is no longer a stepchild of urban planning, just as urban planning is no longer a stepchild of architecture and engineering. With the realization that cities cannot be understood simply as collections of people or as outgrowths of city planning and design have come studies of aspects of city life that were often ignored a generation or more ago. In contrast to these earlier works, which tended to focus on major figures, politics, and slums, are ethnic studies; demographies of social mobility and aspiration; economic studies of the impact of certain kinds of manufacture;

studies of street life, hospitals, dance halls, movie theaters; historical geographies of the relations of cities to their surrounding regions. All these have shown how much is involved in the making of even a fairly small or fairly recent city.

There have been even more striking changes in attitude and interest among nonprofessionals. Historic preservation, now the concern of citizens and governments and not just of historical societies, is no longer a matter of locating log cabins or the houses of famous people, or of erecting plaques to mark historic events. Preserving the past visually is perhaps the first priority, but this means more than keeping old buildings as derelicts or as museums; new uses for such buildings are being found so that neither present nor past is ignored. It is also becoming clearer that we need to create a usable nonvisual past, to make histories of cities in which the past is brought down to the present so that each illuminates the other.

The most recognizable ingredient in these changes is nostalgia, and one can find nostalgia animating the ostensibly cold-hearted analyses of professionals and the desire of many amateur enthusiasts to keep anything that is old, however nondescript and at whatever the cost. The feeling of course is not new, but as old as the first commentary on American cities, or as the expulsion from Eden: here is this slum where once was a quiet street, this manufacturing area where once the sheep could safely graze, railroads where once was frontier, whites where once were Indians. Unquestionably nostalgia is a more popular feeling than it was only a little while ago, and is probably more variously felt, too. The persistent willingness of urban and industrialized Americans to tear down the old in a mindless way has led many people to feel cut off from the past and to want to cling, however simply or falsely, to some image of what once was.

Perhaps the first, but, one hopes, not the only or most important result of this nostalgia about the past of cities is partisanship, a struggle between those who prefer everything old and those who prefer everything new. In Seattle one sees a great deal of partisanship, first because the city has an interesting past and second because it is quite capable of inducing people to believe that all in the present is best and in the best of all possible worlds. The idea of history itself becomes partisan, the Present versus the Past. One major result is a tendency by those who prefer the past to make it a matter of legend and lore, causing their antagonists to scorn the past because it is *only* legend and lore. When I first began discussing the idea of this book with people, I found that they assumed, to their delight or dismay depending on which side they were on, that a book about Seattle's past would be a book about pioneers and famous local sinners. To some that was a boring prospect—surely all that has been done. To others it was an invitation to nostalgia: "You must talk to my uncle who was here during the Gold Rush."

While I don't think this nostalgia or this partisanship has died out, and it may indeed even be increasing, I don't find it to be the only view of Seattle's history currently being taken, either by professionals or amateurs. Another attitude is taking shape, one that does not leave the past as a matter of "study" or "research" by academic scholars or as a matter of legend and lore by people who wish to be nostalgic. It sees that historic preservation must include a more vital relationship between past and present, so that the question is not one of Then and Now but of the ways whereby Then became Now.

Cities really are like trees: they have roots and branches, trunks and old growth and new canes. They can be healthy or sick, they can grow or decay, but they cannot remain still for very long. When they become sick, they send out aimless runners; and when the nature of their disease is understood, they can be revitalized. Great cities are like great trees, secure and yet active, confident that the process of aging yields strengths and beauties as well as inevitable decay. The more one tries to see cities this way, the more one sees people and events and institutions in a city forming a unit which is always changing. A book dedicated to this way of seeing and understanding must constantly be considering the different things going on simultaneously in the city to see how they are related, while also looking forward and backward in time to see how the city as a whole is changing.

If cities really are like trees, then it follows that Seattle will be like other cities, especially other American cities, and more especially still, other young American cities. There is, however, a considerable difficulty in making comparative judgments among cities when one is mainly interested in the way one city's interior parts and events work together: it really is not possible to know more than one city well enough. One can compare component parts easily enough—Seattle's streetcar history as opposed to Cincinnati's, its public schools compared with those of Minneapolis—but the wholes really are different, unique. People are fond of comparing Seattle with Portland because so many of their experiences are similar, whereas they seldom compare Seattle with London or Peking. How would one go about doing it? Seattle is as different from London or Peking as a rhododendron is from a maple or an oak, and different from Portland only as a rhododendron from an azalea. But even the easier comparisons among cities tend to be a little facile, a little too obviously designed as vehicles for proving a point, something that can be helpful along the way, perhaps, but not crucial or central. To know one city well, to see how it took and is taking its shape, is awfully hard, and the more one does it, the more one realizes how little one really knows other cities.

The impulse to write a book like this one thus derives mainly from the fact that I live in Seattle and make my life here. In such a situation one can judge harshly, one can often feel sadness at loss or at missed chances, but one inevitably will feel love, admiration, and gratitude. My basic desire is to understand the city, to find out how it came to be as it is, but it seems to me that one's understanding cannot be, and shouldn't try to be, completely detached and impersonal. What is important to me is not going to be what is important to everyone else. My way of understanding Seattle is probably affected by my background, which is eastern but not urban: upstate New York, suburban Philadelphia, western Massachusetts. The idea I had of urban life was based on the little I knew or could imagine about eastern seaboard cities: Boston, New York, Philadelphia, Washington, D.C. As a result, when I first came to Seattle I wondered where the city *was*. There were so few places where one could find a crowd, city excitement, city danger. I was, of course, looking for a maple or an oak, having never seen a rhododendron.

As I came to know the city, however, it seemed to open up an almost endless series of challenges. One need not have an eastern rural man's sense of city life to come to Seattle and find it beautiful and baffling. I remember distinctly the feeling that Seattle was here, there, everywhere; I remember even more distinctly my first encounters with people who had lived in Seattle all their lives and seemed so unperturbed by all that puzzled me. As I have said, when I began asking questions about Seattle's past, I was told about pioneers and gaudy sinners, and it wasn't until later that I realized most had learned what they knew from Murray Morgan's *Skid Road*. Morgan's book is so obviously the best to date on Seattle that it seemed to convince people that what he deliberately had left fragmentary and impressionistic had to be left that way. At this point my biggest help came from Jane Jacobs' first book, *The Death and Life of Great American Cities*, which, in not mentioning Seattle at all, thereby challenged me to find ways to understand it in her terms. By the time her second book, *The Economy of Cities,* appeared, I had already set out to assemble materials for my book; but it convinced me, perhaps more than anything else, that what I had hoped I could write was indeed possible. Cities are wholes, like organisms, like trees, and my job was to learn what kind of whole Seattle was by learning about its past.

The periods into which my chapters divide the city's history have no special meaning or intention. They are probably the periods and the dividing lines most people would use. The pioneer period runs from the founding in 1851–52 down to the time of the fire and the coming of the first transcontinental railroad in the early 1890s. The pioneers knew that when the railroad came, Seattle would be on the map, a city indeed. What they knew perhaps more instinctively than consciously was that the city Seattle would become after the railroad's arrival depended on what kind of city the pioneers themselves built. It took more than thirty years for the boom to begin, by which time the original settlers were all old or dead, but people were proud of Seattle and, for all its rawness and turmoil, they had reason to be.

The third chapter covers the first great boom years, 1890–1910. In many respects this was the decisive period: Seattle grew six times over within these twenty years and became the premier city of the northwest; the habits of mind which were formed then still play a major role in the city today. Here for the first time we will encounter problems of focusing or orchestrating apparently disparate activities and events, because no single person or business or institution stands out. In this period all the fine old neighborhoods were built, and the parks and boulevards; it was also the era of urban populism and the railroad deals and the beginnings of labor unrest. The way all these were important is the subject of the fourth chapter, "The First Climax," which looks at Seattle as it went into World War I, an apparently healthy young giant of a city, and emerged exhausted, almost a depression city a full decade before the Great Depression itself.

The fifth chapter is about Seattle between the wars, a quiet and static city for the most part. Its major economic impetus lost, Seattle seems almost to have been waiting around for World War II and for the prodigious rise of The Boeing Company. But quiet cities have their virtues, too, and I have here tried to identify some of them by means of a series of portraits, of Vernon Parrington, Nellie Cornish,

Richard Fuller, Mark Tobey, Jesse Epstein—people not native to Seattle but who came and flourished in these years, as much because of as in spite of the city's lack of decisive energy.

The sixth chapter is "The Boeing Years," from World War II down to about 1968, Seattle's second boom period, this time not as the result of extraordinarily diverse growth but as the city was taking on characteristics of a large company town. Yet under the umbrella of Boeing many different changes were taking place, both because of the natives who had grown up in the quiet period between the wars and because of newcomers arriving in a city that seemed, for all its settledness, fresh with possibility. Certainly the quiet was over: the Metro cleanup of Lake Washington, the World's Fair of 1962, the great booms at the University of Washington, in downtown building, in the housing sprawl in the north end and east of the lake.

The last chapter, "The New City," is an attempt to see the extent to which Seattle, in the midst of obviously great changes, has become or is becoming new. All the signs of crisis were here—the racial strife at the end of the sixties, the bursting of the Boeing bubble in 1970 and the long layoffs that followed, the erosion of the public schools, the constant threat of a major taxpayers' revolt. Yet certainly the Seattle of the mid-1970s is not like the Seattle of 1919, a spent force, and in some respects it seems to be fulfilling the promise of its first boom years. It is not possible, of course, to be decisive about the present, but some of the major features of the new city can be outlined and their futures guessed at.

Looking back over the whole period of Seattle's history, I think certain major generalizations are possible. For instance, the city was bourgeois from its first breath, and its major building material is wood. But rather than assemble the evidence, here or anywhere else, to "prove" these or any other generalizations, I have tried to let the patterns emerge as the story unfolds. If I have been able to do this at all successfully, the result will be a series of contexts that ask for, suggest, and make generalizations but which keep the overall sense of the city in the foreground and the generalizations hovering over it. That way one can begin to see how much is involved in the making of a city, how much might be brought into play to support arguments, how much more important is understanding the city than being able to make one or two decisive statements about it. Finally, too, by letting the patterns emerge, I hope to be able to show how much there is that remains necessarily elusive, obscure even, not capable of full proof. No one can pin down with great precision the experience of the millions of people who have lived in Seattle over a century and a quarter, and so one must try to suggest a great deal while demonstrating a great deal.

It is a kind of partnership, then, that I seek with my reader. I would like to think that anyone who has had some prolonged experience with a city, Seattle or another, can constantly be comparing what I have shown and suggested with what he or she knows or believes about Seattle or somewhere else. This is a personal book, one man's understanding of what happened; but I hope that this potential shortcoming can be a source of strength and fun, too, a chance for a reader to play his or her experiences and sense of human affairs against my own. The result will be overlaps and agreements, discrepancies and disagreements, but that is inevitable; the hope is that there will also be curiosity, absorption, even some excitement. Since the history of cities consists of individual experiences becoming collective and collaborative, so it is perhaps appropriate that a book about the history of a city should attempt to be that, too.

Acknowledgments

No ONE who reads beyond the first paragraphs of this book will imagine it is the work of a committee. It is filled with my judgments, my personal reflections, my methods and shifts in method, all chosen and made because I have all along tried to be responsive to what seemed to me most important and characteristic about the past and present of Seattle. It was done without colleagues; its research was constantly punctuated by solitary walks and drives around the city, brooding, looking at this, poking around trying to find that. Its shapes, insights, mistakes, and limitations are mine, and expressive of the kind of person I am.

Yet it also has been a collaborative undertaking, and I could not possibly name all those who have helped me, often without their knowing it, come to whatever understanding I have about Seattle. A city may be something one finds out about by oneself, but never have I felt I could not have written this book without the help of others more than when sitting quite alone, trying to understand what someone else has told me, or led me to.

Fortunately, some of my benefactors are so obvious that I can say this book would not have been written, or ended up as it is, without them. First, I worked in 1969–70 with a sabbatical leave from the University of Washington and with a grant from the National Endowment for the Humanities. That year was indispensable. I did not finish the project then, as I had originally hoped, but the year was time enough to do a great deal of legwork and to give the book its essential shape. Second, various people and institutions at the University of Washington were extremely helpful then, and in the intervening years, especially Richard Berner and his associates in the library's Manuscripts Collection, and Robert Monroe and his associates in the Northwest Collection. Third, there were many people to whom I went for advice and information, none of whom had any reason to be helpful beyond their own kindness: Helen Malson Graves, Arthur Loveless, Elizabeth Ayer, Maynard Pennell, Bernadine Smithea, Dave Beck, Victor Denny, Berthe Poncy Jacobson, Ellen Wood Murphy, Jesse Epstein, Richard Fuller, Miner Baker, Byron Fish. Fourth, there were those, some friends and some strangers, who read the manuscript in an official capacity; those known to me are Murray Morgan, Robert Burke, Victor Steinbrueck, Brewster Denny. They all corrected many errors, criticized severely and generously, did more than they were asked to do to make the book better. One thing I have relearned, but as if for the first time, about both myself and others, is how easy it is to fall into ways of naming people, dates, and events that are simply inaccurate. Errors remain in the text still, I fear, but many fewer than when those who read it for the Press saw it. Fifth, there is Jane Jacobs, who has never, so far as I know, visited Seattle, and whom I have never met, but who guided me into her incomparable understanding of cities and who was never more with me than when I otherwise felt most alone.

At which point I am almost forced to give up, because with so many others official help blended into conversation, or a conversation became a long afternoon's or evening's willingness to talk and to listen. Impossible to list them all, but let me thank, at least, for large and small favors, Harry Burns, Andrew Hilen, Malcolm Griffith, Rae Tufts, James Kimborough, Emmett Watson, Betty Bowen, David Brewster, Paul Schell, Barbara Bronson, James Wilson, Malcolm Brown, Phyllis Lamphere, Roy Noorda, and all the others who will, should they read this book, see how a sentence or a page or more was shaped by something they said. Finally, Barbara Henderson and Dorothy Sale each read the manuscript with harsh and loving care, each talked and listened with intelligent patience, each was never better than when finding how to tell me that perhaps my way was not quite the best way. Of such, one hopes, is the kingdom of heaven.

Contents

Illustrations

SEATTLE, PAST TO PRESENT

I

Gray and Green

SEATTLE is slightly above 47° 30′ north latitude, slightly west of longitude 122° west. It is almost due north of Portland and San Francisco, and due west of Great Falls, Montana; Saint John's, Newfoundland; Basel, Switzerland; and Budapest, Hungary. A position that far north yields sixteen hours of daylight in June, sixteen hours of darkness in December. The chief factor determining the climate is not its latitude, however, but its proximity to the Pacific Ocean. A hundred miles west of Seattle, along the coast, is the wettest spot in the continental United States. At Quillayute the average annual rainfall is about one hundred fifty inches. Between there and Seattle rise the Olympic Mountains, which absorb much of the moisture coming off the ocean, so that Seattle ends up with an annual rainfall of about thirty-five inches. The influence of the marine air is strong enough to moderate the temperature: the thermometer has rarely gone as low as zero or as high as one hundred. When the weather reaches what are for Seattle its extremes, above the low seventies and below the mid-thirties, it is almost always governed by high-pressure systems inland and so is dry. It is a climate often compared to that of southern England, but Seattle's hot weather tends to be much less humid.

It is said to "rain a lot" in Seattle, a statement that is both true and misleading. Its annual precipitation is less than that of all the major eastern seaboard cities, none of which is famous for its rain. The difference is that Seattle gets very little of its precipitation in the form of snow and even less in the form of heavy thunderstorms. A steady daylong rain in Seattle will make everything seem very wet, while the precipitation may come to no more than half an inch. In fact, it is really wet only in the winter; December and January account for almost half the annual rainfall. Between May and October will be a number of two- to three-week stretches with no rain at all. What does distinguish the climate is the general cloudiness. From late fall through early spring the sun is a relative stranger, and on any day of the year a marine push may bring low clouds in at night which last through the morning. Sunrises are more infrequent than sunsets. It is the grayness that gives the essential feel of the climate, that sets off the sudden bursts of sunlight during the spring and fall, that accentuates the relatively short but brilliantly clear and dry summers.

It is magnificent climate for growing things. Its great native tree is the Douglas fir. Before the white men came, the land was covered with these superbly tall and straight trees, mixed with other conifers and evergreen shrubs. The spring is long, running from February to as late as July, and is usually damp and cool, which makes it a paradise for those who love to help and watch plants blossom and leaf. Compared with the inland valleys of California, the growing season is quite short; but compared to most of the rest of the country, it is long. Since the winters are seldom severe and the summers seldom so hot as to leach the soil, evergreen shrubs and trees, rhododendrons, azaleas, and camellias are in their element. Gardening is easy, and almost everyone is growing something.

The city is both bounded by and dotted with bodies of water. On the west is Puget Sound, an inland saltwater sea that leads out through the Strait of Juan de Fuca into the Pacific. This waterway provided the major means of transportation to and from Seattle until the coming of the railroads. On the east is twenty-two-mile-long Lake Washington, a cool and, at present, clean mountain-fed lake at close to sea level. In between the Sound and Lake Washington is Lake Union. The three are connected by two man-made canals, the one to the west involving a lock. These connecting bodies of water, along with Green, Haller, and Bitter lakes in the north end and the Duwamish River emptying into the sound in the south, plus numerous creeks within the city limits convey a sense that water is always near. Consequently, Seattle has more boat owners than any large American city, the boats ranging from unlimited hydroplane racing boats to ocean-crossing cruisers and yachts to kayaks, canoes, and dinghies. Many of the boats are manufactured locally. Probably because the outdoor swimming season is short, there are too few public beaches along the more than two hundred miles of shoreline. Rimming the shores of Lake Union and Portage Bay are colonies of houseboats.

The land between the lakes and the Sound is almost never flat. It moves from sea level to 457 feet on the top of Queen Anne Hill, less than a mile away. Seattle is often referred to as a city of seven hills, like Rome; but there really are quite a few more than that. Downtown is built on what was once steep hillside rising away from a cliff above the sound, and it is surrounded on the east, north, and southeast by First Hill, Capitol Hill, Queen Anne, and Beacon Hill. Other areas are flatter, but the constant rise and fall of the land means one is never far from a great view of water and mountains and other parts of the city. In the winter especially, when the leaves are off the deciduous trees, one is constantly aware of space opening out, to anything from the nearest hill or tall tree a few hundred yards away to Mount Rainier, which is almost a hundred miles to the southeast.

It is a great place for architects, though there is no true local architectural style. Since the major building material is wood, the city is dominated by single-family frame houses, and Seattle has the largest percentage of homeowners of any major American city. Its population density is low. What is usually most striking to a newcomer about the layout of streets and neighborhoods is the great mixing—of architectural styles, of income levels, of pretensions at various levels. People who want to know where "the best part of town" is can only be told "Here," "There," "Over there." There are "good neighborhoods" in Magnolia and Seward Park and Laurelhurst and Windermere and Innis Arden; there are "good old neighborhoods" on Queen Anne and Capitol hills, in Madrona and Washington Park; and in all these places one can find, often on a single street, houses of great elegance and houses of great plainness. There are an enormous number of fine houses, ranging in age from one to eighty-five years, but almost no mansions. Concurrently, though there is a good deal of living at or below the poverty level, it is not very easy to see. There is no single area one can call a slum, and in the heart of the black ghetto, where one can find numerous abandoned or overcrowded houses, one can also see next to them a large house in the process of being renovated or a small one resolutely being kept up with fresh paint and a fine garden.

As of 1975, Seattle's population was 503,500, down from 530,831 in 1970 and from 557,087 in 1960, the first declines in the city's population ever recorded by the United States Census. The population of King County, of which Seattle is the seat, is 1,148,000, and growing slowly. Seattle ranks fourth among American cities in Asian population, fifth in native American Indians, forty-fourth in Jews, and is not among the first fifty American cities in its black population. There is a sizable Scandinavian district in Ballard, a much smaller Italian neighborhood in Rainier Valley.

The excitement of a large city—density, crowded space, danger— these it has, but one must go looking for them. Travelers, visitors, and natives when they are feeling defensive all tend to compare Seattle with San Francisco and end up ruling against Seattle, finding it too bland or complacent, not cosmopolitan, not a "real city." As might be expected, labor unions are strong in Seattle, solid, workmanlike, bourgeois rather than activist in aspiration. Governmental units tend to be not very strong, and generally speaking, honest and unadventurous.

Though everything seems spread out, the water and the hills keep providing focuses and boundaries for the eye, so there is little feeling of what is usually meant by urban sprawl. The topography discourages the street pattern from following a simple grid, and often what seems on a map to be a straight street in fact is a street that rises, falls, stops on a ridge, starts again farther down or up or around a bend. There are lots of streets, especially in the older sections, only one or two blocks long, lots of others that carry on two or three separate existences, divided in between by ravines or lakes. It is perhaps too hilly to be thought of as a great city for bicycles, but it is very good for walking, excellent for driving around. At present there are the beginnings of a badly needed network of trails and footpaths.

Seattle is a soft city, made up of soft light and hills and water and growing things and a sense that nature is truly accommodating. People garden, boat, go to the mountains to hike and climb in the summer and, by the thousands, to ski in the winter. There is no day in the year when it is too hot or too cold to work or get around, and few days when one cannot be outside, in a boat, walking, playing golf or tennis or going fishing. A bourgeois city, capable of sustaining middle-class virtues and middle-class pleasures, large enough to accommodate many variations from its bourgeois norms, comfortable enough to do this without noticing the differences.

Seattle's colors are gray and green.

II

The Founding

ON November 13, 1851, the schooner *Exact*, on its way from Portland, Oregon, to the Queen Charlotte Islands off the Canadian coast, stopped at what is now called Alki Point in West Seattle. Twenty-two people, ten adults and twelve children, disembarked. They were met by two young men of their original party who had come on foot and by canoe from Portland. It was raining. A few Indians were walking around. Some of the women, miserable at finding their promised land a wet, gray wilderness, wept. The men set to work putting a roof on the cabin that had been begun by the advance party, and one of them reportedly said, "They say white women are scarce out here. The best thing we can do is to go to work to provide shelter for those we have."

That is the traditional account of the founding of Seattle. The group is usually called the Denny party after its leader, Arthur Denny, a young man of twenty-nine from Illinois. A monument at Alki Point which commemorates the founding lists the names of the original settlers as follows: Mr. and Mrs. Arthur Denny, Mr. and Mrs. John Low, Mr. and Mrs. Carson Boren, Mr. and Mrs. William Bell, Mr. David Denny, Miss Louisa Boren, Mr. Charles Terry, Mr. Lee Terry. The Dennys had three children, one of whom had been born that fall in Portland; the Lows four; the Borens a daughter; the Bells four girls. David Denny was Arthur's younger brother, and Louisa Boren, who was soon to marry David, was the sister of Carson and of Arthur's wife, Mary. The story of these early days—the landing, the building of four cabins, the establishment of trade that December with San Francisco via the steamer *Leonesa*, the meager Christmas celebration—has been told often, and is usually taught to all Seattle schoolchildren in the fourth grade.

It is never easy, however, to say when something began. Three men had come earlier in 1851 to homestead land a few miles away in the Duwamish River valley. Seattle itself was not founded until the following February, when Arthur Denny, Boren, and Bell plumbed the coastline of Elliott Bay to the east of Alki Point with a horseshoe to find the deepest point in the harbor. It was easy to land ships at Alki, but the prevailing winds from the southwest subjected it to nasty storms, from which Elliott Bay was relatively sheltered. On the south end of the bay tideflats extended from the mouth of the Duwamish, and along much of the east side cliffs rose sharply from the water. But the deepest harbor was there, and at one point, where the cliffs dropped away to the tideflats, an easy landing was possible. On February 15, 1852, Denny, Boren, and Bell each staked a claim along the east side of the bay and their families moved over shortly after. Those who stayed at Alki, led by Charles Terry, had a hard time keeping the settlement going. For a while the new settlement on Elliott Bay was called Duwamps, after the river and the Indians who lived near it. During the summer the name was changed to Seattle at the suggestion of Dr. David Maynard, who arrived during the spring and made friends with the Indian leader, Sealth. Maynard realized that it was too hard for whites to pronounce Sealth's name as the Indians did and felt that "Seattle," being much more euphonious than "Sealth" or "Duwamps," would be more likely to attract other settlers.

So Seattle was founded in November 1851, or in February 1852. Seattle's beginning, however, was part of the whole westward movement and the vast Europeanization of the North American continent that began with Erickson or Columbus or the Jamestown Colony. There is no way to make sense of Seattle's early years unless one tries to work back at least a little way into the years before the Denny party landed. The Denny family itself can be traced, thanks to a handsome four-volume genealogy, to four families of that name who settled in Pennsylvania in the early eighteenth century. Yet one looks in vain through these volumes for some clue as to how members of this family ended up the founders of Seattle. The closest one can come is noting that Arthur Denny's direct ancestors had never settled permanently, having gradually worked their way west, approximately a generation at a time, from Virginia to Kentucky to Indiana, to Cherry Grove, Illinois, where they were living when they decided to come to the west coast. Of course, many people were coming west in those years; but if we do accept their coming as part of a large drift in the population, why did they come to Puget Sound, where almost no white people were? What did they expect to find, or to do?

Our first evidence comes from Arthur Denny's granddaughter, recalling stories told by her mother:

> She remembered family gatherings around the fireside on winter evenings while her father read letters from Farley Pierce, Liberty Wallace and other venturesome souls who had gone out to Oregon to seek their fortunes; she remembered when the neighbors dropped in and discussed the news from their friends. The letters told of the wonders of the Pacific; the grandeur of the mountains; the vastness of the untouched forests; but best of all they told of the mild climate and the fertile soil and the flowers that bloom in the winter time.

Given such descriptions, it is no wonder the women wept when they arrived at Alki Point on a drizzly November day.

Had Cherry Grove been a barren, rocky place, had the Dennys been people who could not easily endure hardships, had they wanted to see mountains and forests, the explanation given to Roberta Frye Watt might explain more than it does. But Cherry Grove was in a rich heartland, and the Dennys were both hard-working and uncomplaining on the one hand and not given to great responsiveness to the beauties of nature on the other. We can perhaps come closer to understanding the situation by noting that Arthur Denny, like his father, had never been strictly a farmer. He had taught school for a while, then learned surveying and became supervisor for Knox County. Though not the least footloose, he was in some way restless, seeking his fortune, and he was drawn to where others seemingly like him, Liberty Wallace and Farley Pierce, had sought theirs, in Oregon. It was a very long and very difficult journey, and Mary Denny was pregnant with their third child in the winter of 1851, but still the Dennys and the Borens decided to come west.

Oregon was their destination, as it had been for two decades of midwestern pioneers, because Oregon was, for all its vast landscape and mild climate, like what they had left. The government had "opened" the area for precisely this reason. Moving west from Saint Louis the land soon grows dry, the rainfall drops to less than twenty inches a year, and farming on traditional forty-acre sections is not possible. Furthermore, this land was inhabited by Indians, themselves driven west as the whites packed themselves into covered wagons, and not given to understanding why they should accept whatever the whites were willing to offer. But in the Willamette Valley in Oregon the land could be settled in something like midwest-

ern fashion. The winters were indeed mild there compared to those
farther east, and the land could be cleared easily and sown well. The
lure of Oregon was not the lure of California at all. Oregon was for
settling, for families, while California was mostly for single men
dreaming of getting rich in a hurry.

So the Denny party set out, upon the Oregon Trail, along the valley
of the Platte, across the Rockies at South Pass in Wyoming, up into
Idaho, where they were joined by John Low and his family, and then
to the Columbia River in what is now southeastern Washington. At
this point, according to Arthur Denny, something happened:

> On leaving home for what we called the Pacific Coast, we had no other
> purpose or expectation than to settle in the Willamette Valley. But we met
> a man on Burnt River by the name of Brock, who lived near Oregon City
> and had come out expecting to meet some friends, failing in which he
> came back with us to The Dalles. He gave us some information in regard to
> Puget Sound, and called attention to the fact that it was about as near to
> the Sound from where we first struck the Columbia River, now known as
> Umatilla Landing, as it was to Portland, but as yet there were no roads
> over the mountains by which it could be reached.
>
> My attention was thus turned to the Sound, and I formed the purpose of
> looking in that direction.

We might blame the existence of Seattle on poor Brock, thinking
there must have been magic in his description, but there is no reason
to think he ever had been to Puget Sound.

All he told Denny was distances, distances that at the time were
very unequal despite their equality in miles. We can only surmise
what Denny was imagining. If all he had wanted was to settle, he
would never have had his attention turned so easily to Puget Sound.
But if the distance from Umatilla to the sound was no greater than
that to Portland, then when a road could be built, future settlers
would be as inclined to come to one place as the other. Denny was
going to the sound in the present, but for something that would or
could happen in the future. Denny would settle, but not just for himself or his family.

The party went on to Portland, where they arrived in August, only
to have many of them come down with the ague so they could not
move on again right away. John Low and David Denny set out to
explore the Puget Sound country, going on foot north from Portland.
In Olympia, at the foot of the sound, they were joined by Lee Terry,
like David Denny a young man of nineteen, and the three went north
by boat and landed at Alki on September 25. Denny and Terry started
to build a cabin and Low returned to Portland, where the party was
reconstituting itself a little. Mary Denny had her baby, a boy. Mr.

and Mrs. William Bell and their daughters, plus Lee Terry's older brother Charles, were added to the group. At the same time John Denny, Arthur and David's father, and three of their brothers, all decided to stay in Oregon, unenticed by Arthur's plans or Low's stories about the water wilderness to the north. So it was that the various Dennys, Borens, Lows, Bells, and Terrys came on the *Exact* to Alki.

If we glance briefly at the other members of the party, and at those who soon followed them to Seattle, we can see why Arthur Denny was the major figure in the founding and early development of Seattle. He, however vaguely, was imagining a settlement here, one large enough to attract people who reached Umatilla and learned Puget Sound was no farther than Portland. By comparison, Carson Boren was not interested in a settlement at all. He was known as Old Dobbins, and he began selling off parts of his land very soon after he, Denny, and Bell staked their original claims. He had the most valuable property, as it turned out, but neither sought nor got much advantage from that fact. Roberta Watt says, "He was a conscientious worker, but unfortunately unhappiness in his home life robbed him of that ambition that actuated the others. It sent him to the woods and away from the habitations of men."

But even Boren seems clearer to us than some of the others. John Low and his family stayed at Alki only briefly, then moved to Olympia and on to California, to return much later to Puget Sound, to Snohomish. William Bell was one of the first to stake a claim in Seattle, but amidst the many accounts of the pioneers he remains faceless. He founded an area north of Denny Hill still known as Belltown, but left when his wife fell ill soon after the skirmishes with the Indians in 1855. He returned fifteen years later and gradually sold his land in small lots for much less than he could have gotten for it.

Lee Terry, who began the first log cabin, stayed only for the winter and then left for New York. His brother, Charles, is much more prominent. He had been in California during the early days of the Gold Rush and had learned that on the frontier one made money in commerce, not in get-rich-quick mining. He stayed at Alki after the others had moved across Elliott Bay; but the moment he saw that he had settled in the wrong place, he traded with Doc Maynard for some of his land. He then bought some more land from Boren, built a cracker mill, became one of the settlement's richest men, and died, at the age of thirty-seven, in 1867.

Arthur Denny's brother, David, was also an important pioneer, but it is perhaps characteristic that when he wrote his brother from

Alki before the entire party had come, he said: "We have examined the valley of the Duwamish River and find it a fine country. There is plenty of room for one thousand travelers. Come at once." His vision of the new settlement, to judge from this, was rural rather than urban, of farming along the river rather than cutting down logs for San Francisco. When he was old enough to stake his claim, he chose land out north, between Elliott Bay and Lake Union. There will be occasion later to give a few more details in his somewhat melancholy story; here it is enough to say that he never understood the kind of place Seattle was, or was to become, as well as Arthur.

Among the earliest settlers not belonging to the original party, Doc Maynard and Henry Yesler stand out, and more has been written about them than any of the others, including Arthur Denny. Maynard is personally the most attractive of the pioneers. He had come west to leave a bad marriage, had fallen in with a group that landed in Olympia, done some trading there, then moved to California, then back to Puget Sound in 1852. His portrait is nicely drawn by Murray Morgan in *Skid Road*. He was tireless, gregarious, hard-drinking, a Democrat, an enthusiast; in all but the first of these qualities he stands apart from the others, and is perhaps most special in his apparently genuine desire to do things for others. He fell in love with the idea of Seattle soon after he came and was willing to do anything to make Seattle grow. Not greedy, he was a buyer and seller, and not a shrewd one, either. He started the first store, made one of the first plats, founded the first hospital—an admirable man.

Henry Yesler was like Maynard in that both were from Ohio and neither claimed to be a gentleman. Otherwise they were opposites, Maynard friendly and profligate, Yesler dour and tight-fisted. Yesler appeared in the autumn of 1852, looking for a place to establish a sawmill. The others, delighted, gave him the waterfront and some of their best hinterland if he would settle with them. He agreed, and so Seattle had its first payroll in 1853. He built the cookhouse that became the town's only restaurant; he built a hall that became Seattle's meeting place; and when the city got its first charter in 1869, he became mayor. He sold out his sawmill in 1876 and dedicated the rest of his life where he knew the real money lay then, in real estate. There is no evidence that he ever saw Seattle as much more than a place that had rich and exploitable natural resources. Had Seattle been settled solely by people like Maynard, it would have died quickly, rich only in legend and lore. Had it been settled by people like Yesler, it would have soon become just another company town.

Seattle in the 1870s, population about 3,000. Above, looking north from First and Columbia (photo courtesy of the Seattle Historical Society); below, looking south from Second and Pike, showing the University of Washington building on Arthur Denny's knoll (photo courtesy of the Photography Collection, Suzzallo Library, University of Washington)

Arthur A. Denny (courtesy of the Photography Collection, Suzzallo Library, University of Washington)

Catherine Troutman Maynard, who did what she could, but could not keep her husband's gravestone upright (photo of Maynard courtesy of Photography Collection, Suzzallo Library, University of Washington; gravestone photo by Philip Christofides)

Chin Gee Hee, the major employer of Chinese coolie labor (courtesy of the Seattle Historical Society)

The Wa Chong Company's advertisement in the *P-I*, February 8, 1886, the day after the Chinese "had left." No one knows where the company found its coolies, or how many it could offer.

Downtown Seattle shortly after the fire of 1889 (courtesy of the Photography Collection, Suzzallo Library, University of Washington)

Pioneer Square as rebuilt after the fire, in the early 1890s. The Pioneer Building, on the left, is still used as the city's datum point; the Brasserie Pittsbourg is now in the basement, and Metro has most of its offices upstairs (courtesy of the Photography Collection, Suzzallo Library, University of Washington)

The Latona and Brooklyn streetcar. At the front of the car, the man on the right is David Denny, who went broke in 1893 mostly as the result of overspeculation in streetcar lines (courtesy of the Photography Collection, Suzzallo Library, University of Washington)

Queen Anne Hill in the 1890s, looking north from David Denny's home at First and Republican (courtesy of the Seattle Historical Society)

First Hill "mansions" in 1900. Only a handful of the buildings in the first of Seattle's "good neighborhoods" still stand (courtesy of the Seattle Historical Society)

The town of Ballard in 1902, before it became part of Seattle, looking north from Queen Anne Hill (courtesy of the Photography Collection, Suzzallo Library, University of Washington)

Brooklyn, to which David Denny's streetcar ran, in 1902, seen from across Portage Bay. At the top of the hill are the first buildings of the University of Washington on its present campus (courtesy of the Photography Collection, Suzzallo Library, University of Washington)

The University Book Store in 1901, still downtown on Third Avenue, a decade after the university itself had gone elsewhere (courtesy of the Photography Collection, Suzzallo Library, University of Washington)

Above, the Natatorium at Alki Beach, about 1910, a perfect watering place for the Employed. Below, Woodland Park and Green Lake in the same period, the Gilded Age's image of quiet retirement (both photos courtesy of the Photography Collection, Suzzallo Library, University of Washington)

There were others. Doc Smith settled at the north end of Elliott Bay, knew the Indians well, and is usually credited with translating Chief Sealth's farewell speech into the orotund English in which we now know it. Thomas Mercer claimed the south slope of what was later called Queen Anne Hill, and did much of the town's moving and hauling. His nephew, Asa Mercer, was only in Seattle a little while, but managed in that time to become famous as the man who went east to recruit single women to come west to settle in the largely male logging community. He also became the first president of, and teacher at, the University of Washington. Archie Binns very nicely reconstructs these people in his *Northwest Gateway* and manages to make them seem engaging and impressive without pretending that they contributed in crucial ways to the development of Seattle.

ARTHUR DENNY'S SEATTLE

Arthur Denny has always been known as the founding father, but his role has been generally underrated and misunderstood. Obviously, almost all the others were important in some way, but Denny is the one who signifies best the kind of settlement that was to be made, the kind of city Seattle was to become. No man was more typical of the Republican era than Denny. A little over six feet tall, weighing around 170 pounds, he was an imposing figure who seems to have smiled only rarely—the late pictures show a solemn face with a long white beard—and never to have laughed. Our glimpses of him in the earliest pioneer days are very brief, like the scene with Brock on Burnt River, so we are forced to look at some things he said near the end of his life and to work backwards from there:

> I am proud of the schools of Seattle to-day, where a high school education is furnished free to every child who chooses to take it. But I regret that it is in many cases so little appreciated by both parents and children that it al-most justifies the expectation that the next step will be to pay children for going to school, and allow them to strike for higher wages and shorter hours, with the privilege of arbitrating the matter in the end.
>
> . . . .
>
> I will presume to say that if the people now possessed more of the spirit that actuated the old mossbacks, as some reproachfully style the old set-tlers, we would hear less about a conflict between labor and capital, which in truth is largely a conflict between labor and laziness. We had no eight hour, nor even ten hour, days then, and I never heard of anyone striking, not even an Indian. Every man who was worthy of the name . . . was found striking squarely and determinedly at whatever obstacle stood in the way of his success.

This gruff, grim, and self-righteous statement typifies, so far as can be determined, Denny's character throughout his career in Seattle, though perhaps the acid in his tone developed only as others started to call him a mossback and still others started to organize laboring people into unions.

We must be careful not to patronize him, though we have no reason to like him, since there is no evidence that anyone ever did. In his idea of work, and of work in relation to his family, his community, and his sense of their mutual future, lies much to treasure, much that is characteristic of the Seattle he helped to build. As he settled he was "seeking his fortune," a phrase that in the present context is worth some pondering. When the three little pigs set out to seek their fortunes, they did not want to become Carnegies or Stanfords. They wanted houses strong enough to resist the attacks of the wolf, and a fortune was not a vast amount of money but a destiny to be found in the building of a home.

For Americans the presence of a huge continent to the west created a sense that one could always move out to the territory ahead. For some, this move was flight; Doc Maynard belonged to this group. For others, emigration was motivated by greed; Henry Yesler and perhaps Charles Terry can be placed among these. For still others, the west was where a destiny could be found in the building of a home, and Arthur Denny was one of these. As one moves west one sees houses and towns that still offer ample testimony to this latter desire. Most of these are eastern and midwestern, in towns like Lowville, New York; Sudbury, Pennsylvania; Washington Court House, Ohio; Princeton, Indiana; Oskaloosa, Iowa; Seneca, Kansas—towns built with stern and usually Anglo-Saxon rectitude still evident in their clapboard houses and tree-lined streets. The model was the small town and the prosperous farm and a way of living that has proven amazingly constant well into this century of almost total change.

West of the Missouri River or thereabouts the land and natural resources of the country become vast and often overwhelming to someone seeing them for the first time. The rivers are few, large, and often dangerous. The forests, especially those on the western slopes of the mountains, are taller, denser, and vaster than any farther east. The mountains are huge, the ranges long and often impassable except in places that are themselves not easy to scale. The land itself is large, especially on the Great Plains and in the Great Basin, where many present-day counties cover more land than half a dozen eastern states. In this country one could not easily find one's fortune just by building a house and settling down, though many tried to do just this.

There were huge profits, or fortunes in the other sense, to be made in the west, but in a land that large and rugged the profits had to be huge in order to exist at all. The Gold Rush miners came out looking for gold, and only a few found it. But the gold ran out quickly and the miners moved on, leaving the mountains for the large companies, which would extract from them copper, silver, lead, tin, uranium, manganese, and aluminum. So too in agriculture. The early settlers came to the Willamette because its valley could be homesteaded, but those who grew rich were in a later period, in eastern Washington and especially in California, where they brought in big machinery to irrigate and fertilize and so make dry-land farming pay. So too in forestry, where big companies did most of the business because they could buy up vast stands of timber and hire a large supply of cheap labor. In each case in order to make the extractive industries work at all, they had to be worked big. If one were to come west and seek any kind of fortune, one had to reckon with this fact sooner or later.

In the west small towns like the stable and prosperous ones of the east and midwest are rare. Much commoner are the company towns of the logging, mining, and farming companies, single-payroll towns, grim in their drabness. Workers here tend to become only interchangeable parts in a large machine; living conditions are seldom more than passable; amenity, grace, variety, and human independence are hard to find, or to maintain when found. These places have none of the virtues of a city, few of the virtues of the good eastern and midwestern small towns. They are the saddest consequences of the presence of vast land and vast natural resources in a capitalist system. Such places range in size from a few hundred in remote farming or logging areas to "cities" like Butte, Montana, or Everett, Washington; but their essential composition is the same. Here only a few can "seek their fortune" at all, and the fortunes even they can seek are in bank accounts, not in permanent homes.

The alternative to the company town in the west is not the small town but the city, and cities were destined to play a much larger role in the development of the west than of the midwest or the south. What cities in the west provide is everything the large and rugged country does not itself yield: depots, ports, railroads, machinery and the expertise necessary for its manufacture and especially for its repair, the expertise to build and maintain all but the crudest refining processes, the banking and legal services, the medical facilities and the doctors, the food processing and distributing, the retail trade above the simplest level. The larger the city, the more it will be called upon to do. The key to how much cities will develop lies in how they develop their capital.

Some of those who came west and began to glimpse the essential facts of its economic development concluded that only huge amounts of capital—which meant eastern capital—could do the developing. But when the growth and security of this capital was the only consideration, the inevitable result was the company town, and the company town was itself helpless without a city nearby. If the city had some measure of economic independence, then its labor and commerce would be diverse and varied enough to meet its own needs and to export its various kinds of goods and expertise to the company towns in its hinterlands. If it could do this, it could develop its own capital, often in surprisingly large quantities. When it could do *that*, it became a destination for people seeking their fortunes, offering not so much the prospect of great wealth, as the prospect of settled homes and plenty of opportunity.

After the cities had been built, especially after the railroads had been built west to them, then it was not so hard to imitate the three little pigs. What we have to try to reconstruct, however, is what Arthur Denny contemplated as he "formed the purpose of looking in that direction" of Puget Sound. We know that he was not like those men from Maine, Pope and Talbot, who settled in San Francisco and then came and cut down trees at Port Ludlow and became very wealthy. We also know that he was sufficiently different from Liberty Wallace and Farley Pierce that he liked the idea of starting an entirely new settlement in a mostly undeveloped wilderness. And finally, we know that he wanted his settlement not just for himself but for a future when the equal distance from Umatilla to Portland and Puget Sound might begin to matter in attracting later settlers. Knowing this much is knowing a lot, really. Denny would seek his fortune in a vast wilderness, and where others coming later were to seek theirs, on at least roughly equal terms. He would settle, they would come, and the result would be a city.

As Arthur Denny staked his claim in the spring of 1852, Portland and San Francisco must have seemed far away, and Chicago or Saint Louis or New York on the other side of the world. In the golden climate of California perhaps even early settlers knew the railroads and millions of dollars of trade and millions of people would soon be on their way. But Puget Sound was darker, with forest and cloud, so it is hard to see how anyone could have known that a city had to be built there. Yet years later, in a brief essay called "The Founding of the State of Washington," Denny wrote: "Forty-one years ago all of Puget Sound north of the mouth of Steilacoom Creek was as wild as when visited by Vancouver in 1792 but even then I expected to see a railroad from the Atlantic Coast to Puget Sound." Whatever his faults, Denny was not given to gloating hindsight. If he said he expected a railroad to come to Puget Sound as he cut his first Douglas fir, then almost certainly he expected just that. Whatever his comprehension of the essential relation between the west, the significance of cities, and the coming of the railroads, he understood what was most important. Others in early Seattle must have realized this too; but since he was a central figure from the beginning, we will not be amiss in letting him stand as the representative for the essential way of settling that would make Seattle a city.

Furthermore, Arthur Denny did not expect the railroad to appear by magic and he did not seek to importune a group of eastern capitalists to build one. Rather, his eye was out for settlers like himself, people seeking their fortunes, people with skills at various things Seattle needed right away. Get them and the city would follow, get the city and the railroad would follow. One of his major disappointments was that these settlers appeared so slowly in the early years; he attributed this slow growth first to the decision to open up Kansas and Nebraska for settlement in the 1850s, then to the Civil War in the 1860s, so that people who might have come to Seattle were farther east still, settling, fighting, or dying.

We can call Denny's dream a dream of a city, if we will, but we must bear in mind that for him it was not quite like that. He remained a small-town person in many ways, and what is most revealing about this passage from his autobiography is that it could have been written in Cherry Grove as easily as in Seattle: "In my life I have endeavored simply to meet the obligations to my family and discharge my duty as a citizen to my country and the community in which I have lived. It has not occurred to me that I have accomplished anything above the ordinary and, if so, I should feel humiliated to claim it for myself." This may seem contradictory when placed next to the previous passage about Seattle becoming a large city, but when the two are put together they show why Denny was so important. In the process of meeting his obligations to his family and of discharging his duties as a citizen, Denny would help make a city out of a wilderness. His sense of obligation and duty would keep him from becoming an exploiter like Henry Yesler, and Seattle from being another company town like Port Gamble. His sense of the future for a city of settlers grown large enough to become a major railroad terminal meant that he welcomed Yesler when he came, just as he had welcomed Doc Maynard, who was unlike him in so many ways. One begins to see why Seattle was a bourgeois city from its first breath.

In his later years Denny was often compared to Abraham Lincoln, another citizen of Illinois who in fact was once a friend of Arthur Denny's father, because both were log cabin frontiersmen who came to prominence in places far from their birth. Perhaps a more telling comparison might be with Brigham Young, who came west as the leader of a party, who dreamed of community rather than exploitation, who saw that making the vast west economically productive would require cities rather than small towns, who personally was austere and not liked by many people. The difference, of course, is that Denny was not the leader of a religious group that could yield itself to authoritarian government, and so Denny could never simply say that his will should be done. A good deal of what he did to make Seattle grow he did himself, but a good deal he did by encouraging others. This is probably one reason why, in his declining years, he really was thought of as an old mossback, and others who came later and got richer faster were given the credit for making Seattle grow. Stories about Seattle's first pioneers usually gave Denny a prominent role, but because Denny was not the head of an authoritarian government like Young, because the settlers did not flock to Seattle in droves, because it was not until Denny's declining years that Seattle began to look like a city and the railroads came, Denny's contributions were underestimated.

In 1916, when Clarence Bagley came to publish his *History of Seattle,* he filled his last volume, as was the custom in those days, with the success stories of the city's prominent citizens, starting with those who had contributed enough to make publication of the *History* possible. One would have thought that Denny, though many years deceased, would be given pride of place, especially by Clarence Bagley, who revered the pioneers and was himself descended from an important early settler. Instead of occupying first place, Denny is twenty-second, fitted between two later nonentities who lack even the gaudy reputation of pirates. By 1899, when he died, or by 1916, when the *History* was published, no one really knew why Denny's narrow vision and peculiar greatness had done so much to shape Seattle.

If one reason for this later neglect of Arthur Denny is that he could not, like Brigham Young, impose his will by fiat or force, another is that he cannot be simply associated with any single event or activity.

He participated in all kinds of commercial ventures but seldom stayed in one for long. He spent a great deal of time dealing in land but he was never Seattle's most important speculator or developer; and since he sold or gave almost as fast as he claimed or bought and platted, he cannot be associated with a particular piece of land or part of the city. He was postmaster, regimental officer, territorial legislator, and congressional representative, but never long enough to be readily identified with a particular kind of public service. In this very busyness lies a kind of key. He equated his own growth and wealth with the growth and wealth of Seattle, in ways that neither denied nor simply served his personal needs, so that if something needed doing, he did it and then stopped the moment it was done, or else got someone else to do it.

We can isolate a few of his activities, however, to see the kind of contribution he made. It is not clear if Denny or others of his party knew that from the beginning Seattle's growth would be tied to that of San Francisco, but it could not have taken them long to see this. A month after the Denny party landed at Alki the *Leonesa* stopped and contracted for a load of logs to be used as pilings for the docks in San Francisco; payment was made in goods brought back on a return visit. After Seattle itself was founded, boats would arrive from California with merchandise, the ship captains selling what they could and leaving the rest to be sold on commission. Arthur Denny built a one-room store, twenty by thirty feet, on the corner of First Avenue South and Washington Street, and became commissionaire. He worked by himself for a while, then took in two new settlers, Dexter Horton and David Phillips, as partners. "It was not long," writes Clarence Bagley, "before Mr. Denny and his partners were able to place themselves on an independent basis, the founder of the house visiting San Francisco to purchase his annual stock." Within five years, then, Denny's firm had found ways to diminish the dependence of the little town on its major market, and in this respect Seattle was different from many other logging towns on the sound. By becoming commissionaire and then entrepreneur Denny both assumed the risk and gained the profit, reducing San Francisco's hold on Seattle from that of maker, shipper, and capitalist to that of maker only. Having established the commercial pattern, Denny sold most of his share of the business to Horton and Phillips in 1855.

In 1860 he was in business again, this time with Henry Yesler in the operation of a store, and in 1866 sold his interest in that. In 1872 he again became a partner of Horton's, this time in a bank situated in a larger building on the site of the original store. Horton was like

Denny, dour, stern, unflinchingly honest, and it is quite clear that the success of the bank, founded long before any federal or territorial banking regulations, was simply the result of everyone's believing in the integrity of its owners. Shortly after, Denny began the Denny Clay Company, which quickly expanded to include the digging and manufacture of all kinds of building materials. Still later he was the moving force behind the formation of the Denny-Blaine Land Company, which was run by Arthur's son, Charles, and Elbert Blaine, a lawyer who later assumed management of Denny's estate.

In all these business dealings, Arthur Denny reveals a number of salient qualities: a desire to get things started, a willingness to work with other people, no thought of building monuments to himself, no marked business sense but an instinctive reliance on his own unshakable integrity to make the right things happen. When one looks at the number of different businesses into which Denny went, and the partners he joined, one might sense someone easy, affable, a gregarious booster, when in fact the opposite was the case. Denny was always aloof, austere. What marks him is his way of seeing his own destiny as tied up with Seattle's; he did not, like Brigham Young or Anaconda, simply impose his personal will on the community, but worked to create a city that one day would be large enough for a transcontinental railroad.

As he managed his businesses both broodingly and variously, so he managed his land. Although the 320 acres of Denny's original claim are now the heart of downtown Seattle, at the time and throughout his life they were not the most desirable parts of the city for commercial or residential development. A year after Seattle was settled, Denny, Boren, and Maynard decided to make a plat of the town for present and future use. Denny describes this with what he thought of as humor: "All had gone reasonably well until the time when we were to record a joint plat of the town of Seattle, when it was found that the Doctor, who occasionally stimulated a little, had that day taken enough to cause him to feel that he was not only monarch of all he surveyed, but what Boren and I surveyed too." The plat made by Denny and Boren covers the land from Front Street (later First Avenue) east to Third Avenue, and from Mill Street (later Yesler Way) north to Seneca Street. Maynard's extended south from this along the tideflats. Later in the day Maynard sobered up enough so all could see that his plat met Denny's and Boren's at an angle, because while both followed the shoreline, Maynard's also followed the compass, as plats, at least theoretically, were supposed to do. The details of this episode are laid out in rather gaudy fashion in Bill

Speidel's *Sons of the Profits*. The discrepancy was never straightened out, so that all the streets south of Yesler Way still are at an angle to those north of it, but no dire consequences resulted.

Perhaps the most interesting fact here concerns not Denny and Maynard but Denny and Boren. Originally, when Denny, Boren, and Bell made their claims, "we divided the territory," says Denny, "so that each could have access to the water." Denny somehow then talked Boren into giving him part of his waterfront property. Denny's primary claim runs east-west along a line askew to the streets as originally platted, running from near First and Union streets to Broadway and Cherry Street on its southern border and from about First and Bell to about Ninth Avenue and Pike Street on its northern border. But it also has a flange running from this, going from about Third Avenue and University Street south to the foot of Yesler Way and extending west over to the waterfront. Denny had built his first permanent home on land covered by this flange, on the corner of First Avenue and Marion Street. Just when or how this flange was created has never been made clear, nor is there any evidence that its existence was ever a source of friction between Denny and Boren. But, since Boren's claim had already been diminished when Denny and Bell gave Yesler some of Boren's land while Boren was in Oregon, Boren ended up with no waterfront property for himself. While one can prove no skullduggery, Denny must have seen an advantage for himself in the fact that, as his granddaughter later said, "Boren was more interested in farm land and in hunting than in town lots." Denny was interested in town lots.

To imagine the topography of the Seattle they were settling is to make an interest in town lots seem strange, or at least premature. Dense evergreen forests came down from the hills to the high bluff above the water. There was just the one place on the shore, where Yesler had his mill, that was neither cliff nor tideflat. It was not forbidding country, and all the settlers must have realized soon that they could succeed at least as long as San Francisco wanted Seattle's logs. It was not easy land to get at, however, even after the trees were down, and to plat streets and lots on a very steep hill full of stumps must have been hard to do and probably seemed, to some at least, a trifle silly. But Denny was imagining a large community, filled with people, and plat he did. He platted with Boren, he platted with Bell, he platted by himself. He bought land from Bell, he sold lots to new settlers. If he was not monarch of Seattle, he was something like monarch of all he surveyed. As late as the 1880s, when Denny was in his sixties, he acquired, first as lessee and then as outright owner, the last piece of valuable land near downtown, and platted it as Denny's Broadway. He seems like someone brooding, not opposed to making money, but not primarily interested in profit, either, looking for ways for the land to be developed, feeling the growth of his own property to be a part of the growth of Seattle. In one sense he was fulfilling his obligations to his family, in another he was fulfilling the terms of a large vision.

I do not mean to imply that Denny was doing anything strangely original or unique, or that his activities alone secured the early health and growth of Seattle. Mike Simmons in Olympia, for instance, owned a ship that he took back and forth to San Francisco to stock his store, and Doc Maynard worked, like Denny, as a commissionaire in the early days. Denny may have been Seattle's leading surveyor, but all towns are eventually surveyed by someone. What Denny offers, rather, is an image of precisely the kind of activity that was essential to achieve the diversity and cooperation among the small city's settlers which in turn could lead to a decreasing dependence on the outside world for Seattle's essential livelihood. He really did think of his own destiny and that of the city as being irrevocably connected, and he had energy and vision enough to do at least some of the things that made the city what he knew it could be.

Nowhere is this clearer than in his dealing with the property that became the original site of the University of Washington. The very idea of a university was a little preposterous in an area that could not provide students enough should it come into being, and there were far more immediately important things for the young people of Seattle and the territory to do than to extend their schooling beyond the practical minimum. But in 1850 Oregon Territory had received a grant from the United States Congress which provided that two townships, one north and one south of the Columbia River, should be given to aid in the establishment of a territorial university. When Washington became a territory in 1854, it was again given the right to settle the site for a university. For a while it was to be in Seattle, then both in Seattle and in Boisfort Prairie, in the Cowlitz Valley in Lewis County, about halfway between Seattle and Portland. Most of this was just talk, since no one was seriously inclined actually to build the school anywhere.

In 1859 a Methodist minister, Daniel Bagley, moved to Seattle and immediately became enthusiastic about building the territorial university. The city's ministers differed from their colleagues in Oregon on this matter. Oregon ministers, for the most part, worked to keep a territorial university from being built because they believed education was properly the job of the church, not the state. Bagley not only wanted a secular university but seems to have glimpsed its potential power for the city in which it was settled. "You go back," he told Arthur Denny, who was territorial legislator for Seattle, "and get me appointed a commissioner to locate and build the university, and I will show you something a good deal better than the capitol."

The "capitol" was that for the territorial government, which had only temporarily been given to Olympia. Originally Denny had dreamed of having the capitol in Seattle and had gone so far as to plat part of the area he called Capitol Hill. Convinced by Bagley, however, that having the university was far more important, Denny made a deal with the representatives from Vancouver, Port Townsend, and Walla Walla. When the legislature met in 1861 they were to divide the territorial institutions among themselves, the capitol for Vancouver, the penitentiary for Walla Walla, the customhouse for Port Townsend, the university for Seattle. Olympia's claim on the capitol proved too strong for Vancouver, but the other towns soon got what they were seeking. The law Denny wrote interested few people, since it required that the university be built and opened within a year, and no one thought that was possible. It said nothing about the kind of school it was to be beyond prescribing a site of at least ten acres. It also enabled the university commissioners, or trustees, to "sell lands donated by Congress to the Territory of Washington for University purposes."

When Denny returned to Seattle he was told that ten acres out on Capitol Hill were too far away from the rest of Seattle. He replied, "Bagley, I'll give the knoll," meaning a tract in the middle of his own best property. Bagley did the rest. He sold land to pay wages, got the help, the materials, the building built, and Asa Mercer to be the university's president and sole teacher—all within a year. The one thing he could not find was students, and the university got along for years teaching elementary and high school students when it was open at all. It did not graduate its first college student until 1876. But it was there, and pictures of Seattle in the 1860s show pretty clearly how much must have gone into its making. Standing on the knoll above a city of stumps, a few functional houses, and muddy streets, it looked quite impressive, if a little lonely and absurd, with pillars and cupola and a good coat of paint.

Denny himself did a good deal more than secure the legislation and give the land. He served for many years as a member of the

Board of Trustees, and when he died in 1899 the university's president, Frank Pierrepont Graves, in his eulogy to Denny gave a good indication of the kind of services Denny had rendered:

> Had he been a university man, his work would have been glorious in that he desired to extend such benefits to others. But that a hardy, rugged, and industrious pioneer who had not had the opportunity of early training himself should seek to furnish an opportunity to the coming generation seems to me a far more glorious tribute. [He was] ever ready to give the institution apparatus, specimens for the museum, equipment, prizes for students, bricks for buildings and, if it were necessary even to don a pair of overalls and patch the leaky roof.

The university thus was for Arthur Denny part of the community he had helped to make and so it became part of his instinctively felt obligations and duties. This was not philanthropic activity in the usual sense, being less grand and more admirable than most philanthropy. It was doing what could and had to be done to make a vision, a sense of the future, real.

Dedicated and hopeful as they were, neither Bagley nor Denny could possibly have known what they were making for Seattle in their work to create and sustain the University of Washington. One hundred years after the school on the knoll first opened its doors, Olympia still had the capitol and Walla Walla the penitentiary, but the University of Washington community by itself was almost as large as the combined population of these two cities. When the university was ready to expand beyond its one building, it relocated on its present site north of Lake Union and Union Bay, and its first building, Denny Hall, was finished in 1895. The university kept title to the ten acres of Arthur Denny's original gift, and it is now prime downtown property, yielding an income of more than ten million dollars a year. We will have occasion later to look at the university and its impact on Seattle. What it has become is more than its founders could have envisioned, but without them it could not have been anything like what it is today; its being in Seattle was a crucial factor in shaping the institution, just as the university's presence in Seattle has contributed a great deal to the character of the city. It was Denny's and Seattle's good fortune that the university became as important as it did, but it was the kind of luck that can only result from the essential city instinct, the appetite for hard work, the sense of slow and rooted growth that mark almost everything in Arthur Denny's career.

I have said little about Arthur Denny as a person, partly because as a person he does not seem particularly striking or interesting, partly because much of the evidence comes from Denny's later years. It is characteristic, perhaps, that the early reminiscences and accounts of pioneer days almost always depict Denny as doing this and doing that, and seldom consider him apart from what he did. When he ran his store, he had customers buy their liquor directly from the San Francisco ship captains because he would not allow spirits on his premises; but that is no more striking or less decisive than his saying "Bagley, I'll give the knoll." He was austere and ascetic, he ate alone in his later years, and he always carried with him a needle and thread so that he might immediately sew on a button if one fell off. While the city grew up around him, he kept his house, his yard, his cow, his barn, his chickens, his orchard, after most of the other original buildings had long since gone and most of the land on his claim was being used for commerce and manufacture. We might have expected as much, however, from someone who was still out surveying in his sixties, and who thought nothing of putting on overalls to patch a leaky roof at the university. There is a world of difference from being urban and being urbane, especially in a small frontier city.

What is needed, really, is not a closer analysis of Denny as a human being but clarification of why the kind of things Denny did led to Seattle's diverse early growth. For that, two comparisons should be helpful, one with Arthur's brother David, the other with Chief Sealth.

Near the end of *Four Wagons West*, Roberta Frye Watt describes the demise of David Denny:

> He grew to be a rich man but he did not stop there. He was in every big city enterprise. He helped to install the water system, the electric lights, and the street railway. To all of these things he pledged himself and his fortune, that he might do greater things for his beloved city.
>
> And then the crash came, the financial panic of '93, and David lost everything that he had crossed the plains to win. In terms of money he died a poor man. Every penny of his hard-earned wealth, which more than paid his obligations, was exacted from him.
>
> Then, broken and sick and old, he turned again to the forest. All that he had left was a place in the wilderness that he had given to his daughter, where Washelli is now. When he had left his city home for the last time he said as he paused at the door, and sadly looked about, "I'll never look upon Seattle again." Then, like a sorrowing father turning his back upon an ungrateful child, he went out of the city to his humble home in the woods.

David was almost ten years younger than Arthur, and he lived far from the waterfront, near Lake Union; it is for him that Denny Way and Denny Park were named. He was like his brother in many ways, enterprising, hard-working, sober, a pillar of his church, generous with his land. In addition, he was one of the few settlers who learned Indian dialects and made friends among the people who had been here when the white settlers first came.

But there were crucial differences between the two brothers. When Seattle began its first boom period in the eighties and early nineties, David Denny became expansive, adapting his methods to those of a younger and more speculative breed like Judge Thomas Burke and Daniel Gilman, who, as we will see, were into many schemes, mostly involving railroads but including mining, water, electricity, and real estate. In those later days David Denny was the pioneer to turn to if one had a plan that would be "good for Seattle" and one needed a re-spectable tone and a willing investor. But unlike his brother, David Denny did not make his money off his claim, and, unlike Thomas Burke, he did not have real estate holdings at the ends of the streetcar lines to keep him solvent when the streetcars had to be sold at a loss. He overextended himself badly, and during the panic of 1893 he was left holding numerous empty bags when his friends or debtors fled or pleaded poverty. The bank that finally foreclosed on David Denny was Dexter Horton and Company, whose vice-president still was Arthur Denny. David's grandson, Victor Denny, has told me that though his grandmother was very bitter about the abandonment of her husband, she did not place the blame on Arthur, who by this time was over seventy, in semiretirement, and in no position to dictate bank policies. At the time the controlling interest in the bank was held by a Portland man, William S. Ladd. But Arthur Denny did not rush in to bail out his brother, either, as he must have been in a position to do.

This story shows more than one reason why no one is on record as ever having liked Arthur Denny. It shows also his unshakably solid way of doing things. David Denny was no profligate or dreamer, but he did not have Arthur's sense of city land and city business. For Arthur, Seattle was never something about which to speculate; he would have risked its future no more than he would have risked his family's or his own. Let others make the big fortunes, let David try to enhance his that way. Arthur's fortune, such as it was, remained like that of the third little pig, the outcome of fulfilling his obligations. David's fortune came from buying and selling companies doing, or pretending to do, business all over the county, so that when the pinch came, David could not see where he was and Arthur could, having based all he did on what he could see by looking out his window. In the earliest days, to be sure, he had little choice but to do this, because his land claim was the basis for his fortune and for his own ways to contribute to the growth of the settlement. But he stuck to that choice, not tight-fistedly, but in a way that kept the future to a scale of what he could see.

A comparison with Chief Sealth gives us a chance to look briefly at that remarkable man and to see the same point from a somewhat different angle. This is a book about the city made by the white settlers and so it does not look hard at the Indians who were here when the Dennys landed. But since we have been so much concerned thus far with the way the land near Elliott Bay was developed, we can gain something by comparing the development of Seattle as a city with the way the original inhabitants were living on the Sound when the first whites arrived. The story of the Indians is inexpressibly sad even as imperfectly as it can be pieced together, and fortunately we have a quite good picture of Chief Sealth, mostly from his magnificent farewell speech.

Sealth stands out like a mountain. Since he was willing to be friendly with the white settlers of Puget Sound, he is vulnerable to the charge that he did no more than sell out to a group willing or determined to ignore, revile, and render his own people impotent. Just who or how many Puget Sound people Sealth represented has never been established. What is clear is that these people were much more loosely knit than many more warlike tribes farther east so they may have felt very little need for chiefs or leaders. Sealth, through his friendship with the whites, had come to the settlers as the Indian leader, and it was with him that they dealt when, after various skirmishes in 1855, they determined to isolate the Indians on a reservation at Suquamish, on the Kitsap Peninsula across the Sound.

As the Indians left, Sealth made a speech that inevitably is paralleled in certain ways by the sad farewell gestures of David Denny almost forty years later. Fortunately Sealth was more articulate at this moment than was David Denny, and his speech, in spite or because of the florid Victorian rhetoric into which it was translated, probably by Doc Smith of Smith's Cove, is justly famous as one of the great Indian farewells. As Archie Binns says in *Northwest Gateway*, "As the amiable follies of the white race become less amiable, the iron rumble of old Seattle's speech sounds louder and more ominous":

A few more moons. A few more winters—and not one of the descendants of the mighty hosts that once moved over this broad land or lived in happy homes, protected by the Great Spirit, will remain to mourn over the graves of a people—once more powerful and hopeful than yours. But why should I mourn at the untimely fate of my people? Tribe follows tribe and nation follows nation, like the waves of the sea. It is the order of nature, and regret is useless. Your time of decay may be distant, but it will surely come, for even the White Man whose God walked and talked with him as friend cannot be exempt from the common destiny. We may be brothers after all. We will see.

We will ponder your proposition, and when we decide we will let you know, but should we accept it, I here and now make this condition that we will not be denied the privilege without molestation of visiting at any time the tombs of our ancestors, friends, and children. Every part of the soil is sacred in the estimation of my people. Every hillside, every valley, every plain and grove, has been hallowed by some sad or happy event in days long vanished. Even the rocks, which seem to be dumb and dead as they swelter in the sun along the silent shore, thrill with memories of stirring events connected with the lives of my people, and the very dust on which you now stand responds more lovingly to their footsteps than to yours, because it is rich with the blood of our ancestors and our bare feet are conscious of the sympathetic touch. Our departed braves, fond mothers, glad, happy-hearted maidens, and even the little children who lived here and rejoiced for a brief season, will love these somber solitudes and at eventide they greet shadowy returning spirits. And when the last Red Man shall have perished, and the memory of my tribe becomes a myth among the White Men, these shores will swarm with the invisible dead of my tribe, and when your children's children think themselves alone in the field, the store, the stop upon the highway, or in the silence of the pathless woods, they will not be alone. In all the earth there is no place dedicated to solitude. At night when the streets of your cities and villages are silent and you think them deserted, they will throng with the returning hosts that once filled them and still love this beautiful land. The White Man will never be alone. Let him be just and deal kindly with my people, for the dead are not powerless. Dead, did I say? There is no death, only change of worlds.

Had Arthur Denny heard those words, he probably would not have understood them. Denny was well known and honored among the Indians because he was one who always kept his word; Denny's yard was camped on by certain Indians at the time of his death out of respect for his departed spirit, but Denny's was too narrow and too determined a spirit to understand. Of all the books on the pioneer period his is the only one that does not quote or allude to this speech. The whites who lived beyond Denny, out in the woods, like Doc Smith, Thomas Mercer, and David Denny, almost certainly better knew what Sealth meant than did Arthur, who was not one to lift his eyes up unto the hills, to say nothing of believing that the rocks thrilled with memories of stirring events.

Denny's land was to be a city, a place for planning, hard work, and making money, all of which are alien to Sealth's sense of the same land. Sealth did not in the least like having the city of the white people named after him, because he believed that no one's name should be spoken after his death lest the departed spirit be disturbed. Not even Maynard seems to have understood that. But in its white person's way Arthur Denny's life was as devoted to the land as the Indians', as careful, as adherent to itself.

White people do not leave the land alone in America. They have been uncomprehending of the Indians partly because the Indians did not ever seem to *do* anything with the land. If, however, whites are going to do something, it then becomes crucial what they do. In the west they built cities, the necessary hubs of transportation, commerce, and manufacture, and much of the time they have built these cities badly. A bad city is not one that cuts down trees, builds buildings, and paves streets, but one that tries to forget that indeed a city is being built. The ecology of an urban area is as important and often as mysterious as the ecology of the wilderness in which the Indians moved and lived. Often people came west fleeing urban life and never realized that cities are even more essential here than farther east. They came to build a sweet little nest out there in the west so they could let the rest of the world go by. The result, we know, is often nests that are not sweet, suburbs and freeways, people neither going nor staying but twitching with restlessness, despoiling the land with a wantonness all the more destructive and saddening because unintended.

There was to be a city on Puget Sound, whether or not Arthur Denny ever came. The question was always what kind of city it was to be. Cities can have relations with their land as good in their self-conscious and changing ways as the Indians in their more passive ways. What is most required is the constant realization that cities generate power and that this power, like all other, should not be ignored or deified. To ignore the power of cities is to move to the wilderness and build a suburb, to deify it is to build temples of Mammon in the heart of downtown.

Arthur Denny neither ignored nor deified the power of the young Seattle. He used it, rather, to build commerce that created an independent base for business, to survey and buy and sell land whose ways he could see and understand, to create a university. A small city is terribly fragile, subject to economic changes, booms and busts, elsewhere. Denny had to wait much of his mature life for the country to change so that the settlers he expected in 1851 were finally there in the 1880s and after; under the circumstances, there was little Seattle could do but wait. What defenses it could build against the inevitable changes in the outside world were built by people like

Denny, who made the city a real place because they were as respectful of the land in their ways as Chief Sealth and the Indians had been
in theirs.

TOMBSTONES

One final note on this earliest period of Seattle's history is offered
us by Roberta Frye Watt when she describes an incident that occurred just before she published her book in 1931: "I read my notes
to a friend and she said, 'Yes, interesting, but why so sad?' Then I
began to think that perhaps I had omitted the comedy of pioneering.
I went to an old settler and asked him to tell me of the fun they had in
the early days. He looked at me and then said, as he slowly shook his
head, 'It wasn't funny.' " We have no way of knowing how bone-
wearying and dispiriting a life could have been whose present was
dedicated to endless work and deprivation. It was mostly a sense of a
future that drove them on. That their labor was finally fruitful makes
the lives of these people no less sad.

Cemeteries offer glimpses of the grimness of frontier life. There is
no pioneer cemetery as such in Seattle, and one can find the tombstones of early settlers scattered in two or three graveyards. A wet
winter morning is perhaps the best time to go, since such trips
should not be undertaken lightly. One can find the rather grand arrangement of tombstones made to honor Arthur Denny and his descendants, with those of Carson and Mary Boren lurking somewhat
uncomfortably in the background. But more moving by far than
these are the sequences that read like this:

Gardner Kellogg	Sarah B. Kellogg	
February 26, 1839	June 2, 1848	
June 24, 1918	October 28, 1906	
Sarah Bonney Kellogg	Chester Ferry Kellogg	Baby Kellogg
March 9, 1880	May 24, 1869	May 24, 1869
October 10, 1906	November 3, 1875	

or this:

Samuel Francis Clise	Nancy McKenzie Clise
1824–1868	1830–1903
Mary Clise	Charles Frank Clise
1858–1858	1862–1876

Under such circumstances, a short life may be a blessing, or a curse,
and so too it may be with a long life. Perhaps one knew that lives like

that of the Kellogg twin who did not survive his or her first day, or that of Mary Clise, were part of the understanding their parents had of life as a whole; it is less easy to see how to understand or accept those of Sarah and Chester Kellogg, of Charles Clise, of those of their parents who so long outlived them.

In Thomas Prosch's *Life of Catherine T. Maynard* is a picture of Doc Maynard's beloved second wife at the tomb of her husband, whom she outlived by many years. The stone is standing upright, its letters clear. At present one must hunt to find it at all, near the top of the tallest hill in the Lakeview Cemetery, and not only are the letters faded, but, stranger still, it is now embedded in the ground. Next to it is the grave of Catherine Maynard, who had lived in Washington Territory and State for fifty-six years. Her grave, its letters still clear, gives this inscription (an adaptation of Mark 14):

Catherine Troutman Maynard
One of the Founders of Seattle
July 19, 1816
October 20, 1906
She Did What She Could

She did what she could. She had come west with her husband, Israel Broshears, and he had died on the way. Doc Maynard had joined their party, and some years after she had settled in Olympia, he obtained a legislative divorce from his first wife and married Catherine Broshears. She lived for over a year on the Indian reservation in Suquamish, then on Alki, a collection of stumps and faded dreams, after Maynard traded some of his best land away to Charles Terry. Later still, back in Seattle, the Maynards were paid a visit by his first wife, who had come out, among other reasons, because Maynard had filed half his original claim in her name. The three lived in apparent harmony for a while, even as the land in question underwent the strains of legal wrangling. Maynard himself drank more and more until he died, in 1873, and Catherine still had thirty-three years to live. She opened a reading room, which Dexter Horton and some others soon turned into the first YMCA in Seattle. She later lived variously in Ellensburg and Medical Lake, east of the Cascades, as well as in Seattle, and she is remembered as being able to ride a horse as well at eighty as most people could at twenty. She had a huge funeral when she died. But she could not keep David Maynard's tombstone upright, though perhaps even in this "she did what she could." It is a riddling phrase. It implies that she did a great deal, and also that what she did was not enough.

The phrase in its very elusiveness, furthermore, can warn us not to try to read much more than the patterns of these people's lives, lest we allow ourselves to become sentimental or scornful on the basis of what can only be imagined, not known. We can read the city the settlers built better than we can read them. One of the reasons we can be so moved in cemeteries is that they can show us how little we know.

THE SEVENTIES AND EIGHTIES

Like Catherine Maynard, Seattle in its first generation did what it could, but increasingly it must have begun to seem that what it could do was not enough. For Denny, and presumably for the others, the community could be pronounced a success when it was strong and large enough to become the western terminus of a transcontinental railroad. In 1853, when Washington became a territory, its first governor, Isaac Stevens, had rashly predicted a railroad would come to Puget Sound from across the Cascades in five years. The others, knowing that no transcontinental railroad then existed anywhere, or was even imminent, may have known better, but they were committed to hoping.

The Indian skirmishes in the mid-1850s sent some settlers away from Seattle and presumably kept others from wanting to come. Kansas and Nebraska were opened up for homesteading, and then came the Civil War. By the time Seattle could once again begin to expect an influx of settlers and a railroad, most of the original settlers were middle-aged, looking back on lives they had built on hopes, hopes that had had to be renegotiated, perhaps many times. Thus, when Jay Cooke took over the Northern Pacific in 1870 and the road west from Minnesota began to be built and a branch line from the Columbia River to Puget Sound was underway, the hopes were raised once again. The Northern Pacific was one of the greatest land swindles or giveaways in the Republican Era that Vernon Parrington later called the Great Barbecue, for, railroad or no, the company had acquired the rights to millions of acres of land from the federal government, and, once it saw how to claim its right-of-ways, it never tired of getting more. Perhaps the people in Seattle knew what scoundrels they were dealing with, but they did not have much choice, and in 1873 they made a handsome offer to the Northern Pacific if it would build its terminal in Seattle: $250,000 in cash and bonds, 7,500 town lots, 3,000 acres of undeveloped land, and half the waterfront. An arm and a leg, as we would say.

The Northern Pacific was not interested in just an arm and a leg when it could get the whole body, and it replied by announcing that it was going to build its terminal in Tacoma, on Commencement Bay, thirty miles to the south of Seattle. Tacoma was then little more than a huddle of shacks the railroad could develop entirely as it pleased. Seattle's response, as Archie Binns has said, was both very foolish and very wise: it would build its own railroad, and not south to Tacoma to link with the Northern Pacific but east over Snoqualmie Pass to Walla Walla. There was a famous May Day picnic in 1874 at which the citizens came out and started building the road; it was a nice solidifying gesture, but not one designed to lay much track. The road was called the Seattle and Walla Walla, and Arthur Denny was its president. In the best of times Seattle would not have been able to raise enough money to do the job, and in 1873 the first feverish speculations in transcontinental railroads collapsed and no capital was available anywhere. Jay Cooke went broke. The Northern Pacific had managed to complete its spur road from the Columbia to Tacoma, but it was nowhere near able to tie that up with its transcontinental road.

There was indeed wisdom in the little city with its population of eleven hundred setting out to build its own road, as there almost always is when a city tries to keep control of its own destiny. Coal deposits had been discovered east and south of the city, in Renton, Newcastle, and the Cedar River valley. In 1876 a quiet Scottish businessman, James Colman, came to town, bought Yesler's wharf, and took over construction of the Seattle and Walla Walla. He extended the road to Renton, on the south shore of Lake Washington, and Seattle had its second major export. By this time Seattle itself had close to exhausted its own supply of timber, and within a few years would actually become an importer of wood. But Seattle, Portland, and especially San Francisco provided a good market for the coal, which was plentiful and close to the surface, and for the next ten years coal was Seattle's leading export. Furthermore, the building of the railroad, if only as far as Renton, began the process of securing the Puget Sound hinterland for Seattle business so that later, when other roads were built, and logging and farming were begun, all traffic came in and out of Seattle.

The development of the little railroad and the hookup with the coal mines is like the original cutting down of the natural dependence on San Francisco, like the opening of the Dexter Horton Bank, like the securing of the University of Washington, in that it represents an embryonic city doing all it can for itself. Though the population was only a little over a thousand, when Colman built the Seattle and

Walla Walla to Renton everything but the locomotive and the rails had been made in Seattle, including the car wheels and the castings for the one passenger car. The original settlers had been independent people and had attracted independent people—if not very many—to join them. Such individuality almost inevitably leads to diversity of local commerce and manufacture, and, in turn, economic independence.

By fair means and foul the Northern Pacific did get its railroad across the country, and in 1885 cars could leave Tacoma and find their way eventually to Saint Paul, Chicago, and New York. Tacoma itself boomed, and its population grew from 1,098 in 1880 to 36,026 in 1890. If those in Seattle had been right in thinking that the placement of the terminus would by itself decide which city on the sound would become dominant, Seattle's fate would have been sealed. Not so. Even during the decade of Tacoma's phenomenal growth, when almost all the lumber and wheat was exported from there, Seattle was growing too, because the settlers were at last coming west in sizable numbers. It boomed from 3,553 in 1880 to 42,837 in 1890 and 80,671 in 1900, while Tacoma quickly flattened out, gaining only a thousand new people between 1890 and 1900. During exactly the same period when the Northern Pacific had apparently put Tacoma in a commanding position, Seattle was in fact securing its pre-eminence.

What made Seattle was not its original location or the placement of the railroad terminus—nor was it, incidentally, the Alaska Gold Rush—but what happened inside the city itself. Here are a few sentences from *The City That Made Itself* by Welford Beaton:

> The community was small, in the scheme of things it amounted to little, yet it faced the mighty task with a grim smile that never left its face until, a score of years later, the fight was won. The struggle developed giants. No help came to the town from the outside except in the shape of new settlers whose decision to make Seattle their home was influenced by the fight she was making. Thus the city grew on her own strength and enrolled recruits with each succeeding year. . . . The reason for her growth lay in the stout hearts of her warriors.

Most successful cities have citizens who enjoy rhapsodizing as Beaton does here, but beneath his complacent boosterism lies a truth that must not be ignored just because the language is self-serving.

Seattle's first great attributes would seem to be her harbor and her forests, and of course they were essential. But harbors and trees exist all over Puget Sound, and everywhere else they yielded company towns: Tacoma (much the largest), Port Townsend, Port Ludlow, Port Gamble, Everett. Again, the presence of coal fields in eastern

King County helped Seattle, but as many places in the Appalachians show, the nearness of coal is seldom a blessing for a community. In other words, while Seattle's economy in its first generation was primarily extractive, in no way do the mere facts of forests and coal and a harbor account for Seattle's growth. I have focused on the career of Arthur Denny as a means of defining the young city's strength, partly because Denny himself was very important, partly because the kind of thing that Denny helped to do is the kind of settling that made Seattle a diverse city very early on, that made others, as Beaton says, gravitate toward Seattle when they came to the northwest.

In 1880 Seattle was still a small place of 3,553 people, but it had already developed, even as it stood fearful of losing out to Tacoma and the Northern Pacific, a remarkably sophisticated economy. There were the coal and the port, there were meat packing, carpentry, and furniture manufacture, there were foundries and bakeries and breweries, retail stores, banks, law offices, doctors, all of which operated within the city and also exported to the logging towns, mining outposts, and farming communities that were performing single operations and so were forced to rely on Seattle to get much of what they needed. Of course Seattle had to rely on San Francisco and Portland and Chicago for a great deal, but every year it was cutting down on its original dependence upon older and larger cities. That was the major impetus for the city's growth—people working in a place, seeking and making opportunities, diverse because human beings and human needs are diverse.

From 1880 on Seattle was visibly changing, and while there were significant recessions or depressions in the mid-eighties and again in the mid-nineties, it was coming into its own. Soon a man like Arthur Denny would become not so much a leader of a community of settlers as a leader of a class of people who were Republican, righteous, sober, capitalistic. Some of the newcomers soon joined that class, but many others were more transient, often recently emigrated from Europe and living according to traditions and habits that a person of limited imagination and tolerance like Denny could not easily understand. This group would include not just artisans and laborers and clerks but people of some means who were more quicksilver than Denny, more speculative or reckless. In the eighties and nineties Seattle was evolving from a hard-won settlement into a booming city, and the people who had made the settlement began, perhaps inevitably, to seem old-fashioned, mossback. But all this could happen because Denny and the others had done what they had done.

Their rootedness and their diversity were essentially the same thing; and because they were the same, Seattle could eventually become a city that might see them as mossbacks.

It is Henry George, of all people, who offers perhaps the best way for us to understand and evaluate the achievement of the founders and their generation. Had Denny ever heard of George's ideas he would have thought them heretical or treasonous, but here is a passage which marvelously describes the activities of Denny and Terry and Maynard and Bagley and the others:

> The habit of looking upon capital as the employer of labor had led both to the theory that wages depend upon the relative abundance of capital, and to the theory that interest varies inversely with wages, which it has led away from truths that but for this habit would have been apparent. . . . Capital instead of first is last; instead of being the employer of labor, it is in reality employed by labor. There must be land before labor can be exerted, and labor must be exerted before capital is produced. Capital is the result of labor, and is used by labor to assist it in further production. Labor is the active and initial force, and labor is therefore the employer of capital. Labor can only be exerted upon land, and it is from land that the matter which it transmutes into wealth must be drawn. Land therefore is the condition precedent, the field and material of labor. The natural order is land, labor, capital, and instead of starting from capital as our initial point, we should start from land.

"Land is the condition precedent, the field and material of labor"—thus Arthur Denny thought and acted, thus Seattle began and first grew. There was a constant worry that Seattle had to depend on large quantities of capital generated elsewhere: we see it in the worrying about the Northern Pacific, we will see it in the anti-Chinese episode, we will encounter it whenever we look at the development of the city's economic power.

No one has said how much money the Denny party had when they landed at Alki; it could not have been much, and it does not matter, because what the settlers needed was not money but land to be "the field and material" of their labor. Given the marvelous land, given the great and diverse labor, the city would become established and the capital would inevitably follow, "to be used by labor to assist it in further production." A sawmill, a store, a bank, town lots, a university, a railroad to nearby coal fields—small things, but everything else follows from them. Whenever Seattle has acted as though it believed this, it has prospered; and whenever it has looked elsewhere—to the east or to the government or to San Francisco—for its capital, its ideas, its essential definitions of its destiny, it has floundered. Arthur Denny's Seattle and Henry George's economic formulations are one, and in the following chapters we will have more than one occasion to use them for our guide.

Helen Malson, who later became the mother of the painter Morris Graves, was born in Seattle in 1872 and first lived at the corner of Second Avenue and Cherry Street. As she grew up, her life centered on home and church. She recalls that while she was never told where she could not go in town, she understood that south of Yesler Way was another Seattle, more transient, lower in class, more openly or gaudily sinful than her own. Something like that division had probably been in Seattle since the first sawmill, but as the city grew, the division became more marked. A young woman in the 1870s and 1880s would have known about it even if no one ever explained the hows and whys of life in a logging and port community.

Within Helen Malson's "own" community, changes were taking place too. Seattle's twelve thousand inhabitants in 1885 could be found almost entirely within ten blocks of Yesler Way. There were still stumps on parts of the original land claimed by Bell, Boren, and Denny. But the town no longer belonged to those first settlers, who were getting on in years. They had waited while they worked for the new people to come, and now, in the eighties, they were coming in some numbers. Many came and stayed only awhile, and most of these lived south of Yesler Way or near the logging operation on which they worked. Others came and settled, and they tended to live north of Yesler Way. By 1885 a good many of the twenty-one people Clarence Bagley would put before Arthur Denny in his biographical section of *History of Seattle* were already in town and beginning to make their presence felt. The dividing line of Yesler Way was there, however unstated, and one might well expect clashes or at least antagonisms between those who lived on either side of the line. The anti-Chinese incidents are representative, and a hasty look at the affair might show only this superficial division. What is most interesting, however, is that even in the midst of turmoil there was more to Seattle than class lines, capital and labor lines.

By 1885 the Chinese had been immigrating for more than a generation. A series of treaties, mostly designed to protect American interests in China, had guaranteed the right of people of either country to immigrate to the other. Most of the Chinese who came to America worked for low wages, did tasks more dangerous than others would undertake, lived under conditions others found intolerable. The whites called them coolies, and they were treated as a nameless, faceless, interchangeable mass. Eventually they began to pose a threat to white workers coming to the west because they would do as much or more for less pay. As a result, in 1882 Congress passed a Restriction Act prohibiting further immigration and denying permanent residence to Chinese already here who were not citizens. But the law was sporadically enforced because white workers did not complain while they could still find work and because the large companies, especially the railroads, continued to find the coolies useful.

The labor movement was just beginning to be organized during and after the Civil War, and it developed in the west later than elsewhere. Representatives from the Knights of Labor played a part in the anti-Chinese incidents, but as yet no union existed anywhere in Seattle. Agitation was the most the Knights could hope to accomplish. Even that represented new and often terrifying possibilities for employers, and one recurrent fear was that agitation, disturbance, or whatever would give the area a bad name and eastern capitalists would not invest here. The presumption was that capital is the "condition precedent" when there is an abundance of land to labor. If this folly represented the worst the employers could think up, the worst the agitators could do was to refuse to distinguish between coolies, employed as a slave class by large companies, and other Chinese in the area who were more settled, as launderers, houseboys, merchants, and farmers, and who posed no decent threat to anyone.

Neither side had a monopoly on callousness, on racism, on fears of a Yellow Peril. On both sides the Chinese were "an evil," "a curse," "heathens," and both agreed that sooner or later, under some conditions, the Chinese must go. What aroused the white people, really, was each other, not the Chinese.

On September 2, 1885, the Seattle *Post-Intelligencer,* the city's only real newspaper, carried two stories involving Chinese. In one a Chinaman (the term invariably in use then), having been put off a boat in Seattle because he did not have fare to Victoria, was told he must leave town or be killed because "the unfortunate fellow belongs to a company that is in bad odor with the Seattle Chinamen." In the second a man calling himself John Smith was arrested for the fatal stabbing of Chin Ah Kin. From these stories we can presume that the Chinese were in town and were not invisible, though they were obviously separate; also while they might not be citizens, their civil rights were observed to the extent that John Smiths could not get angry at one with impunity.

On September 4, the *P-I* reported an anti-Chinese incident in Rock

Springs, Wyoming, at a Union Pacific coal mine. A group of whites there set fire to houses occupied by Chinese, tried to drive the Chinese out of town, and in the process killed some and wounded others. The Republican and conservative paper had an interesting editorial about the incident four days later: "The Boston philanthropist who welcomes this alien race and calls its people his brothers, forgetting that their coming means the ruin and death of others whose white faces and Saxon speech give them a right to be called his brothers that is far stronger . . . probably feels no twinge of conscience when he reads of the massacre at Rock Springs." So while there was a "massacre," it was not just its perpetrators who were to blame. Furthermore, "it is absurd to blame the individual Chinaman for the difficulties and dangers of the Chinese question, as it would be to blame the individual negro for the rebellion and its calamities." A small city newspaper that can see this well around a problem is one that can be trusted a long way as a guide to the subsequent events.

Soon comes word of a similar incident in Squak, now Issaquah, fifteen miles east of Seattle, on the hop farm of the Wold brothers. Again, a group of whites set fire to shacks lived in by Chinese workers, killing three. For the rest of the month the *P-I* reported news of companies, in Coal Creek, Black Diamond, Bainbridge Island, and Seattle, that were either firing Chinese and hiring whites or else closing down altogether. Inevitably the Chinese and the unemployed whites gravitated from the hinterland to Seattle.

Then the meetings began. A group called the Liberal League met on September 21 at the behest or with the aid of the Knights of Labor. One of this organization's men, James McMillan, said the Knights were opposed to violence; and another, Daniel Cronin, rumbled that if the Chinese were not out of the area soon, there would be trouble. It was a low-keyed meeting, but enough to call out "taxpayers and property owners" to a countermeeting two days later, which the local paper reported much more fully. Judge Orange Jacobs, District Attorney J. T. Ronald, Governor W. C. Squire, United States Attorney Cornelius Hanford, attorneys James McNaught and J. C. Haines all spoke, and while each found ways to support law and order, the range of attitudes was wide. On one end, Hanford: "The destruction of property here by a mob would be the means of advertising us all over the world as a lawless community." On the other, Haines: "Most of the Chinamen are here in violation of the law. Three years ago the Restriction Act was passed, and since then the country has been overrun with them." Hanford was speaking about unknown capitalists in an unknown future; Haines was making an important point, one which could be used throughout the affair to divide the Law and Order people into those who wanted to defend the rights of capitalists and those who could seriously ask what the law was and what order was most wanted. Since most of the Chinese were in the country illegally, it was precisely people like Judge Jacobs, District Attorney Ronald, Governor Squire, and United States Attorney Hanford who could enforce the Restriction Act.

The next meeting of the Liberal League, by now called the Anti-Chinese Congress, heard opinions at least as diverse as those of the Law and Order people. Mayor R. Jacob Weisbach of Tacoma suggested the presence of coolie gangs on Puget Sound could be attributed to a plot by San Francisco people to keep the northwest servile by throwing its whites out of work. A Mr. Thornell complained he could not sell his cabbages because Chinese farmers sold theirs for less. A Dr. Taylor wanted to boycott all companies employing Chinese, and a Mr. Magill wanted to know how the Northern Pacific could be boycotted. A Mr. Turner said he once supported Leland Stanford for the Senate but now he thought Stanford ought to be in jail.

While these speeches were being made, a committee was in another room trying to draft resolutions that might bring order to this potential chaos. The committee's speaker was Mary Kenworthy, a fiery, resolute Seattle widow whose own ideas can be detected in the resolutions she read:

> No government can be just where elements are permitted to exist which by their nature are not fully responsible to all the duties of citizenship, and whose productions flow not in a collective fund to enrich the commonwealth. . . . They become factions in our institutions, conducive of conditions which are . . . in direct opposition with every principle of true republican democratic government, are in opposition with every law of political economy and are opposed to our homes, families, health, decency and morality.

The resolutions that followed called for all citizens to discharge their Chinese employees, for mass meetings in every community on October 3, for the congress to meet again in Seattle on November 6, and for the United States Congress to be informed that the Western Washington Congressional Association misrepresented the people when it called for a repeal of the Restriction Act.

If we can assume that it was Mary Kenworthy who drafted the resolutions, we can say she was still living, figuratively, in the Seattle of Arthur Denny. She was concerned with labor and production, not with capital; she saw her commonwealth being mutually responsive in all its elements; she saw threats to productivity as threats to "homes, families, decency, and morality." All this is consonant with the Seattle Denny had worked to settle. It is only when Kenworthy organized women to go around house to house insisting that all Chinese domestic help be let go that it is not so clear whether she was more concerned with democratic republican government or more simply against the Law and Order folks.

It is perhaps inevitable that two sides should have formed in response to the Chinese problem, perhaps inevitable too that before any settlement could be reached each side had to bring to the surface whatever suppressed feelings it harbored. We can see a good deal of this in an exchange of letters to the *P-I* on October 1 and 2, between pioneer David Denny and a shoe salesman named John Keane. Denny's letter poses questions, Keane's makes replies. (1) Denny says he spent two thousand dollars during the past year hiring foreign born, but non-Oriental laborers, because times were hard. Did he do the right thing? Keane answers that anyone who intends to become a citizen should be hired, but "the coolie slave defies the land he treads upon." (2) Denny says there are 2 million unemployed in the country, and only 150,000 Chinese. After the Chinese are evicted, who will be next? Keane's reply is ingenuous at best: if 150,000 unemployed whites are hired, they will feed the economy so that soon there will be jobs for the remaining 1,850,000. (3) Denny wants to know who can tell him whom he can and cannot employ. Keane says he should be told "if the people you hire are obnoxious or injurious to the general welfare. You say that though the Chinese take their money from the country, they leave their labor. To whom do they leave it? The parties and corporations who are more injurious to the country than the Chinese themselves. To parties whose profligacy knows hardly any limits, who spend the money abstracted from the people in the saloons of the demi-monde of Paris and the gambling dens of Baden-Baden. . . . To corporations who use the money to bribe and corrupt the legislature, both state and national, in order that they can more effectively rob and plunder the people."

That Keane's last outburst was addressed to the sober and industrious David Denny only shows how easily the argument, otherwise well enough conducted, could leave the local arena and thereby become gaudy and unreal. But Keane was usually better than this. At the first meeting of the Liberal League he had called for a general meeting of all citizens. At the next meeting of the anti-Chinese he got up to ask if it were true that the other side wanted the Chinese to stay "because Wa Chong and his crowd have mortgages on a large amount of their property." Wa Chong was the most important Chinese factor on the coast, and his local agent, Chin Chun Hock, placed an advertisement in the *P-I* every day and throughout the worst of the troubles announcing that the Wa Chong Company would contract for cheap labor on short notice. Keane's was a question no one answered satisfactorily, though the fact that the Chinese stayed long after they said they would go shows Keane may have hit a real target.

What Keane, like everyone else on both sides, did not say was that if a peaceful settlement were to be reached, it would be the Law and Order people who would reach it, by trying to enforce the Restriction Act, by determining which Chinese were legally in the country and deserving of full civil rights, by firing the Chinese coolie labor they employed. The anti-Chinese party could only threaten, although it could hardly threaten more than local covert acts of eviction. Yet, as both sides got increasingly skittish, the Law and Order people seemed inclined to worry only about mobs and about the possibility that "business prosperity will be scattered to the four winds if this country is to be published to the world as the place to which social agitators can safely resort to try their experiments of mob law," as Judge R. S. Greene intoned to a grand jury. No wonder that G. Venable Smith, a lawyer in the anti-Chinese group, told his people: "I don't know how it will be settled. It may be conflict of arms; I hope not. It may be by destruction of property; I hope not. But it is coming like a war."

Late in October came the trial of Perry Bayne, accused of being the ringleader of the group that had burned and killed in Squak in September. Clearly, the prosecutor, J. T. Ronald, really wanted a conviction, yet he managed to act so as to guarantee an acquittal. Ronald offered three witnesses immunity from prosecution—two Indians, Jim Graham and Jim Youdepump, and one white, Sam Robertson. Robertson testified that he and Bayne had met at the Wold store, gotten guns, picked up a group of Indians, gone to the tents of the Chinese, and killed three people. The Indians corroborated only to the extent of saying they were armed when arrested. J. C. Haines, the defense attorney, who was as much a member of the Law and Order party as Ronald but who understood a good deal more about both law and order, brought out the fact that it was David Denny who had made the offer of immunity to the Indians, and then he paraded a host of witnesses, all of whom testified to Perry Bayne's quiet nature and good reputation and to Sam Robertson's volatile hot-headedness. Finally, Bayne himself testified that he had gone to the Wold farm, unarmed and at Robertson's insistence. He had warned the coolies of possible violence if they did not leave and was rewarded with a shot from a Chinese tent and a volley from Robertson's group.

The jury was out for only half an hour before it brought in an acquittal. The conclusion that Ronald had tried to frame Bayne is inescapable, and it also seems certain that David Denny had bribed the Indians. There is no way of knowing what Bayne did to incite Ronald to mess up his case by going after him instead of Robertson. Bayne was not a worker displaced by the Chinese but a local blacksmith. He had indeed gone to Ingebright Wold and demanded eviction of the Chinese two days before the attack, but whatever his motives, they were not selfish or crudely partisan. Hardly a hero, but a good person, certainly. We will see his like later on, as, unfortunately, we will see the likes of J. T. Ronald.

November 6 had been set as the deadline for the departure of all Chinese from the area. On the third a large group of Tacomans, including Mayor Weisbach, apparently organized by Knights of Labor agitator Daniel Cronin, evicted all Chinese from their homes along the Tacoma waterfront, marched them to suburban Lakeview, and put them on a train for Portland. No one was hurt, but the Law and Order people were convinced that mob rule had come. Officials in Seattle wired Governor Squire in Olympia for troops, and Governor Squire in turn asked Secretary of the Interior Lucius Lamar for federal soldiers. Lamar replied that Seattle officials should try to handle the situation, and Law and Order trembled.

Mayor Yesler called a mass meeting of all citizens for November 5, and met earlier that day with some of the Anti-Chinese Committee of Fifteen, some Law and Order people, and with the presumed leader of the Chinese, Gee Hee. The mayor told the Chinese he could not prevent violence if they did not meet the November 6 deadline, and Gee Hee said all coolies were leaving immediately and all others would go as soon as they could dispose of their property and collect debts. Everyone agreed that Gee Hee's information should be announced to that evening's mass meeting, which would be attended mostly by anti-Chinese people but would be held in Frye's Opera House, where the Law and Order people usually met, and would be run by Mayor Yesler.

Unfortunately the meeting did not open with the announcement of the Chinese people's plans, but with speeches. J. C. Haines sought to smooth over differences by attacking the Yellow Peril; G. Venable Smith cautiously said that if an agreement were not reached and approved, the present meeting was a mistake. Then came Thomas

Burke, a lawyer with working-class clients who also had friends among the Law and Order people. His speech was all wrong, filled with just the sort of ignorance and innuendo that Law and Order could not recognize or appreciate but that would infuriate the anti-Chinese:

> There is no division among the people. We are all laborers, and the attempt to draw class lines is false and malicious. . . . I am a poor man, and I don't have much help, but I have not had a Chinaman in my house for two years. I pay a white woman five dollars more a month than a Chinaman would do the same work for, but it is a matter of principle with me, and I feel it my duty. . . . It has not been twenty years since I carried water on the railroad, and less than that since I worked on the dump. My brothers are laborers, and why should I speak against the working man.

The crowd quickly got restive, though Burke seems not to have seen why, even though with every word he was drawing class lines he was insisting did not exist. When he launched into Tacoma the crowd began to boo and hiss:

> The mayor of Tacoma is a foreigner and can hardly speak the English language. I have read how Germans rose up against the Jews and drove them from their homes. I remember how they drove the Russian peasants out; but what am I to think when only thirty miles from where I stand, in the Republic of the United States, such atrocities have been committed. It could not be done under an American. It was done under a German.

As a speech to an audience already split, made with the intention of showing that everyone present was everyone else's brother, this is almost incomprehensible. Murray Morgan says in *Skid Road* that "Burke's speech may well have been the greatest ever made in the Puget Sound area" because "nothing is so painful as truth told by a former friend, nothing so infuriating as an unanswerable argument." That there was pain and fury is evident. G. Venable Smith got up to ask everyone to keep listening, and Burke interrupted: "I need no one to intercede for me with a Seattle audience." The whole performance seems to me not so much courageous as aggressive and obtuse. Whatever dark feelings lay within anti-Chinese people, they had a real complaint and a real argument, which Burke could not see. In denouncing Weisbach as a German he could only bring those dark feelings to the surface, not because the argument he offered was unanswerable but because he did not seem to know what the other side was talking about. The anti-Chinese were less vulnerable to the charge that they were a mob than to the charge that they saw all Chinese in the area as coolies and so failed to separate the racial from the economic issue. Burke gave the anti-Chinese people a member of the other side they could call a villain.

Still, though they were not about to forget Burke, the crowd went home after John Leary announced the agreement reached earlier in the day; when they met the following night, the Anti-Chinese Congress contented itself with progress reports, laughter at the mayor's proclamation urging everyone to stay home, and agreement that Chinese business people should be allowed to wind up their affairs. It was announced that all Chinese had left Newcastle, Renton, and Tacoma, and that upwards of two hundred Chinese had left Seattle already. The congress apparently felt it had won or was winning, and was pleased without gloating.

Everything died down for two months. The grand jury charged by Judge Greene back in October had returned an indictment against the Anti-Chinese Committee of Fifteen and they were to be tried in January, but in its year-end summary of news the *P-I* spoke of the anti-Chinese incidents as a thing of the past. Many Chinese were still in town, and neither Gee Hee nor the Law and Order people were making any serious effort to get them to leave in an orderly fashion. Thus, when the Committee of Fifteen went on trial, and prosecutor Ronald proceeded to bungle this one as badly as he had the Perry Bayne trial, trouble was brewing again. One defendant, it turned out, was not even a member of the committee, and others had only newspaper accounts offered in evidence against them. Still others, who admitted meeting to plan something along the lines of the expulsion effected in Tacoma, claimed that at no time had violent or unlawful expulsion been contemplated. Since the group was charged with conspiring to deny the civil rights of the Chinese, one of Ronald's difficulties was that no one could say precisely what their civil rights were, especially for those who had entered the country illegally. But without even foundering on these reefs Ronald had troubles enough. The case against some of the committee was dismissed and the others were acquitted. Once again, incidentally, J. C. Haines had served as attorney for the anti-Chinese people.

But Wa Chong continued to advertise cheap labor on short notice long after whatever time others would have needed to wind up their affairs. Most estimates of the number of Chinese remaining in Seattle are based on the February outbursts and so are not fully reliable, but 350 is a minimum figure. Clearly the anti-Chinese people had failed in their primary aim, and some decided, finally, to act.

On the morning of February 7 a group of white men entered Chinatown. They were led by men named McMillan, Metcalfe, Kidd,

Rochester, and Winscott, none of whom except McMillan had been prominent in the Anti-Chinese Congress in the fall. The group claimed they were investigating violations of the city's cubic air ordinance and, wherever they gained admission, they ordered the Chinese to pack, while various teamsters hauled movable furniture to the steamer *Queen of the Pacific*. The operation had been well planned and was in its first stages quietly executed. When Chief of Police W. C. Murphy arrived an hour after evictions had begun, he could only run from group to group and watch.

Near the end of the morning John Keane, on his way home from church, saw a huge crowd at the dock and learned for the first time what happened. Sheriff John H. McGraw was at the dock and told Keane he and his men would not interfere as long as the Chinese were not being forced onto the boat. Keane found a young man named Wah who spoke English and told him to ask everyone on board if they had been forced to leave. Wah returned and said no. McGraw had Wah repeat the operation several times because he wanted to make sure he adhered to the law. United States Attorney Hanford appeared and insisted that there was a difference between not being forced to leave and wanting to leave. Wah went back on board and returned saying yes, some wanted to stay.

Meanwhile Governor Squire wired for federal troops and issued a proclamation urging people to stay home. A number of Law and Order people were deputized: George Kinnear's group, the Home Guards; the Volunteers; the Seattle Rifles; Company D of the territorial militia, headed by J. C. Haines. Judge Greene issued a habeas corpus writ ordering all Chinese to stay to appear in his court the next morning. Captain Alexander of the *Queen of the Pacific* said that whatever the law decided, he could not take more than two hundred Chinese on board. At seven o'clock the following morning the leaders of the eviction group were arrested, including, for some reason, John Keane, who had been in church at the time. The Chinese were then escorted to Judge Greene's court, where each was asked if he wanted to stay. Of the eighty-seven there, seventy-two said they wanted to leave. The whole group was taken back to the dock, and when news of what had happened passed among the Chinese left on the dock, many said they would gladly go if their way was paid. Various people—including Mary Kenworthy, John Keane, and Sheriff McGraw—made pledges totaling fourteen hundred dollars. Two hundred Chinese boarded the ship and the others were told they would have to wait for the *Elder* when it docked in a few days.

The sticky moment had arrived when the Chinese who were not leaving had to be taken back to Chinatown and protected. The Chinese started down Main Street with McGraw in front and Kinnear's Home Guard in the rear. Kinnear, in an account he wrote many years later, remembered that "the street was packed full of raving, howling, angry men, threatening revenge on those who were interfering with their lawlessness." Obviously a crowd was milling about, ignorant of the agreement that had been reached at the dock, pushy, angry, but unarmed. The crowd closed in, shots were fired, and five of the crowd were wounded. A fireman later said he saw a deputy clubbing a man and a member of the mob trying to wrestle a gun from a deputy. A man named Mulrane was shot in the lungs by an officer or deputy. Another, Charles Stewart, said he confronted officers with, "Hold on, gentlemen. What are you going to do with these Chinamen?" and was told, "You come along with us." When he refused, he was grabbed, thrown to the ground, shot twice, and fatally wounded.

Shortly after the shots were fired, J. C. Haines tried to explain to the crowd the agreement reached at the dock. Some shouted back: "Burke! Burke! Give us Burke!" Burke was a leading deputy and some had not forgotten the November speech. Then John Keane told everyone to go home and the crowd began to disperse. There was a lot of invective later about mob rule, but it is clear that the crowd was angry primarily because it thought it had been betrayed, perhaps even by its leaders. It is also clear that the deputies and volunteer militia, understandably edgy, had been more violent than the mob.

Federal troops arrived the next day, the city quieted down, and a week later about seventy-five Chinese went on board the *Elder*, while maybe as many stayed. Wa Chong continued to advertise that cheap labor could be contracted for on short notice.

Perry Bayne of Squak was a blacksmith, John Keane sold shoes, G. Venable Smith was a lawyer (about to embark on an ill-fated utopian adventure on the Olympic Peninsula), Mary Kenworthy, a widow. These people were artisans and bourgeois, not themselves threatened by coolie labor, but caring nonetheless. The salt of the earth, and every city has such people, but in a crisis in 1885 in Seattle they could in effect prevail, not by controlling events or masterminding them, but by speaking for concerns that were not simply partisan. The sides taken in this dispute could be ugly, but they were never allowed to become so fixed that these people, and their counterparts on the other side, could be overlooked or overcome.

John Keane, though the least known of the group, seems the most impressive. It is a shame that he should otherwise be so anonymous, a name only in city directories and perhaps on a tombstone somewhere, but the fact that he can be located now only in connection with this incident may be the best illustration we have of the man he was and the circumstances, and the city, by which he is known at all. For all his florid talk about the saloons of the Paris demimonde in his exchange of letters with David Denny, he came out best there. Along with Smith and Kenworthy he consistently could see how to take the Knights of Labor talk offered by Cronin and McMillan and make it a local argument about local matters. Keane helped keep matters in hand on the dock on February 7, and helped get them back in hand on the streets the next day. It says much that such a person, forceful, unknown, without recognizable personal interest or connection, could play so large a part in such potentially destructive circumstances. It was people like Keane who kept the affair from being a clash of the self-interests of capital and labor, fueled by racial hatreds. So long as he could be heard there would be no mob. He and the others like him were the best possible repudiation of the fears of the Hanfords and the brutal antagonisms of the Cronins.

On the whole the Law and Order people come out looking less good. Theirs was the opportunity to do the best that the instincts of law, order, and property could wish them to do, and they muffed it. Arthur Denny may have been given to denouncing the lazy, but he would not, at least in his prime, have fallen into the moral arrogance of George Kinnear, R. S. Greene, and Cornelius Hanford, or the pugnacious obtuseness of Thomas Burke. The very fact that Denny's most obvious "heirs" could have failed so fully to see that land and labor are the conditions precedent tells us much to be on guard for in the next generation, the boom years. Yet, during the worst of the February troubles Sheriff John McGraw was consistently sensible, cool, and strong (he later went on to become governor in 1892). J. C. Haines, furthermore, is worth matching against John Keane, and, as with Keane, it is a pity he is not better known and now not very knowable. He showed by his successful defense of people on the "other side" that he knew the civil rights essential to law and order; his Company D played a major role in controlling the wilder elements in the mob and among the deputized volunteers. He was given to haughtiness, and to virulent attacks on the Yellow Peril, but he instinctively practiced aristocratic virtues that are the hardest qualities to find in a small frontier city.

Given the nature of the anti-Chinese incidents—unrest, factionalism, threats and fears and counterthreats—we need not be surprised that there was much in the story that is ugly. It was not Burke or Cronin who ruled the day, but Keane and Haines, Smith and McGraw, and, we might add parenthetically, the *Post-Intelligencer*, which did a good job of keeping its Republican head through most of the fall and winter. Seattle was growing quickly now, becoming more amorphous, more powerful, more capable of generating strife, but when the pinch had come it had remained strong in its strongest virtue, which was a diverse and not easily labeled citizenry.

III

Premier City of the Northwest, 1890–1910

On June 6, 1889, a fire started in the basement of a store on First Avenue near Madison Street and quickly spread throughout downtown. By the time it was contained that night it had destroyed sixty acres covering more than thirty blocks, and Seattle's downtown was in ruins. Damages were estimated àt ten million dollars.

In a stagnating city such disasters can deal a death blow, but in a healthy one they are almost always spurs to new and greater growth. San Francisco recovered quickly from its earthquake, Chicago from its fire, Japan and Germany from the devastations of World War II, because the essential ingredient had not been lost: people with energy, expertise, and no desire to leave. The worst things that happen to cities happen slowly, and Seattle had no intention of giving up just when it was enjoying its first great spurt of growth. Within a few years downtown Seattle was rebuilt, in stone and brick rather than wood. The reconstruction can be considered a badge of youthful pride, because Seattle was now more than able to build in such a manner. It had passed from a city whose major business lay in the export of logs and coal to one that imported its raw materials and exported mostly manufactured goods. It had enough brickmakers, masons, ironworkers, foundries, electrical workers, plumbers, cement manufacturers, and roofers so that the fire was in fact a boon to an expanding and increasingly diversified economy.

The story that can be derived from statistics is very revealing here. Since this period, roughly from 1880 to 1910, was the period when Seattle and Tacoma were in closest competition for the claim to preeminence on Puget Sound, and therefore in the entire state, a comparison between the two should be helpful. First, a rehearsal of the population figures:

	1880	1890	1900	1910
Seattle	3,553	42,837	80,671	237,174
Tacoma	1,098	36,006	37,714	41,801

Seattle's figures resemble Portland's, Los Angeles', or Chicago's in their first decades of great growth. Tacoma's are like those for Holyoke, Massachusetts, Bridgeport, Connecticut, or Scranton, Pennsylvania. In Seattle a first burst was followed by a second decade of steady growth and a third of explosive growth. In Tacoma the first burst, between 1880 and 1890, was the only significant one. By the nineties the company-town quality of Tacoma's urbanization was taking its toll. In the Panic of 1893 all but one of Tacoma's banks failed while Seattle's survived by pooling their resources and soon were prospering again. In the panic it became clear that the business community and the public no longer trusted the railroads, and so Tacoma was in deep trouble. Seattle's business, less tied to speculation, withstood the original shock of the crisis and was strong enough to profit nicely from the shot in the arm given it by the Gold Rush in Alaska.

A brief comparison of the manufacturing figures for the two cities is revealing here. In 1890 Tacoma had 225 mechanical and manufacturing industries, which took 4,000 employees to turn an investment of $7 million into manufacture worth $10.5 million. Of this last total, more than a quarter was in lumber. Ten years later the total number of establishments had grown to 381, but there were many signs that all was not well. The total invested in manufacture had risen only slightly, as had the number of employees; the value of goods produced had risen from $10.5 million to $12 million, but the increase had come only because of an increase in flour milling, the one industry besides lumber that had grown because of the new transcontinental railroad. Elsewhere was sag or collapse. Bread-making had fallen in value from $218,000 to $90,000, plumbing and gas fitting from $703,000 to $117,000. While the industries directly connected with the railroad and the harbor had held their own, all the others had fallen off, which meant that essential goods and services, either for the manufacturing establishment or the general citizenry, were either less available or expensively imported. Very obviously, everything that Tacoma was less able to do for itself Seattle would benefit from if it could be the source of supply.

This it undoubtedly was able to be a good deal of the time. In the same ten-year period Seattle's number of manufacturing establishments grew from 331 to 953, its invested capital from just under $6 million to just over $10 million, its value produced by manufacture from just over $10 million to just over $26 million. Bread-making and plumbing and gas fitting, as well as many other industries that were sagging in Tacoma, grew, but, more exciting and important, hosts of new products and services were being offered in Seattle that had never existed in the territory or state before: awnings, tents, and sails; bicycle and tricycle repair; bottling; boxes; bridge-building; factory-produced cheese and butter; factory-produced women's clothing; spices and roasted and ground coffee; lock and gun smithing; looking-glass and picture frames; mattresses and box springs; mineral and soda water; optical goods; oyster canning; paving and paving materials; plastering and stucco work; window shades.

Perhaps the saddest fact about Tacoma between 1890 and 1900 is that those most responsible for its leveling off suffered least. However much major investors lost in the 1893 panic, by 1900 they were, if they had invested in railroads, lumber, and flour, doing better than in 1890. It was everyone else who had to struggle. In a locally famous 1894 *Harper's Weekly* article a man at Seattle's Rainier Club is quoted as saying: "Well, gentlemen, if I were a man of wealth seeking a home and investments on Puget Sound, I would live in Tacoma and invest in Seattle." In 1894 there were many large houses in Tacoma on the bluffs above Commencement Bay, and the city had become sufficiently quiescent that people living in these houses would not have to worry about nouveau riche pushiness for another two or three generations. There would be no new wealth in Tacoma; the rich would get richer while the rest of the city stagnated.

Seattle, by contrast, was taking advantage of its new transcontinental railroad line to aid not just those who already were doing major business. It was making for itself, and for export to places like Tacoma, what all cities in the area had previously had to import from elsewhere. It was taking on some of the finer aspects of a barter economy, in which a carpenter builds a home for the tailor who made his clothes and the tombstone sculptor is paid by the person who made his mattress. Given all this, one can see why the boost Seattle received from the Gold Rush was not a major contributor to its essential economic development. Of course the Gold Rush was exciting and of course it did help, but if it had been the crucial event it often has been taken to be, we would expect a falling off in Seattle when the gold ran out, as it quickly did. In fact, the opposite happened. If prospectors came to Seattle to buy goods and a steamer ticket, they did so because the goods were available and the ships were already here, going to Alaska. Erastus Brainerd was back east doing lavish public relations work for Seattle; but Bellingham, or Port Townsend, or even Tacoma could have had five Brainerds and would have gained little from them. Being closer to Alaska than Tacoma, Portland, or San Francisco may have helped Seattle, but not enough to have made a great difference. Seattle's relation to this gold rush was actually like San Francisco's to the Gold Rush of 1849. In both cases the cities profited because they were already in existence and were able to provide essential goods and services when the miners arrived. In both cases, when the gold ran out and the mining towns folded, the cities went on to periods of greater and stronger growth.

Perhaps the most revealing of the Census manufacturing figures is the one called "all other industries," which designates the horde of small establishments, probably only one or two to a product, that dot any healthy city's manufacturing life. "All other industries" in 1900 had much the largest amount invested, was the third largest employer and the fourth largest in dollar value added by manufacture. Money in large amounts was being invested in these small establishments even though many of them were new, operating on hope and perhaps a shoestring, and were necessarily inefficient as they learned how to make artificial limbs or to refine molasses. Land and labor being the conditions precedent, capital was following where the labor was best being expended, and on land that therefore was becoming increasingly valuable. People were coming by the thousands, looking for and finding new work, creating in the process still more opportunities that would lead to another decade of explosive growth.

Seattle in the nineties, to judge by the standards of old cities or even of Seattle no more than ten years later, must have been a crude, somewhat primitive place. It must have been, nonetheless, a very exciting place. Give me back the days when I was still becoming, still to be, says Goethe's Faust—*that* was the great time.

Let us take a look at the layout of Seattle then. The year I have chosen to work with is the year of the Gold Rush, 1897.

SEATTLE IN 1897

The city was moving out from its original center in all available directions. Since Elliott Bay was on the west and the tideflats were on the south, expansion had always been to the north, east, and southeast. After the fire of 1889 came a very gradual shift in the center of business activity away from Yesler's Wharf and First Avenue South and up toward the land of Arthur Denny's original claim, where many established settlers had their homes. The core of the city was still the five blocks on either side of Yesler Way, between First and Third avenues. The big office blocks were there, the leading hotels and banks, the municipal buildings, almost all massive, brick and stone, about five stories tall, with large, high-ceilinged rooms and few windows. Even within this core, though, there was a great deal of variety: rooming houses, grocery stores, a cigar maker, a women's clothing factory, a wholesaler, a few one-family homes.

North and east of the core the number of large buildings declined and the small stores, small factories, and frame houses increased. Arthur Denny's house was on First, near University Street; Dexter Horton's was at 1206 Third Avenue, between Seneca and University; George Frye, Arthur Denny's son-in-law and owner of Frye's Opera House, had his home on Pike just off Fifth; James Colman lived on Fourth, and Henry Yesler's mansion was just north of the Skid Road itself. These houses were large, but not set off in splendid isolation; Arthur Denny may have maintained his status as founding father by always keeping a cow in his backyard, but his house was surrounded by boardinghouses and small stores. The outstanding building on Denny's old claim was still old University Hall. The University of Washington itself had moved out to a large tract north of Portage Bay, and the downtown building in 1897 was used only as a dormitory by students who commuted by streetcar out to the new campus.

An ordinary promotional picture of Second Avenue during this period, such as might be sent out by the Chamber of Commerce or used by Erastus Brainerd to promote Gold Rush business, would show crowded streets filled mostly with well-dressed people, streetcars, and a few automobiles, in order to dispel any notion that Seattle was just a rough frontier boom town. Such pictures were not staged; but the life of downtown, including the life of Second Avenue just north of Yesler, was not restricted to shoppers and wealthy business people. If downtown included no heavy industry, it did have furniture and cabinet makers, machine shops, groceries, laundries, dressmakers, meat and fish merchants, and in a great many instances the owners and employees of these businesses lived there or nearby. The boardinghouses accommodated not only transients like salesmen and sailors, but also jewelers, engineers, teachers of anything from the violin to penmanship, clairvoyants, midwives, retired couples. There were rooms not just for the single and the childless but for whole families and groups of families. The city directory estimates the total population of Seattle in 1897 to be 65,000, and of that number as many as 15,000 lived downtown. There were of course many transients and laborers—by 1900 most of the downtown dwellers would have moved to somewhere else in Seattle while an equally large number took their place—but most unskilled workers lived nearer the sawmills, shingle companies, packing plants, and railroad lines at the edge of the city, and most of the transient population was made up of people on the move rather than drifters. In the downtown area the fishermen, sailors, and the apparently unemployed tended to live west of First Avenue, near the water. Nearer the heart of the city one found not just cooks, waiters, domestics, hotel managers, and janitors, but many others who obviously did not have to live there: doctors, lawyers, real estate and investment brokers, office managers, stenographers, and bookkeepers. The office blocks were not all offices; many had apartments adjacent to and above offices and showrooms. Five adult men, all named Lock, each working at a different job, lived together in a boardinghouse on Seventh Avenue. Oscar Atwood was treasurer of the Globe Wallpaper Company at 907 Second Avenue and lived three blocks away at 1103 Third Avenue; his widowed mother ran a boardinghouse across the street from Globe Wallpaper, at 904 Second Avenue. Starting just from that information, one can begin a novel. The alleys between the streets, now seldom used because office buildings have little use for them, were hives of activity then. In one stretch of alley between First and Second avenues were a print shop, a contractor's office, a painter's office, and a shoe outlet.

Of course there was some distinction between business and residence, rich and poor, but it was never so absolute or clearly defined as to prevent a constant mixing of people and types of activity. First Avenue had the bulk of the older hotels and business blocks, of which the Arlington Hotel and the Colman Building are good existing examples. Second Avenue had the big retail stores, the Bon Marche and Frederick, Nelson, and Munro, and the two major newspapers, the *Post-Intelligencer* and the *Times*. In just a few years the first of the "skyscrapers," Louis Sullivanesque buildings of structural steel and many windows, would begin to be built along Second Avenue. Third Avenue had a quiet, pastoral air, created by a row of trees and the presence of a number of churches.

But these separations of activity were small, and the overall impression one gets is of variety and heterogeneity. There were no zones, no restricted areas, so light industry and office work were next to each other, and both were next to all kinds of residences. People who, according to politics or economic level or religious persuasion, were "natural enemies" lived and worked and shopped side by side, and the evidence is strong that this led not to irritation or exacerbation of differences but to tolerance and tolerable harmony. From the anti-Chinese episode we know that there were many in Seattle who distrusted or disliked Judge Thomas Burke. He lived, when his wife was on one of her frequent trips, at the Rainier Club, the Mecca of business people, on Fourth Avenue, and his office was in the Burke Building, which he had built, on Second and Madison. Many of those who thought of themselves as Burke's enemies lived and worked right there, and would have seen him pass by once or twice a day. When one's enemy is just another person who lives nearby, one is less threatened than by an institution, a building, or someone who lives miles away, in a world one cannot enter.

The most densely populated areas outside downtown proper were on either side, to the north and south, because it was easier to build parallel to the water, on grades less steep than those facing any development to the east. Just north of downtown rose Denny Hill, on which was the Old Washington Hotel but on the slopes of which little building was possible. North of Denny Hill was the land originally claimed by William Bell, Thomas Mercer, and David Denny, which extended to five natural barriers: Elliott Bay on the west, Queen Anne Hill and Lake Union on the north, Capitol Hill on the east, Denny Hill on the south. Since the land east and west of Denny Hill was relatively flat, however, there never had been serious impediments to building in this area once the city began building north of downtown. There were no tall buildings here, few large hotels, office blocks, or stores. Compared with downtown, everything was on a smaller scale: a few large houses, many boardinghouses, small businesses, and one-family homes. Some of the oldest houses still standing in Seattle can be found here, between Fairview and Eastlake avenues. Dave Beck, later labor boss of Seattle, grew up in various locations in this area, and he gives the impression that the residents of the neighborhood were largely artisans and working-class people. But the area was not so homogenized that people making good money in trade were prevented from living there, near where they were making their fortunes, in furniture manufacturing, in hay and grain dealing, in farm equipment manufacture and repair, in retail stores. Frederick's two partners lived here, Nelson on Fifth near Lenora, Munro on Pontius, as did Edward Nordhoff, manager of the Bon Marche; the head of the Salvation Army; the owner of the Rainier Beach Railway; the widow of William Bell. In the larger houses we find instance after instance of a carpenter, a streetcar conductor, a schoolteacher, and a clerk, all related, all living together. It was an area where populist and progressive ideas grew, ranging from middle-class causes like women's suffrage and prohibition to trade unionism of various shades of radicalism and militancy.

South of the Skid Road was different, as it had always been. The tideflats began to be filled as early as 1895, and the small area bounded by them, the steep hills to the east, and downtown, had from the beginning been the roughest and presumably the most sinful section of Seattle. There were almost no single-family houses in the area, but, rather, a great many residential hotels, occupied mostly by transients; the sailors' and longshoremen's unions and housing facilities; shacks huddled for a few blocks around the American Log and Shingle factory; The Parlor, and its competitors in the saloon and brothel businesses. The anti-Chinese "riot" took place here, and, by reputation, the militant anti-Chinese lived here, though John Keane and Mary Kenworthy and G. Venable Smith and others whose names have survived did not. No one of prominence lived in this area, though many prominent people worked here, along First Avenue South below Yesler Way, in what had been the city's central commercial district, with the Dexter Horton Bank, the Kinnear, the Terry-Denny, and the Maynard buildings. By 1897, however, only the older firms were here, and new businesses were settling north of Yesler, away from the warehouses and flophouses and seamen's hotels.

The Chinese who had been evicted had not returned, though the Wa Chong Company was still operating, and Gee Hee had his store on Washington Street. Japanese had begun to immigrate to Seattle and had settled here, as had the Filipinos, and, perhaps more surprisingly, the Jews. It was not a ghetto in the usual sense, because many gentile whites lived here; but almost no minorities lived anywhere else, except the more affluent Jews, like Kline, Rosenberg, and Gottstein, who had stores on First Avenue just north of Yesler. The impression one gets is that racial or religious discrimination was something assumed rather than thought about or acted upon. One finds in the speeches and writings of whites of all classes and backgrounds easy stereotypes of Asians, Jews, and blacks, and quite obviously enough racial segregation implicitly existed that the stereotypes did not have to be questioned. The clerk or machinist who might come to know Judge Thomas Burke because the two lived and worked near each other might never even see a Jew, a Japanese, or a

black, and so could feel free to think of them simply as types: Shy-
lock, or sly and inscrutable, or lazy and shiftless.

The residential nature of this area south of Yesler Way probably
meant that it was not as wild and dangerous as many who lived elsewhere in the city thought. Single women who were not prostitutes
did not walk the streets here, but this is not to say they could not
have done so. It was the sort of area that a booming seaport town had
to have, the sort that could be denounced if need for righteousness
arose, or indulged if it came time to think of Skid Road as colorful. A
number of later Hollywood films about the Klondike open in a
theater-saloon-whorehouse here; a leading character in John Dos
Passos' *The 42nd Parallel* gets drunk and is rolled here; Murray
Morgan's tale of John Considine in *Skid Road* offers lots of colorful
sights and sounds. In 1897 the Skid Road area was probably quieter,
less gaudy, and less pretentiously sinful than it was to become a decade or so later, when Seattle had more than tripled its population
and was veering more sharply from wet to dry, to radical left and to
radical right. If there were illegal activities, they were almost certainly taking place more out in the open here than anywhere else in
the city, but it was nonetheless primarily a residential section and so
more ongoing and orderly in its day-to-day living than its reputation
gives it credit (or blame) for.

First Hill, the name given to the area directly east of downtown,
was the first of Seattle's efforts to make a "good neighborhood." As
we have seen, the older settlers, like Denny, Colman, Yesler, and
Horton, did not move out of the downtown area as they grew older;
but the newer rich wanted to be able to use their neighborhood as
well as their house as a badge of their status. First Hill was an obvious choice, because it was close to downtown without being part of
it and because it occupied a commanding position. Anyone who
lived in the first eight or ten blocks could look east, up the hill, and
see the houses of the newly important.

The roll call of First Hill residents is almost a roll call of Seattle's financial muscle at the turn of the century: James T. Hoge, secretary-
treasurer of the *Post-Intelligencer* and later president of Union Savings and Trust and builder of the Hoge Building; Cornelius Hanford,
now United States district judge; Jacob Furth, president of Seattle
National Bank and a little later manager of the streetcar lines for the
Boston firm of Stone and Webster; Charles Frye, of Frye and Bruhn,
meatpackers, and later founder of the Frye Museum; August Chil-
berg, banker, shipowner, manager of an immigration service for
Scandinavians (a kind of Gee Hee for the city's largest immigrant

population); Eugene Semple, former territorial governor and long-time promoter of tideflat and canal companies; Morgan Carkeek, the city's leading contractor; Crawford and Conover, real estate developers; James Lowman, of the city's leading stationery store and publisher, Lowman and Hanford; John McGraw, former sheriff, former governor of Washington, and president of the First National Bank; John McDougall of the department store, McDougall and Southwick; Charles Malmo, who later made a small fortune in nurseries; William Pigott, later founder of Pacific Car and Foundry.

Yet for all the largeness and impressiveness of the mansions built by these people, there was obviously something fragile about the neighborhood, and within no more than two generations almost all the great First Hill homes were gone, while the other old "good neighborhoods" then coming into existence lasted. Of the thirty to forty mansions on First Hill, only Joshua Green's home on Minor, the University Club on Boren, and a handful of others remain. Most of the original builders moved away when something apparently better or farther from downtown Seattle opened up, most notably The Highlands in 1909, with its fence, beautiful golf course, and five-acre lots. The First Hill houses were apparently not an attraction for people moving into Seattle or money later on, and one by one they came down and First Hill became the city's hospital district. It is as though these mansions were built as a kind of show, so that when the show moved elsewhere, the buildings and their assertive wealth no longer seemed attractive.

All the other neighborhoods coming into existence in the 1890s were the result of streetcar lines moving north and east from downtown and providing opportunities for settling that were obviously attractive to all but the poorest. The First Avenue line ran north from downtown and part way up Queen Anne Hill; the Yesler line ran out to Leschi Park and the Taylor sawmill on Lake Washington; the East Union line started at 14th and eventually wound its way down to Lake Washington at Madrona Beach; the East Madison line went out to Madison Park on the lake; the Broadway went north from Yesler out Capitol Hill to City Park (to be renamed Volunteer Park after the Spanish-American War) and Lakeview Cemetery.

Along or near these lines one could find houses as grand or pretentious as any in Seattle proper, and often they were only a few yards or a block away from a simple carpenter's or contractor's house. On Queen Anne and Capitol hills, which had been completely logged off, not far away would be the house of a farmer, dairyman, or blacksmith, and the sheep might safely graze. The Kinnears lived on

Queen Anne near the land they had given the city for a park, as did David Blaine, who had come to Seattle back in 1853 and had been the city's first minister before becoming wealthy in various partnerships with Arthur Denny. The lumberman A. S. Kerry had a large house on the west slope of Capitol Hill; Judge J. J. McGilvra, who had developed the area almost single-handedly, lived in his mansion in Madison Park; the fumbling prosecutor during the anti-Chinese incidents, J. T. Ronald, now Judge Ronald, lived in Rainier Heights on a bluff above Lake Washington near Jackson Street. One interesting fact about these and similar houses, incidentally, is that when they sought to command views at all, they faced toward the city: it was Seattle, not Mount Rainier or the Olympics, one wanted to be able to see. All this was to change quite quickly in the next ten or fifteen years, when the "democratic" mixing of rich and bourgeois and settled poor was replaced by a more self-conscious sorting out of neighborhoods into good and not so good. At that time the commanding view of the city was given up for a house less easy to spot from the street or the streetcar and whose view was of a lovely garden in the backyard, of water and mountain.

These areas constituted Seattle in 1897. Except in the dream of speculators, there was no Magnolia, no Montlake, no Washington Park, no Mount Baker, little development on Beacon Hill or south of Jackson Street. But there was a great deal outside the city limits that is worth mentioning, especially since most of it would be annexed to Seattle within fifteen years. Once again the development was along streetcar and railway lines. The Rainier Avenue Electric Company ran from Twelfth Avenue and Washington as far south as Rainier Beach just north of Renton, but as yet it had not become the artery for much business; the Italian truck farms that were to fill Rainier Valley came a little later. Except for a few farms and small lumber operations near the railway's stations—Wetmore, Columbia, Matthiesen, Dunlap—the land was almost empty of people. Columbia City could pretend to be a little more than a train stop because it had stores, a church, and a school. It also had what may have been a very interesting resident, a man named Reeves, Professor Reeves because he was a professor of Romance Languages at the University of Washington, which in those days was almost two hours away from Columbia City. He was also president of a firm called the Co-op Irrigation Company, which may have occupied him a good deal more than his teaching. Due south of the city, beyond the tideflats, farming villages along the Duwamish—River Park, Van Asselt, Duwamish, Georgetown, South Park—were distinct from the city and from each other until the tideflats were filled in. A ferry ran to West Seattle from downtown, and a trip across Elliott Bay was a favorite Sunday excursion; but West Seattle itself then did not have many more people than when Charles Terry had named it New York–Alki.

A good deal more was happening to the north of Seattle. Ballard was a town of about twenty-five hundred people, a company operation owned and operated by the Stimson Mill. Situated at the east end of Salmon Bay, Ballard had not yet become the fishing port and Scandinavian enclave it was to be within a generation. The people who worked for Stimson lived in Ballard, or Ross (now North Queen Anne), or Fremont, and seem during this period to have been almost as isolated from Seattle as were the millworkers across the Sound. Just east of Ballard a strip of land running north from Lake Union to 85th Street had become part of the city of Seattle as early as 1891, mostly as the result of the gift of Woodland Park, which a little later contained the zoo. A streetcar ran north from Lake Union to Green Lake, and the whole area offered rich prospects for speculators. W. D. Wood, Seattle's mayor in 1897, lived near Green Lake; B. F. Day had built near where a school was given his name; a journal called the *Pioneer Weekly* was published here. Mostly, however, the people who lived in this area worked for Stimson in Ballard.

Farther east, along the railroad line of the Seattle, Lake Shore and Eastern, was the community of Brooklyn and the University of Washington, both of which were just beginning a quick development as the result of a streetcar that ran out from downtown along the east shore of Lake Union, over the University Bridge, and out to Ravenna Park. Students at the university could commute from almost every part of Seattle, and if none came as far as Professor Reeves of Columbia City, many came from Ballard, Queen Anne, downtown, and First Hill. The university as yet consisted of only a few buildings, and was at the time wrangling with Governor John R. Rogers about control of the school. It was gradually throwing off its high school and finishing school image, having 303 college-level students enrolled full-time. East of the university and north of Ravenna Park the land was still in the process of being logged off; James Colman owned the mill community of Yesler, at the north end of Union Bay near what is now Laurelhurst. The land had all been bought up, to be sure, but the loggers were just getting to it.

The city was all very new, not just at its fringes, but everywhere. Seattle had gained about four-fifths of its 1897 population in the preceding ten years. No wonder, then, that there were more carpenters than members of any other identifiable trade; no wonder Seattle was an importer of lumber. A host of schools had to be built, streets and sewers had to be put in, the water system had to be revamped, the public transportation had to be developed—Seattle had to begin to think like a city. It was building on a very strong base, and as the earlier comparison with Tacoma shows, it was developing its opportunities in healthy ways. Perhaps, however, our geographical survey can show us other ways of understanding this urban health, even though they are less definite than statistics and more subject to speculation and error. The most striking single fact about Seattle in 1897 is that, with the exception of First Hill, different land uses and economic classes everywhere were being mixed. This mixing had not been planned, and probably could not have worked well if it had been. Instead, it had resulted from the great variety of work being done, which gave people mobility and opportunity, which mottled the economic scale with so many variations and changes that class lines could not easily form or harden, which perhaps just gave people so much to do that they could not afford the luxury of worrying or being contemptuous of their neighbors.

In any city most of the people one meets are strangers, and in no city is there only one class or caste of people. The clearer and stronger the class lines, the stronger the tie one feels to the people of one's own class or caste—or style or race or religious belief. Under these conditions one is more apt simply to label those not of one's own class. "They" are the bosses, or the workers, or the people who live on Skid Road or First Hill. When work and place of residence easily mix people, however, "They" no longer seems an appropriate label, and when the mixing is of genuinely and variously different people, the labels disappear. This mixing has nothing to do with liking other people, nothing to do with civic spirit; it has to do with feeling at home in a community of people who are strangers one to another and going separate ways. In a healthy city the outside world is not of one's own making or choosing, but one is not threatened by it and indeed one can easily find it exhilarating. Seattle in the nineties can be imagined as a place where in the course of working, living one's life, securing one's family and privacy, one also could learn a great deal about all that lay outside, and feel one's sense of freedom expanded by the number of opportunities available. It was not a refined place, a cosmopolitan place, a neat or a particularly clean place: even in the downtown area there were unpaved streets; outside there must have been a good deal of mud, a fair amount of poor lighting and primitive plumbing; landscaping must have been an indulgence of the wealthy, like stables or an automobile. As we usually measure cities, then, Seattle was altogether young, raw, and crude. But the truly essential needs of cities are diversity and opportunity, and these Seattle had, mixed and unplanned.

In such a city as Seattle in 1897, problems are going to pile up quickly: there are the practical and immediate ones like control of the "natural monopolies" of water, sewage, electricity, transportation, schools, ports, and terminals; and the national issues then coming to the fore, including unions and the rights of workers, women's suffrage, prohibition, restrictions on business, the federal income tax, restrictions on immigration, the democratic or antidemocratic intent of the United States Constitution. In a company town such issues need never be fought, or, if they are, the outcome is likely to be acrimonious and defeating. In a stagnating city small groups usually raise the key issues and are met with entrenchment and apathy. In Seattle, young, leggy, prosperous, filled with energetic people, one need not look for peace or harmony. One might find, however, a balance being struck between parties or factions. What was really a process—first land, then labor, then capital—would not abort into fights between capital and labor; that way the rights of individuals could be harmonized with a generalized sense of the public good. Seattle in 1897 had a great opportunity to achieve such balances and harmonies, but it was growing quickly and so would have to act quickly, too.

RAILROADS

Through a series of deals Seattle's first railroad, the Seattle and Walla Walla, became the Columbia and Puget Sound and was bought by the Oregon Improvement Company, a subsidiary of the Northern Pacific. In 1885 a group of twelve Seattle people, led by Thomas Burke and Daniel Gilman, decided to have another try at a Seattle-based road, the Seattle, Lake Shore and Eastern, which was to run from Seattle through the Cascades to Spokane. Like the Seattle and Walla Walla, it never got near its destination, but was a success anyway because it got far enough to secure for Seattle's business a significant part of the Puget Sound hinterland.

Its depot was on the waterfront, at Western and Columbia, and the line ran north through Interbay to Ballard, east along the north shore of Lake Union and through part of the present University of Washington campus, around Union Bay to the logging town of Yesler, then north along Lake Washington, down the Sammamish Slough to Squak, and east to Snoqualmie Falls. At Woodinville, near the north end of Lake Washington, the line moved north into Snohomish

County. From there the plan was to build north to Sumas on the Canadian border, where a connection could be made with the Canadian Pacific and thereby give Seattle a transcontinental line independent of the Northern Pacific.

Gilman and Burke had little money and so were forced to borrow from local friends to secure loans from eastern money. They dickered with the stock, they organized subsidiaries that could be separately financed, they borrowed on what was not there. The road was constantly beset and was of consequence only for a little while. Gilman had iron mines near Squak that yielded little; a proposed ironworks on the east shore of Lake Washington did no more than get its promoter, Peter Kirk, a town named after him; the northern extension got no farther than Arlington, halfway to the Canadian border. By 1890 the road was so badly overextended that its backers wanted to sell out. The only offer they got was from the despised Northern Pacific, which wanted the road not so much for its own use but to keep it from James J. Hill, whose Great Northern was coming steadily west. At this point Burke and Gilman turned their attention to Hill, who, they figured, could get them what they wanted after all.

The little line did more than get Burke and Gilman into the railroad business. These were the years when Tacoma alone had a transcontinental line, when Tacoma was gaining almost a corner on the wheat and flour market and was exporting many more logs, although it was never more than slightly ahead in its total volume of exports. Seattle was, as we have seen, the more sophisticated manufacturer, and Seattle had a much better developed small transportation system: two railroad lines and what was called the mosquito fleet, small boats making runs all around the sound. In addition, the Seattle, Lake Shore and Eastern had gotten from the city council what turned out to be a valuable concession. Burke and Gilman had developed an idea called Railroad Avenue, a manmade road along the waterfront to be used by all trains coming into Seattle, and they got the council to give their road the right-of-way to its inner and most valuable thirty feet of track.

The trouble with Burke and Gilman was not their energy or enterprise; they really had done rather well with their little line. But they were conditioned to forget that land and labor are precedent conditions to capital and so were too afraid and too respectful of big bankrolls farther east. Seattle needed a transcontinental road badly, and these men were willing to do anything to get one. What they forgot was how much Hill or any other builder of roads to Puget Sound needed Seattle. Hill had built his way across the plains slowly, ruthlessly, and thoroughly. He did not build one section until the previous one had been completed, towns established, and immigrants brought in. He thus did not have to commit himself to his western terminus until he was practically there, so he could play towns off against each other, looking for the best possible deal. He kept saying maybe he would come to Everett, or to Seattle, or to the barely existing village on Bellingham Bay, Fairhaven. He hired Judge Burke to be his Seattle attorney, and Burke worked to get Seattle to give anything he wanted: a sixty-foot right-of-way on Railroad Avenue, land for his terminal, no interference from city or state governments.

Ironically, those who most wanted to fight Hill and Burke originally were not from Seattle but from east of the Cascades. During the constitutional convention of 1889 people from farther east, who had had experience enough with the Northern Pacific and the Great Northern, kept warning that the Elliott Bay tidelands, which included Railroad Avenue, should be kept in the hands of the federal government. That way, they argued, local governments could not be enticed into making deals with the railroads.

Hill could move his line into Everett if he liked, or swing it north to Bellingham Bay, but he in effect had no choice, for Seattle was where the people and the facilities were, where everything Hill needed was except the tracks, cars, and immigrants he could bring with him. If the Great Northern's western terminus were to be anything like what it had in Saint Paul on its eastern end, it would have to come to Seattle. Seattle people could have ignored the cries coming from eastern Washington and still have realized this.

In *Mill Town* Norman Clark makes quite clear what Hill was capable of. The Panic of 1893 hit Everett even harder than it did Tacoma, and the Rockefeller interests that had been controlling the town decided to cut losses and run. Hill waited a few years while he acquired majority rights in the Northern Pacific, then came back to Everett and spruced the town up. He then sold nine hundred thousand acres of Northern Pacific land grant timber to his friend Frederick Weyerhaeuser at six dollars an acre, and allowed Weyerhaeuser to build the biggest sawmill in the world in Everett. Hill could not have inflicted that kind of economic imperialism on Seattle, but he could count on Burke to get him a great deal, and on his own patience to get him a lot more. He wanted to locate his own terminal and to have as much right-of-way as he needed. Give him that and he could control railroad business in Seattle. He had to contend against an odd and uncertain combination of forces: local people who did not want to give the city to Hill; the Northern Pacific, which had bought the old Seattle, Lake Shore and Eastern and so had the best thirty feet of right-of-way on Railroad Avenue; the populism throughout the state that wanted to fight any kind of capitalist imperialism.

The Great Northern entered Seattle in 1893, along an outer right-of-way secured for Hill by Burke, to a ramshackle terminal at the foot of Columbia Street. Hill was not satisfied, because he wanted his terminal farther south, near the tideflats, where he figured to control railroad business more easily than he could along the legally tangled Railroad Avenue. He talked to the city engineer, Reginald H. Thomson, who was opposed to giving Hill everything he wanted along the downtown waterfront, but who thought a tunnel could be built underneath downtown so that Hill could have his road to his terminal without taking over Railroad Avenue.

It is not clear what Hill thought of Thomson's idea, but at least for a while he was content to go on squabbling about his terminal, his Railroad Avenue, his terms. The legal and commercial problems were so tangled that he could not simply have things his own way. Robert Nesbit, Judge Burke's biographer, describes the situation:

> The squabble involving the Great Northern, Northern Pacific, Oregon Improvement Company, and some lesser roads on the ram's horn and Railroad Avenue franchises, like radio soap operas, went on and on. Almost any Seattle newspaper during the nineties would report a battle between the Oregon Improvement Company and the police and city street crews over a stretch of track being torn down or put up. Failing that, either the Great Northern or the Northern Pacific, with appropriate newspaper fanfare, would be revealing plans for a depot or terminal calculated to freeze out the other road. Or the supreme court at Olympia would be reversing a favorable verdict obtained for the Great Northern in a local court by Judge Burke. Or Jim Hill would threaten to leave Seattle and put his terminals at Everett or Fairhaven on Bellingham Bay. Or the ram's horn franchise would have been abolished finally and forever, only to pop up again as legally sound as ever.

The ram's horn franchise Nesbit mentions here, incidentally, was the original right-of-way obtained by the old Seattle and Walla Walla, which followed the meander line of Seattle's waterfront at high tide and whose status became cloudy when Railroad Avenue was built out over the water.

What Nesbit shows is the way Hill and Burke kept running into the complicated fabric of a city. R. H. Thomson had told Hill that the city would fight him as long as he thought only of picking a terminal site and driving his line there without regard for any general plan or the interests of the city and other railroads. So Hill waited, while

Burke bought up property for him south of Jackson Street, while the Northern Pacific itself bought up property along the waterfront for its version of the city's terminal, while the legal wrangling went on. Hill began buying Northern Pacific stock, but that process was slow and difficult. In 1900 he decided to return to the plan for a tunnel under downtown that Thomson had suggested seven years earlier. That too involved difficult negotiations and fights with the city council, which continued to mistrust Hill and Burke; but the tunnel was started in 1902 and finished in 1905, by which time Hill also had gained sufficient control over the Northern Pacific that he could prevent it from blocking him further. During the long wait the Union Pacific and E. J. Harriman had appeared on the scene, building north from Portland and settling an impressive terminal on Jackson Street next door to where Hill planned his. But by then Hill was satisfied: if he was not the complete master of Seattle's railroads, he was close to it.

The conclusions we can draw from this story are not clear or one-sided. That Hill was forced to negotiate his entry, to delay it, and to spend much more money than he would have liked to achieve it was entirely to the city's credit. That Hill finally got pretty much what he wanted was not a disaster, either, since no one disputed the importance of the Great Northern to Seattle. What we can say is that if Seattle could have been impeded in its healthy growth, and if one person could have done it, Judge Burke would have been the person. The moment he became Hill's Seattle agent, he assumed unblinkingly that what was good for the Great Northern was good for Seattle, a frame of mind totally antithetical to all that had made the city what it was. Hill's treatment of Everett, and of many smaller towns along his line farther east, shows how ruthless Hill could be; and anyone who, like Burke, took such ruthlessness as a sign of greatness was bound to be indifferent to all of Seattle's qualities that could and did distinguish it from a fiefdom of a railroad baron. We can also note the presence of R. H. Thomson. Had Thomson adopted a political stance, he would have stood alongside men who built railroads and lawyers who did the railroads' fighting. His actions, however, were governed not by politics but by a practical engineer's sense of the possible. We can also note, finally, that Hill and the Great Northern met more resistance in the first decade of their presence in Seattle, in the nineties, than they did in the following decade, when many of the people and groups who were suspicious of what they called "The Interests" gradually split off, found other causes, both progressive and radical, that were nearer to their hearts.

As for the final price exacted by the railroads, we can quickly move down twenty years, to 1918, to see what sort of power they could gain when Seattle was no longer contesting the terms of their presence. In that year the Seattle Chamber of Commerce formed a committee to report on the Port of Seattle and the terminal. By this time not only the Great Northern and the Northern Pacific (the Hill lines) but the Union Pacific and the Chicago and Milwaukee all had major routes coming to Seattle. What the chamber's committee found first was arrogance: "The various railroad companies entering this city were invited at the outset of our investigations to assist the work of this Commission by furnishing data possessed by them . . . but we regret to say that we have failed to receive the slightest aid from any of them." The chamber and this committee contained, we may safely assume, many who had fought hard to get the railroads what they wanted when they first were coming to Seattle; this was their predictable reward. When the committee went on to investigate on their own, they found some interesting practices: "If, for instance, the Milwaukee wants to move a car from Pier 6 (Milwaukee dock) to Pier 5 (Northern Pacific dock) the Milwaukee must take it to the Stacy Street interchange yards, a mile south, notwithstanding the distance from Pier 6 to Pier 5 is only about 150 feet, and in due course of time, probably 24 hours, the Northern Pacific will set the car in to Pier 5." The railroads were subject to greed and power so strong that they did not care how foolish they looked or inefficiently they acted. Some track could be used only by one road, some by only two of the four; there was only one commonly shared line in the city. Shippers, wholesalers, and teamsters were at the mercy of the railroads, and delays and inflated prices were the inevitable result.

All this was a long time after Hill first came, but it showed that those who had wanted the city to exert as much control as possible over the railroads had been right.

R. H. THOMSON

The trouble in dealing with the arrival of such large entities as the Great Northern was not simply that Jim Hill was rapacious or that Seattle people were sycophantic. Another complication was that at a time of great growth, changes came at a bewildering rate, so that it was easy to believe that no real control was possible. Let the railroads come, and the power industries, and the huge new ships, and the boom will continue indefinitely—such was the voice of naïve optimism at a time when it was easy to be optimistic and when everyone was a little naïve. But in a diverse city such voices will not be the only ones heard, and many of those who are cautious or suspicious will not be politically revolutionary either. The presence of such other voices shows us that if Seattle was not the toughest city that ever faced rapid growth, it was not the softest either, and of all the tough people, city engineer R. H. Thomson was perhaps the most important.

Thomson was born and raised in Hanover, Indiana, had gone to Hanover College, and, before coming to Seattle in 1881 at the age of twenty-six, had made one attempt to settle in California and had taught for a while back east. When he came, however, he soon saw that this was where he wanted to stay, and set out immediately to discover which would eventually become the dominant city on Puget Sound. Typically he saw the problem strictly as a matter of topography and transportation, and so he concluded rather quickly that Seattle was in some danger of losing out: "Looking at local surroundings, I felt that Seattle was in a pit, that to get anywhere we would be compelled to climb out if we could." He worked briefly for the city engineer, then for the Seattle, Lake Shore and Eastern, then for various people interested in coal and iron deposits in eastern King County. All the time he was looking around, seeing problems and solutions, developing a loathing for sloppy work and half-baked schemes, of which the little railroad and its various stopping points must have offered a fair number of examples in the eighties. He became city engineer in 1892 and immediately began making lists of the jobs to be done, in sewers and sewage disposal, street pavings and street lighting, water, electricity, transportation, and those hills around downtown Seattle that for him made the city a pit.

The urban populists of the time used the phrase "natural monopolies" to refer to those functions so essential to the city that it could not exist without them and which they felt the city should thus control itself. Some of these, like law enforcement, the judicial system, and public education, seemed so "natural" to Americans that they could not imagine them in the control of private parties. Others, like sewage disposal and water supply, were often left in private hands, though the general sentiment preferred public management and ownership. Others still, like public transportation, electricity, and the telephone system, certainly did not seem like "natural monopolies" to everyone. As might be imagined, there were private people and firms that were interested in claiming that governments should never do more than they absolutely had to, letting private companies, whenever possible, develop the technology essential for the running of the monopolies and having those same companies run these monopolies like any other private business. To them the urban populists were just "The Pops," loud folks who did not understand business. The populists themselves saw public ownership and control of the natural monopolies as an essential protection of the people from "The Interests."

One advantage enjoyed by R. H. Thomson was his total lack of instinctive political sense, so that he could never be claimed by The Pops or The Interests. In the course of a given day almost all his dealings would be with people of business and commerce, yet he was always insisting that the city look out for its own public weal. His imagination was an engineer's drawing-board imagination, more filled with straight lines and solutions than with awareness of complexities and consequences. The Interests often fought him bitterly, but seem to have believed in him and respected him; The Pops seem never quite to have trusted him, though in an either-or situation he was almost always on their "side." He was one of the true heirs of Arthur Denny, a man who would not have been needed had Denny not done what he did, but whose efforts to keep the city healthy and growing were of more permanent value than Denny's.

Thomson's first concerns when he became city engineer were with sewage and water. In 1890 Seattle had hired a Chicago engineer named Benezette Williams to survey the city's sewage and water problems and to plan possible solutions. Williams did a workmanlike job, but Thomson was scornful of him because Williams never imagined, as Thomson did, that the Seattle of forty thousand could grow fivefold in the succeeding twenty years. As a result, Williams saw no harm in allowing individuals and businesses to dump their waste into Lake Washington, while Thomson was alarmed because the lake provided no natural outlet for the dumped material. Looking over the whole area, he decided that West Point, at the edge of Fort Lawton on Magnolia Bluff to the west of Queen Anne Hill, was the one place where a constant and deep current could discharge sewage well out into the Sound and away from the city. He then entered into a long and involved series of negotiations with the army people at Fort Lawton to allow him to take his sewers out to West Point. The army delayed, then it fought, and when Thomson got the city to bring congressional pressure, the army, in 1904, asked to be shown what Thomson had been trying to show them for ten years. So he proved his point, and soon Seattle stopped using Lake Washington as a cesspool, although many did not really see why the city should spend so much money to take its sewer lines to West Point. Thanks to Thomson, however, it was fifty years before anyone saw the danger, and then it was not as a result of Seattle's sewage but that of the many towns and sewer districts outside Seattle that were discharging their waste in the lake. At that time Thomson was praised for having been visionary; it probably is more accurate to say he was a good and careful engineer.

The water question, and the related problem of electricity, was a good deal more thorny and interesting to people in Seattle during the nineties. The city had assumed control of the water supply before Thomson, but it simply continued the operation of the Lake Washington pumps built by the Spring Hill Water Company. Benezette Williams, and then Thomson, both showed that it would be cheaper and cleaner to stop pumping and to rely on gravity to bring water from the Cedar River, which flowed out of Cedar Lake in the Cascades and, forty miles later, into Lake Washington. A man from New York named Edward Ammidown wanted to develop Seattle's water supply from Cedar River through his Seattle Power Company, while Thomson wanted the city to do the work. The city unfortunately had already reached the limit of its bonded indebtedness, but this potential snag was brushed away when the state supreme court decided that cities could sell bonds to construct local utilities without such bonds creating a lien on their general credit. Thus the question became simply a matter of public versus private construction and management, and was fought in 1895 in the first of a series of elections on the "natural monopolies."

Though the plan for Seattle's Cedar River water was Thomson's, he was far from alone in supporting it. Silver Republican Judge John McGilvra, Burke's father-in-law and not the likeliest of prospects, claimed to like Thomson's plan and to dislike the idea of outside ownership. In the nineties we have our first significant showing among established business people of a sentiment against the outside capital that had been so coveted by Burke and others. Urban populism in Seattle was at its peak and was enjoying the kind of broad-based support that rural populism had had ten and twenty years earlier elsewhere. There was a citizen's group called the Committee of 100 and its membership ranged from Professor J. Allen Smith of the University of Washington and tidelands radical maverick Robert Bridges to various working people who would emerge ten and twenty years later as Socialists and supporters (if not members) of the I.W.W. Colonel Alden Blethen of the new newspaper, the *Times,* was in these days an advocate of local control. Yet it shows the strength of The Interests that while they lost, 2,656 to 1,665, they were far from trounced in the 1895 election.

Thomson's next step, the development of hydroelectric power on the Cedar River, was really contingent upon the water supply issue. Everyone realized that this was a more difficult problem, technically and politically, and so had willingly sidestepped it in 1895. There was no tradition of municipal ownership of hydroelectric power, since such power was generally unavailable to cities elsewhere. There was also a private company, the Union Electric, a division of General Electric, represented locally by Jacob Furth, president of Seattle National Bank, who was the most powerful single financial figure in Seattle. Furth was not someone his antagonists hated, the way they hated Burke; but the power company, later called the Seattle Electric, was for a long time the most conspicuous target of those who distrusted The Interests.

A great many of the streetcar lines noted in the survey of Seattle in 1897 had been created primarily as part of a real estate venture by someone who had land near the end of the line. Among Seattle people mentioned thus far, Burke, Gilman, and David Denny all were involved in one line or another. Many were undercapitalized, and of all the Seattle activities affected by the 1893 panic, the streetcars were hardest hit, many having gone into receivership. It would have been an ideal time for the city to take over the management of the street-cars, but the financial and legal tangles seemed too great, and the opportunity quickly passed as the Boston firm of Stone and Webster, with Furth as their agent, moved in, formed the Seattle Electric, and gradually acquired the streetcar companies, then the power plants that had been generating the electricity, then the Union Electric Company.

It was at this point, around 1900, that Seattle Electric had something close to a monopoly on electric power and public transportation, and first encountered R. H. Thomson as a potential antagonist. Thomson wanted the city to build a hydroelectric plant at Cedar River; the Union Electric already had acquired land there, and after the 1895 election, it bought more land upstream from the city's. The first showdown came in a 1902 election to decide if the city power plant should be built, but it was only the first of many. Seattle City Light, as it came to be, was still a long way off.

In 1902 the base of support for a public power plant was so strong that there was little doubt as to the actual outcome of the election. But some wanted the city just to generate enough power to operate street lights, others wanted the city to sell power only to those outlying residential areas that needed too little power to interest Seattle Electric, and still others wanted the city to enter into sufficient competition with the private power people to keep their rates honest and their profits reasonable. Each group had sufficient numbers that the city won the election by a margin of close to seven to one. But this decision, the guarantee that the city would have some hydroelectric power, was only the beginning, and for the next generation the battle over the details was fought over and over. While Seattle City Light became more powerful, Seattle Electric—or Puget Sound Traction, Light and Power as it came to be, or Puget Sound Power and Light as it is now—did not necessarily become less so. Thomson's primary concern was that the city have a plant to generate its own power for its own public uses, and most of the later fights he left to others. He never did see the need for the city to enter into the street-car business, and in this respect he was like many others who saw that Seattle Electric had put the streetcars on a sound financial basis, had extended the lines, had kept the operation running smoothly, and insisted there was no need to interfere.

By the first years of this century, then, Thomson had procured new sewer lines and disposal stations, a new water supply that could serve a city many times the size Seattle then was, a new hydroelectric power plant that was ample to light the city streets and could easily be expanded to meet other needs. He still had three major projects in mind: regrading the hills to dig Seattle out of the pit he saw it in, shifting the primary location of waterfront business from downtown Seattle to the tideflats farther south, and constructing locks to build a waterway from the sound to Lake Union and Lake Washington.

Sewage disposal, water supply, and electric lighting were in certain obvious respects the public's business, and Thomson could easily gain urban populist support for his projects in these areas. The regrades were different in that they involved primarily business interests and private financing, though all the earliest regrades were so essential to simple public access that no one thought of them as anything other than public projects. The first regrading was done long before Thomson, as a matter of putting in streets running north from Yesler Way along the hillside on which the original Denny land claim was situated. First Avenue had been regraded in the 1870s, and the others had some work done on them as downtown moved north, and carriage, streetcar, and finally automobile traffic got heavy. Thomson had to redo some of the early work, on Second, Third, and Fifth avenues especially, to accommodate increased use in the years between 1903 and 1910. This was all very delicate work not only because it was done near surrounding buildings but because the Great Northern was building its tunnel underneath downtown at the same time.

Such projects did not contribute anything to Thomson's plan to dig

Seattle out of its pit, however. The sides of the pit still remained: Denny Hill, to the north of downtown, and the ridge between First Hill and Beacon Hill, to the south and southeast of downtown. In this passage, quoted earlier, from Arthur Denny's *Pioneer Days on Puget Sound*, we get a sense of the spirit with which Seattle would approach this problem: "We had no eight hour, nor even ten hour days then, and I never heard of anyone striking, not even an Indian. Every man who was worthy of the name (and I am proud to say there were few exceptions then), was found striking squarely and determinedly at whatever obstacle stood in the way of his success." Thomson, in his memoirs, could not understand anyone feeling otherwise: "Some people seemed to think that because there were hills in Seattle originally, some of them ought to be left there, no difference how injurious a heavy grade over a hill may be to the property beyond that hill." Both Denny and Thomson believed in private property and in success, and the civic vision of both is closely tied up with the success of men of property. Both enjoy the image of the human bulldozer—there is an obstacle there, says Denny, that obstacle is a hill, says Thomson, and what you do, say both, is to strike at it squarely and determinedly. It is not man who proposes and God who disposes, but the other way around: don't move the man, move the hill. We all know now a great deal about the potential dangers of setting such people loose on a landscape, but to see hill movers simply as dangerous people is to do damage to them. In the first place, something of their spirit is truly essential to the success of the life of any city, where some strenuous and determined action is essential. In the second place, it is important to judge such people not just by their spirit or attitude but by what they achieve. For R. H. Thomson the regrading was his pet, the project he had dreamed of since first moving to Seattle. Others, he could well feel, might have done his work with the sewers and the water and power supply, though perhaps not as well, but the regrades precisely expressed his vision of what was wrong and what had to be made right. As so often is the case with pet projects, they turned out to be not as important as the projector thought.

The regrades to the south and southeast of downtown, the Jackson and Dearborn Street jobs, were tied up with the tideflats. The tideflats in turn were tied up with the plans of many people, but mostly Eugene Semple, to build a canal between Elliott Bay and Lake Washington across the tideflats and through Beacon Hill. Semple, former sawmill owner, former governor of Washington Territory, began in the early 1890s to get legislative and financial backing for his Seattle and Lake Washington Waterway Company. His plan was to dredge two waterways through the tideflats and to use the excavated material to fill in the flats, then to move east with his canal to Lake Washington. As it turned out, he had many more backers, including Thomson, for the tidelands filling than for the Lake Washington canal building, but even the first stage ran into enough trouble that the second never got off the drawing board. Thomson's major contribution here was his authorization for a Semple firm to sluice down the north side of Beacon Hill to allow for the building of Dearborn Street between Fourth Avenue South and Rainier Avenue. Thomson then got property owners closer in to agree to assessments that would allow for the regrading of Jackson Street so that, between 1900 and 1910, the whole south end of the city was redone: a cut was made between First and Beacon hills to open up the Rainier Valley; tideflats were filled from Beacon Hill to West Seattle, largely with land from the Dearborn and Jackson Street projects; two large waterways were constructed south from Elliott Bay, leaving between them Harbor Island, the largest man-made island in the world. All this in addition to the new Union Pacific and Great Northern–Northern Pacific terminals south of Jackson Street. Thomson had overseen almost all these changes and had been directly responsible for some. As a result, no one could possibly see Seattle as being in the bottom of a pit.

No one, at least, except Thomson, who all along had wanted to level Denny Hill at the north edge of Arthur Denny's claim. As early as 1894 Thomson had his assistant, George Cotterill, call on all the landowners on and around Denny Hill to get their support. In 1897 he undertook the first step, regrading First Avenue between Pike Street and Denny Way. It took only a small part of the hill, which he used as fill in various small ravines between First Avenue and the water. With that work completed by 1899, Thomson then wanted a regrade of Second Avenue, which would involve a much deeper cut into the hill. One of Thomson's men, V. V. Tarbill, gave the property owners the following argument: "Property on Second Avenue at Pike Street was worth perhaps $2000 a front foot; but 120 feet away from that, where the hill was very steep, Second Avenue property was worth only $100 to $200 a front foot, and values were still less farther up the Hill. The incentive was very strong for these property owners to grade their lots down and cash in on these values."

So the west side of Denny Hill was sluiced down into the bay. The work began in 1902 and was finished in 1904. At this time the old Washington Hotel was still standing on top of the hill, about a hundred feet above Second Avenue, and its position was beginning to seem precarious. Land values boomed along Second Avenue, just as Thomson and Tarbill had predicted, and soon others wanted more regrading, even though property owners had to pay the entire cost. The hill covered sixty-two city blocks originally, but piece by piece, over the next eight years, it was leveled, in a vast and complicated engineering feat: twenty million gallons of water a day were pumped from Lake Union to the top of the hill, working with force enough to move boulders weighing more than twenty-five hundred pounds, sluicing clay and rocks down into flumes and then into a central tunnel. Houses were simply undermined and then burned with no danger of the fire spreading.

The regrading of Denny Hill was R. H. Thomson's *pièce de résistance*, his demonstration that Seattle could continue to grow only if it removed the hills surrounding the hole in which it had originally been built. In odd places one can still find reference to this idea, and even Murray Morgan is willing to endorse the notion that Seattle grew because Thomson got rid of the hills. It is as if, since such a project were going to be undertaken, people forever after had to find ways of being happy with it. Yet when compared with Thomson's other doings, the regrade of Denny Hill turned out to be of little benefit and may well have been positively harmful. Denny Hill was an imposing sight, relatively small, very steep, and the old hotel at the top was one of the finest monuments the city ever had to its growing aspirations. Given the still lovely steep southern slope of Queen Anne Hill, given especially what was done with the equally steep and imposing and impeding Telegraph and Nob and Russian hills in San Francisco, one can imagine enduring wonders on Denny Hill had it been allowed to stay. Instead of that, we have what is still called the Regrade, a chronically semiblighted area, at its best the home for small service industries and a nice faded apartment or two, at its more frequent worst the home of car lots and garish motels and claims that Jesus Saves placed next to cut-rate furniture and clothing stores. Downtown was indeed moving its retail core north through the period after the fire of 1889, but, as if to spite Thomson, it has resolutely refused to move in any significant way into the Regrade. Pine Street was the northern extent of downtown in the old days and still is, really. People learned then to name the downtown streets by saying Jesus Christ Made Seattle Under Protest and doubling the first letter of each word to come up with Jefferson-James, Cherry-Columbia, Marion-Madison, Spring-Seneca, University-Union, Pike-Pine. They still do.

As I have said, R. H. Thomson was one of the great heirs of Arthur Denny, and what he did that was "good and proper for the city" was a great deal. At a time when others were being the real heirs of Henry Yesler and James Colman, exploiting Seattle's growth into great personal fortunes, Thomson was constantly inspired only by an unselfish goal of a greater and more capacious city. Without him the sewage and water systems might never have been as good as they were, and are; without him City Light would have had to struggle a great deal harder to become established; without him the more necessary regrades might not have been done as quickly or as well; without him the tidelands would not have been filled, the Duwamish not dredged, Harbor Island not created, and the cuts and locks to make a water passage between the Sound and Lake Washington not constructed. All these would have been done later, or done worse, or not at all. It is a wonderful record.

But the legacies of such successes are never simply on the plus or minus side of the ledger, and one of Thomson's most enduring legacies has been the habit of mind which thinks that all the problems of any city can be solved by more and better engineering. Near the end of his autobiographical memoir Thomson surveys the Puget Sound area and dreams of the day when there can be not two but four, five, or six major highways built through the Cascades. If Seattle was a pit, the entire area was just a larger one, and an engineer's mind like Thomson's must assume that when an obstacle presents itself to the eye, the obstacle must be removed: don't move the man, move the mountain. In later years the points of contention were not to be those that engaged Thomson, but questions of "access," and Thomson's unblinking heirs have persisted in believing that "access" means more and bigger roads, which is what Thomson would have thought. Perhaps Arthur Denny, had he faced Thomson's problems and been given Thomson's power, would have done just as Thomson did; perhaps Thomson, had he landed at Alki in 1851, would have done what Denny did. Perhaps both, faced with the Seattle of the sixties and seventies of this century, would simply advocate more and bigger roads. Theirs were simple, powerful, problem-solving minds. The land gave Denny problems he could solve modestly and superbly; Denny's Seattle gave Thomson problems he too could solve, often superbly.

There were more problems, however, which a mind like Thomson's either could not see as problems or could not begin to solve. But that is hardly surprising, since one person cannot be expected to see or know or understand everything in a burgeoning city. It perhaps is not surprising either that the Seattle of the nineties was able to bring out the best in someone like R. H. Thomson; that it did is something for which everyone coming later might well be grateful.

BOOM AND BLOSSOM

In the first decade of this century Seattle had so far outstripped Tacoma that a comparison between the two cities shows little. Instead it is a comparison with Portland we need now. Here are the population figures:

	1880	1890	1900	1910
Portland	17,000	46,385	90,426	207,214
Seattle	3,553	42,837	80,871	237,174

Portland was older, more settled; Seattle had "caught up" in this period of major growth for both. It is usually argued that since Portland's founders came from New England, and Seattle's were from the midwest, Portland ended up being somewhat more staid and Seattle more flamboyant or boosterish.

But whatever their origins, and whatever their distinctive differences, the key fact is that both cities experienced major and similar growth in their crucial decade between 1900 and 1910. The fact of relatively easy transcontinental railroad travel does much to explain the huge increase in population; the fact that each had built thriving small cities before the railroads came explains why the people came there rather than elsewhere in the northwest. In both cities there was not so much a great increase in exports as a vast increase in import replacement, work done for local consumption that hitherto had been done elsewhere and imported. In both cities there was no marked increase in one or two major industries, but there were significant gains in the number of smaller industries, so that the economy did not fundamentally change, but instead achieved a maturity and diversity in manufacturing that moved each city forever out of the class of a city like Tacoma. In Seattle, for instance, the small manufacturing establishments listed in the census as "all other industries" grew in number from 82 to 222, and from $2 million to $12 million in total value of products. That is how a city begins to provide for itself, and when it does, it begins to look and act like a city. It takes two or three such flowerings for a city to become great, but without the first there obviously will be no other. Since such days of new possibility or reckoning are only now, in the 1970s, approaching for both Portland and Seattle, it is too soon to say what their outcome will be. But each has reason to be proud of its first flowering.

In Seattle the most obvious visible sign of the new decade was the new building downtown. The older buildings, put up after the fire of 1889, were massive piles of stone and brick, and it takes a special taste, I think, actually to like their outside appearance. It is easy, however, to admire their interior space, and to see how adaptable they are to storage and light manufacture, to offices and showrooms and apartments. Because they are so adaptable, they can be used for different purposes in different eras. The new buildings of 1900 to 1915 were different in design and tone from the older ones. Most of them were built by people as monuments to their new status as wealthy citizens: the Alaska Building, the Hoge Building, the Dexter Horton Building, all on lower Second Avenue, the new center of downtown; the Cobb and White-Henry-Stuart buildings in the metropolitan tract opened for development by the University of Washington during this period; the Joshua Green Building at Fourth and Pike; the Moore Theater in the Denny Hill regrade; and last and best, the Smith Tower at Second and Yesler, at the time the largest building west of the Mississippi.

They are all monuments to pride and confidence, some financed from outside, most from inside, all attesting to Seattle's boom. When Clarence Bagley and Welford Beaton came to write their admiring histories of Seattle, they included pictures designed to create an effect Bagley and Beaton never tired of: side-by-side photographs taken from a particular spot downtown in 1880 or 1890, then from the same spot in 1910 or 1915. Second Avenue, then and now; looking up Cherry Street, then and now; Fourth and Union, then and now. This is the city that built itself, and here are the pictures to show it.

On the whole they are excellent buildings, more attractive than those built earlier or those to come later. They are distinguished architecturally from the postfire buildings by their steel frames, so their brick and terra cotta exteriors do not have to do all the support work, so there can be many more floors and many more windows, so strong vertical lines are possible. They stand with a sense of skin being pulled taut against the body, and flush to the street, but they are so light in total effect that even when they are quite high they don't ever seem to overwhelm the pedestrian on the street.

Their difference from the buildings of the nineties extends beyond their architecture. These are office blocks. Elsewhere would be the retail stores and apartments, all roughly in the same style, but each with its dominant function carefully isolated and fixed. James Hoge and Joshua Green and Horace C. Henry did not intend to live in the buildings they built, but in mansions on First Hill or in The Highlands. The mixed living that we identified as one of the dominant qualities of downtown Seattle in 1897 was carefully being replaced by people who had no use for such mixing. Soon the Bon Marche and Frederick and Nelson would put up attractive new buildings at the north end of downtown, leaving the office buildings farther south to be the business end, and leaving downtown segregated by sex as well as by function. The new apartments were built outside of downtown entirely, on the slopes of First and Queen Anne hills, on Broadway and Tenth Avenue East on Capitol Hill, in Brooklyn out near the university. This separation of function was not accidental but a source of pride, and downtown living was left to the less affluent.

The new private homes were equally important and impressive, including many not built for the new rich. In this decade hundreds of new tract houses were built along or near the streetcar lines, on the east side of First Hill, on the top of Capitol Hill, in the area north of Lake Union in the Fremont and Wallingford districts. The Capitol Hill homes were a striking example of good tract development, many built with the financial backing of a man from Syracuse, New York, J. A. Moore. Pictures taken of Capitol Hill sometime between 1905 and 1910 show rows of houses, on land shorn of growth—precisely the kind of development that has so often been deplored in suburban America after World War II. The houses have only two or three architectural variations on a box: living room, dining room, kitchen, and hall downstairs, four bedrooms at the corners upstairs, perhaps a third floor with gabled windows, perhaps a front porch with overhanging roof extending the entire width of the house. The sight they presented when first built was hardly pretty, but seventy years of weathering and different owners show what aging and landscaping can do to individualize a tract house provided the house itself is well built in the first place.

But the houses of the more well-to-do are one of the great features of the decade, and most of what are now known as fine old homes in Seattle were built at this time. Where only a few large houses had been built before the turn of the century now grew up whole neighborhoods—on the south and west slopes of Queen Anne Hill, on the west slope of Capitol Hill and around Volunteer Park, all along the ridges above Lake Washington. The general rule was the farther from the streetcar the more expensive the house, and the ideal was not show but seclusion or retirement. Once again, the intervention of seventy years of landscaping has done much to foster this ideal, but it was there from the beginning: these houses were not meant to be seen or fully enjoyed from the street or from a distance, but to be lived in by people who might themselves never see the street. The styles are elegant and traditional: Colonial, Tudor, Georgian, never adventurous, often with fine expensive custom work in the windows, the fireplaces, the porches and balustrades. Here is a brief and totally characteristic description of the Washington Park home of Mrs. A. M. Donahoe, made in 1912:

> The placing of Mrs. Donahoe's home is particularly a happy one, for while it is in the city, there has been left enough trees and other foliage to give the effect of a country place. The home itself stands out in the open, but is sufficiently removed from the main thoroughfare to insure privacy. It has all the charming qualities of the rural English home, and while it follows the English style in general, it has been changed to meet modern conditions. A fine view over Lake Washington is had from the rear.

The main thoroughfare in question is the Madison Street streetcar, and the house is four blocks away up the hill, on what has always been an almost totally silent street. The view from the rear is also typical, showing that what one wants is to see, not to be seen. Throughout these new neighborhoods one is aware of quiet and expensive taste asserting itself in an ideal that blends urban and suburban: streets that bend and dead end, stables and garages the size of houses, careful landscaping on lots that seldom are larger than an acre and often much smaller, secluded public stairs on the hillsides.

The apotheosis of this kind of new house and new neighborhood was, and is, The Highlands, miles away from the city when it was first laid out by the Olmsteds in 1909, and still remote, hidden, excluding. Following a financial crisis in 1907, caused largely by overspeculation in land-grant timber property, a number of large landowners started selling land, and the Puget Mill Company, Pope and Talbot's northwest firm, sold a large tract along Puget Sound, well north of Seattle, to a group of Seattle people who then got the Olmsteds to design it into The Highlands. No lot could be smaller than five acres; there was to be a golf course; and a fence around the entire property would keep out the unwanted. The ideal had changed almost completely from the First Hill mansions and their commanding view downtown. To have "arrived" to the extent of having a home in The Highlands was to have hidden oneself, and no one living there could worry greatly when, or if, they got to work in the morning. For a long time The Highlands stood as the ultimate in living as part of an aristocracy in the region, an assertion of status so assured it did not have to be made more than once, and need not be clearly or loudly announced ever. It was not until after World War II, when rising taxes forced The Highlands residents to agree to divide their lots into smaller sizes, that there was any compromise on this ideal. Thus, while neighborhoods throughout the city and eventually throughout the entire area were seeking quiet, elegant seats of retirement, The Highlands stood as what they were all aiming for.

Closely connected with these new neighborhoods of the rich, and with the ideals embodied there, was the creation, almost within the single decade, 1900–1910, of the city's park and boulevard system. The first generation in Seattle had no need of parks, really, as long as the children could get lost in the semiwilderness that lay around the settlement by the shore. In 1884 David Denny and his wife gave the city a five-acre tract on their original donation claim that first was used as a cemetery and then became Denny Park and the headquarters for the board of park commissioners that was established in 1890. The board made two important acquisitions rather quickly: the land on the north end of Capitol Hill which became City Park and later Volunteer Park; and the large tract west of Green Lake, outside the city limits, which became Woodland Park and the site of the zoo. Since both tracts were well outside the city limits at the time, they needed streetcars to afford access, and hence they became streetcar parks, places where families of all classes could go on a Sunday afternoon. An elderly black woman with whom I talked a few years ago remembered Woodland Park as one of the great places of her early maturity. She lived down in the Rainier Valley and it took close to two hours to get to the park, but she could go there and feel free, as she could not in many other parts of the city.

By that very token, however, when the new rich were building their elegant homes and beginning to concern themselves with boulevards and parks, they sought places where the black woman would not go and no streetcar came near. In the nineties the only such place was Kinnear Park, a fourteen-acre tract given to the city by George Kinnear in 1897 near the family estate on the southwest slope of Queen Anne Hill. But the next ten years saw the acquisition, through gift and purchase, of almost all of what now constitutes the city's parks: Washington Park (now the University of Washington Arboretum) was acquired in 1900 as part of a deal with Puget Mill; Cowen Park was given to the city in 1907; Leschi Park was bought in 1908; Schmitz Park in West Seattle was given in 1908; Ravenna Park and Bailey Peninsula (to be renamed Seward Park) were acquired by condemnation in 1911. In addition, four million dollars in bonds were sold between 1905 and 1912 to develop the parks and build the boulevards designed by the Olmsteds to connect them.

The Olmsteds in question were the sons of Frederick Law Olmsted, the planner of New York's Central Park, and in many provincial cities in the country the Olmsteds represented something like patron saints of new and elegant wealth. It was a sign of serious intention that the park board hired J. C. Olmsted in 1903 to plan a boulevard system, and the board had no reason ever to be disappointed in what they got. Olmsted's plan was perhaps the single most important product of the period. The 1903 design created a winding parkway of about twenty miles which would link most of the existing and planned parks and greenbelts within the city limits and their immediate surroundings. It began on Bailey Peninsula, ran along the lake shore going north, climbed the rise to 31st Avenue South near Jackson Street, swung around to a view park at the end of 35th Avenue and then back to the lake at Madrona Beach, up again to the Firlock Club (the site of The Bush School), across to Washington Park, along the shore of Union Bay to the University of Washington campus, through the campus and north to Ravenna Park, then west to Green Lake and west again to Woodland Park, southwest down Phinney Ridge and then across the valley to the northwest corner of Queen Anne Hill and the Mount Pleasant Cemetery, south through Interbay and over to Magnolia Bluff, and so to Fort Lawton. Spurs or branches were planned running from Washington Park up Capitol Hill to Volunteer Park and from Mount Baker Park on Lake Washington into the Rainier Valley and up to Jefferson Park on Beacon Hill.

Most of what Olmsted planned came into being, and very shortly after he first made his design. The parts that never were—the parkway and view park on the slopes above Lake Washington, the link between Washington Park and the university, the westward extension from Woodland Park to Fort Lawton—came close to existing in some substitute form and do not represent any serious compromise on the plan's major outlines. It was a major achievement, and it remains only to ask what kind of achievement it was and how that can show us the essential qualities of the decade of its outline and basic execution.

Here is a passage that is invaluable in understanding certain qualities of early twentieth-century Seattle. Its author, H. A. Chadwick, owner, editor, and writer of the weekly *Argus* for many years, is referring to Madison Park, which very definitely was not one of the new parks but a public carnival easily reached by streetcar from downtown:

We have a Coney Island now, a playground for the Industrials, a breathing spot for the Employed. . . . The whole show is one inharmonious medley of sounds, and therein lies the charm of the resort for the people who go there. It is all cosmopolitan to a degree, mixed, unexclusive—it is of the people, for the people, by the people, a democratic arrangement to always appeal to certain kinds of Americans. But you don't see family parties there to spend a quiet day out of doors, nor mothers with nervous children, nor society girls with their fiancees.

The tone of *that,* one might say, does much to express and justify the stance of the newly rich; its snobbery is elegant and assured. Of course there were "family parties" at Madison Park, and no doubt nervous children—but not Gibson Girls, not clean-shaven young men with their eye on the main chance, not "Meet Me in Saint Louis" families arriving by automobile.

The sorting out was taking place; Madison Park and Volunteer Park and Woodland Park for what Chadwick calls the Employed, and the new parks for the "family parties" and the "society girls with their fiancees," who could now go where the Industrials would not go because the streetcars could not take them there. There is also a certain sameness to all the new parks and boulevards. For all their profusion, for all their unbroken loveliness, they are created only for retreat, for quiet, they are idyllic, unexciting. Being in one of these parks is often very much like being in another, even more than half a century later when the expanded use of the automobile makes them easily accessible to everyone. At any time but a weekend afternoon in summer, these places are as they were originally meant to be, which means in effect that they are modestly used, and all are used in the same way.

In his report to the park board, J. C. Olmsted used a flat prose for the most part, but he allowed himself a note or two to indicate his sense of his goals. Here is a passage about the slope above Lake Washington in Rainier Heights: "Undoubtedly it would be a wise policy for the city to acquire the whole of this hillside. There is every probability that if this is not done it will be occupied by cheap houses, the existence of which in the proximity to one of the best residential districts in the city would tend to retard the rise in value of that district which its natural advantages should otherwise ensure." That is not the voice of Arthur Denny, or R. H. Thomson, or of anyone else quoted thus far in this history. It asks that it be public policy to segregate by as great a distance as possible "cheap houses" from "the best residential districts," as though the city could have no other interest than that of its wealthier people. To create parks and boulevards for the carriage trade was the highest possible aspiration. The appeal of the parks was not an aspiration to being like San Francisco, not a matter of lavishness, or elegance; except in the wildest of fantasies no one driving on Lake Washington Boulevard or walking in Ravenna Park could feel that he or she was approaching or even faking royalty. The appeal was genteel, not so much a style as the absence of another style that one wishes to avoid.

The newly rich needed ways of establishing themselves, and if travel to Europe or college education in the east would help, it would not distinguish people from Seattle from a similar class of people in Saint Paul or Saint Louis, or Tacoma even, if it came to that. What the parks could add was something close to unique: refined retirement along with a sense of a beautiful and unmanufactured landscape, open without ever being wild, civilized without being urban, showy. If other cities could offer this, they probably could not do so in such profusion. Seattle became a city with hundreds of vistas, turns in the path or the road that offer views in every direction, each slightly different from the one just before or just after; and these were wonderfully exploited in the Olmsted boulevards and the new parks they connected. In a city that was a little more than fifty years old one could claim to find something older cities could not match.

To repeat, what the parks and parkways created is similar to what was created in the new affluent houses and neighborhoods and analogous to the new downtown office blocks, and in each case it was done with a grace and a charm that later ages must cherish and seek to retain. It was, if not a golden age, at least a beautifully gilded age, and did much to set a style and a tone which the city has not lost. Put most simply, the legacy of this decade is the idea and the fact that Seattle is a wonderful city in which to lead a quiet and comfortable private life. The sense of the frontier town is replaced by a blending of houses and roads with evergreen landscape and soft climate that is perhaps the major reason people have loved to live in Seattle.

What the land had given so abundantly was not so much variety as mere profusion. Seattle is not a city in which one can take visitors to see *the* view or *the* park or the best part of town, because these can be found almost everywhere within the city limits of old Seattle, the Seattle of 1910. There are houses and vistas and streets hither and yon that can convince a visitor or a native that this one is *the* one. Someone standing on the front porch of our house, on a one-block street in Madrona, once said, "This is one of the great streets in America." It may well be, but it could be easily rivaled by dozens of others in old Seattle, and it doesn't matter if the assertion even comes close to being true. There are streets that make one want to say such things, and where they seem as reasonable as they do extravagant.

In describing the Seattle of 1897 I stressed the advantages that could accrue when people and function were mixed rather than sorted out, and in the succeeding ten or fifteen years it was precisely this mixing that people were cheerfully giving up. Since what they achieved is on the whole so very good and so totally integral to Seattle as people came to know it, we should not be surprised that what was achieved carried with it a good deal of what became the city's limitations. The ideal of a withdrawn private life makes for comfort, and when best achieved makes for hope, but it can yield indifference to everything outside, and this indifference can cost the community dearly in the way of cohesion, or a common sense of problems and solutions. To retire is to abdicate, and in this decade the people of wealth began to do just that, enabled by the investments of their prosperity to believe that nothing could ever go wrong.

THE MIDDLE-CLASS DILEMMA AND GEORGE COTTERILL

A city that was as land-owning, house-building, and root-making as Seattle was from the beginning is "middle-class." A city of diverse economic activities is always creating a large middle-class population that blends without demarcation into the "working" and "upper" classes. The newly rich I have just been discussing were entirely middle-class in outlook and aspiration, as were many skilled artisans and office workers. Furthermore, while one might describe Washington Park as an "upper-class" neighborhood and the areas around the sawmills as "working-class," there was a great deal of the city where no such easy descriptions could be made, where a person of wealth built a house because it commanded a lovely view of the lake and very ordinary houses could be found next door or on the next street. We can, nonetheless, note that there was a decline in rooming and boardinghouses during the 1900–1910 period, a decline in the number of people living downtown, a tendency on the part of the bank teller to imitate the banker and to move into his own home and out of downtown. We can infer, thus, a bourgeoisie expanding by including more and more wage-earning or working-class people.

When we look at the politics of the period, however, we can do more than infer, though the evidence is more suggestive than full. The first two decades were politically the most interesting and decisive in Seattle's history; before that politics was pretty rudimentary, and after that, for reasons the period itself can offer, politics became quiet, caretaking, seldom the arena for the most active or interesting city energies. But the politics of this period is important, especially in seeing what was happening to middle-class people; and the best way to see the politics is through the career of George Cotterill, who was at once one of the most and one of the least successful people in the city at the turn of the century.

Cotterill was, like R. H. Thomson, a civil engineer, and worked in Thomson's office from 1892 to 1900. Both were teetotalers and staunch members of their churches, both were endlessly energetic and felt strongly about what should happen to Seattle. Neither was interested in becoming wealthy. Thomson succeeded by staying out of politics until it served his utilitarian purpose; Cotterill failed, at least comparatively, by trying endlessly to make politics work. He was by temperament entirely respectable, but by conviction he fought The Interests, fought the railroads, fought the Seattle Electric Company, fought the Republicans who were his natural constituency, became a Populist, became a Progressive, became a Prohibitionist, became a part of the Democratic party he distrusted. He ran for all manner of office: city councilman, mayor, state senator, port commissioner, governor, and always for the "public" interest against the power of money.

The son of an English gardener, Cotterill was born in Oxford in 1865 and was educated in Montclair, New Jersey. When the elder Cotterill moved to a stump farm east of Lake Washington, George went to work surveying in eastern King County with F. W. Whitworth. He spent eight years in Thomson's office and then went into partnership with Whitworth, all of which gave him the same careful detailed knowledge of the city's land that Arthur Denny and Thomson had. He laid out a system of bicycle paths, he mastered the waterfront—who owned it, who wanted to do what with it. After the major portion of his public career was over he was on the Board of State Land Commissioners and later, as highway engineer, he laid out the beautiful Chuckanut Drive north of Seattle, between Mount Vernon and Bellingham. Still later, he was commissioner for the Port of Seattle, and near the end of his life he wrote *Climax of a World Quest*, a book about the original explorations of Puget Sound that is redolent with the conviction that this area was created by God to be the best that Europeanized white people, at least, would ever know.

It was a long career, one that Cotterill could well be proud of, but nothing ever added up for him as it had for Denny and Thomson. Thomson's practical intelligence got things done; whatever ideas he had were quite rudimentary. When he thought he might lose the

Cedar River water election in 1895, he went to Judge McGilvra, a denizen of the established interest, and showed him he had a sound plan. At the same time Cotterill was writing notes from speeches about the undemocratic nature of the United States Constitution, joining the Non-Partisan League, the Populist party, and the Committee of 100, a local group pushing for municipal ownership of natural monopolies. All this brought him into dealing with people Thomson would never have had anything to do with.

Between approximately 1895 and 1902 the political center of the city was a series of parties and fusions and coalitions, the basic ingredients of which were middle- and working-class Democrats and Populists. Issues counted more than candidates, generally, and candidates more than any party structures. The heyday of populism in the country was over, the victim or beneficiary of an alliance with the Democrats under William Jennings Bryan. But in Seattle the regular Democratic party was weak and the Populists could enlist support for local issues among people who would not ordinarily have allied themselves with populism at all. If the ideological heart of Seattle urban populism was Henry George's single tax, that was too little supported to be of great importance. The real issue was municipal control of the natural monopolies, and here the Populists could fuse a broad spectrum of people ranging from reform-minded Republicans all the way over to less-than-doctrinaire Socialists.

Initially this fusion did well, but with each success some adherents got what they wanted and the remainder tended increasingly to split up. The high point for the urban populists, perhaps, came with the elections in 1902 and 1903, which created and then financed Seattle City Light. But already, in 1900, the Populists had not been strong enough to prevent Jacob Furth's Stone and Webster from gaining a forty-year franchise for operation of the street railway system. And in 1902 George Cotterill was defeated for mayor by a nondescript Republican, Tom Humes, and the reasons for Cotterill's defeat reveal many of the inherent weaknesses in the Populist-Democrat coalitions.

Cotterill had two main interests or goals: municipal control of natural monopolies and Prohibition. Many who supported him on one issue were lukewarm or in opposition to him on the other, and Humes managed to defeat Cotterill and sidestep the municipal control issue by stressing the fact that Cotterill wanted to run a sin-free Seattle. Knowing what we do now of the country's experience with liquor prohibition, we can be amused or dismayed at Cotterill's staunch stance against booze, and we can wish he had seen more clearly that liquor is mostly a private issue and municipal control a public one. The more he fought liquor and saloons and sin, the more he was working to divide the populist coalition into middle-class and working-class factions. But for Cotterill it was all a single question of fighting powerful machines in the name of the common citizenry. The enemy on the one hand, for him, was The Interests and the Republican party, and on the other it was the liquor distillers and saloon keepers and the ward heelers of the Democratic party. Cotterill ran as a Democrat when he had to, but he never stopped distrusting the regular party machinery and never stopped antagonizing it by his opposition to liquor.

The Populist-Democrat coalitions, though powerful, were fragile. The great weapon of the Republicans and The Interests was patience, because their power was entrenched while their opposition was constantly reshaping itself. It may have seemed to some that by 1903 the significant populist battles had been won with the securing of the water supply and the creation of City Light. But in many ways the battle had only been joined. City Light had only begun to gain parity with Seattle Electric, and its subsequent history shows that City Light gained control over the private power interests only at the price of having to become more like them. But the sticking point was the streetcar issue. Throughout the 1900–1910 decade the urban populists attempted to mount one attack after another against the Seattle Electric franchise and in 1906 did achieve passage of an eight-hundred-thousand-dollar bond issue for the building of a publicly owned street railway to run from Ballard to Renton. That was as far as they got, however, and just as Jim Hill had gotten most of what he wanted by sitting tight and watching the opposition dissolve, so did Seattle Electric. When the city finally did assume control over the streetcar system, in 1918, it was at Seattle Electric's price: the city paid a vast sum for a fleet of outmoded cars and a set of deteriorating tracks.

George Cotterill worked harder than anyone, and longer than anyone, to keep this kind of thing from happening. By 1910 a lot of the old urban populism fervor had died and begun to seem faintly old-fashioned to many people, and Cotterill was still insisting that the great enemy of city government was the graft-inducing system of granting franchises to private companies for what the city should be doing itself. His was not exactly a voice crying in the wilderness either; the coalition had been splintered pretty badly, however, and in a way no one was more to blame for this than Cotterill himself. He saw no disharmony between his fight for municipal control and his fight for Prohibition, and thus he failed to note increasing signs of disharmony in others.

The two horses Cotterill was riding were moving in different directions. The middle-class reformers increasingly were turning from Populists into Progressives. This meant an emphasis not only on Prohibition and on running a city closed to sin, but also on clean government—and clean government turned out to mean something as close as possible to no government at all. Securing the right for citizen initiatives and citizen recalls meant that politicians and political parties could and should always be held in check. In 1910 a Progressive named George Dilling ran for mayor on the platform of his inexperience in politics. "Dilling is running on his record as a good husband," said Colonel Blethen of the *Times,* and Dilling was barely defeated. The middle-class reformers, in other words, felt themselves to be sufficiently established that they need fight only to hold other forces, on the right and left, in check; they themselves need be for nothing more than clean living and honesty in government. In such a climate the wealthier on the right could retire to their homes and parks in comfort, and those in the middle and working class who still were looking for strong political action were gradually driven leftward, toward socialism and the I.W.W.

Cotterill had no inclination to turn left, though no fear of the left either. But the ingredients necessary to make him, or someone like him, into a successful political force were increasingly not there. The proper role of fusion or coalition politics was to provide a political counterweight in the middle class against the increasingly powerful economic force of the wealthy and outside capital. Urban populism and municipal control of natural monopolies need not be its only concern, but that concern was probably the best one to unite enough people so the Republicans and The Interests could not simply wait them all out. Most needed, perhaps, were leaders who saw how delicate the whole matter was, how every success achieved by the coalition tended to weaken it by giving some people what they wanted. The subsequent weakening then discouraged others, who began to look for other solutions than coalition politics. The two most obvious solutions were, for the middle class, a government that was clean, decent, orderly, noninterfering, and/or, for the still unhappy, the drift to the left. This trend then led to the apparent paradox of a city simultaneously becoming more settled and more bourgeois and yet more radicalized. And that led to the series of clashes we will consider in the next chapter, which led, in turn, to a gradual disappearance of politics as a significant force in the city.

None of this, of course, could be seen at the time, though the precariousness of the balance was apparent at least to the more honest and alert. Here is part of an editorial that appeared in the Seattle *Star* in 1912. The *Star* was at the time a small Scripps-Howard paper that combined sensational news with populist politics, and the editorial offers the best statement I know of the position of the new middle-class and newly settled working-class people at the time:

> We, the common people, are really just emerging from the darkness of ages. We are suspicious and fearful, we still fear the power and selfishness of rulers; we fear injustice from those who make and those who interpret the laws; we cannot make laws fast enough to protect ourselves from the fear of rapacity at the hands of business combinations. We have discovered the use of confidence in democratic rule, but we have not learned to inspire that confidence in others.

It is a statement both frightening and inspiring in its honesty. It sees that people "just emerging from the darkness of ages" are united in fear and mistrust, and that somehow this fear must be transformed into "confidence in democratic rule." It hardly needs to be said that these people cannot be best served by the ideal of a clean, weak, caretaker government, by George Dilling running for mayor on his record as a good husband. Or that if these people cannot gain confidence in democratic rule, their fear and mistrust will tend to turn into sullenness and nastiness.

On the face of it, the period between 1905 and 1912 might be seen as a constant series of steps toward the creation of that confidence in the people. Certainly there were those on the right who believed this, and feared it. George Cotterill, for instance, did not discourage easily, and ten years after his first unsuccessful campaign for mayor he ran again and was elected, defeating the wet, open-town Democrat, Hiram Gill. That same year, 1912, Washington cast its presidential vote for Bull Moose Teddy Roosevelt and elected Progressives to all its seats in Congress. A majority of those elected to the city council were reformers of one kind or another running without the backing of any political party. The Socialist candidate for mayor, Hulet Wells, got only a few thousand fewer votes than the Republican candidate. One might have thought that George Cotterill and all he stood for had at last gotten their chance.

But the appearances were deceptive. By this time "reform" for middle-class Progressives tended to mean Prohibition and weak government as a means of getting rid of political machines, while "reform" to working-class people tended to mean labor legislation or radicalism. Cotterill, fighting both The Interests and liquor, could satisfy some of the needs of both classes, but the coalition had split and Cotterill could not take advantage of his greatest opportunity.

In an earlier day the moneyed right might have seen in Cotterill a strong expression of public and private decency. One would like to think that Arthur Denny, for instance, could have seen this. No longer. By 1912, furthermore, many others had moved so far to the left that they looked upon any middle-class reformer like Cotterill as someone who was trying to put band-aids on a torn and gushing artery. Cotterill himself, and others like him who insisted on stressing the question of a city open or closed to sin, did not help either. There had been, in effect, too much sorting out of people into different classes, each mistrustful of the other, for Cotterill to become a successful leader.

This failure to develop a strong, workable city politics should not keep us from seeing what a remarkable period had just passed. The frontier city that had fought its way into existence and economic prominence on Puget Sound had boomed and blossomed. Economically it had achieved parity and even pre-eminence over the older and securely established Portland. Socially it had achieved a strong bourgeois existence, able to express itself in houses, streets, parkways, and parks of an elegance and dignity that could match the splendors of the landscape. Politically it had fought for and achieved public control over its great natural assets of water and hydroelectric power.

Much was wrong, and the decade to follow would expose the city as being much more powerless and ordinary than it might have been, than it went on claiming to be. There were those who in the flush of Seattle's success dreamed that Seattle could become one of the great cities of the world, the Venice or the London of the Pacific. That was not to be, and we have already seen some reasons why. But the city that in sixty years had created a thriving metropolis out of a wilderness had earned some extravagance in its dreaming:

> When in 1909 Seattle held its Alaska-Yukon-Pacific exposition it announced to the world awareness of the elements which should, by geographic placement, determine its development and give it its quality: Alaskans, Indians, Canadians, Eskimos, and Russians, the Pacific Islanders, and the Chinese and Japanese. These were Seattle's neighbors and her business associates. They might also have been her teachers as well as her pupils. Seattle, near the century's turn, gave promise of becoming a really unusual American city.

Thus wrote Nancy Wilson Ross many years later, in 1941, about the era of her childhood in Seattle.

Ross does not draw a very accurate picture of Seattle's possibilities at the turn of the century. Its citizenry was almost all westward-moving and frontier-settling, therefore instinctively like the Europe or the America farther east from whence it had come. When it built, it built as others had, in Chicago, or New England, or Virginia. When it made a politics, it was a politics dominated by The Interests and populism, as America had been for decades. When it was proud of itself, it was not for its cultural achievements or its rich inheritance of the ethnic traditions of the people of the Pacific Rim, but for its pioneering spirit in making a city out of a wilderness.

If Ross was wrong in her assessment of the potentialities of the Seattle of her childhood, perhaps in another sense she may turn out to be right. The Seattle not of this century but of the next could well become the city she dreams of here. And the right to dream such dreams for the city had been earned, back then, in the period we have been discussing. Seattle had been blessed in climate and landscape, Seattle had been very well built indeed. It soon lost much, gave much away, refused many chances, but what it had done best remained, and remains still. Perhaps it can still have teachers as well as pupils.

IV

The First Climax

THE Alaska-Yukon-Pacific Exposition of 1909 on the University of Washington campus proclaimed to the world that Seattle had arrived. The Olmsteds laid out the plans for the grounds, President Taft opened the fair by telegraph and later put in an appearance himself, people came who had barely heard of Seattle or the northwest, the university inherited a number of permanent buildings, and a theme was announced that expressed some of the sponsors' aspirations for what then seemed an unending bright future. Yet no more than ten years later Seattle had reached a dead end. Its business and manufacture reverted to an emphasis on basic extractive industry, its active and varied labor movement was smashed, its politics had become moribund, and its growth was at a standstill.

The major event in the intervening years was the Great War of 1914–18, and the war played a decisive role in accelerating the pace of events so that what took ten years to accomplish might have taken much longer had there been no war. It did not, however, by itself change anything, and in order to find out what was happening to Seattle between 1909 and 1919 we cannot ask the war to offer an explanation. What went wrong was the result of local and not national and international conditions. What went wrong was the result of the way the boom years themselves had been experienced and understood. As we explore what happened in this crucial decade we will also be understanding more clearly the Seattle of 1890–1910. The second decade of the twentieth century, especially because of the war, heightened every blemish, exposed the defects of every virtue in the way Seattle had taken its apparently triumphant shape.

In the municipal election of 1910 Seattle voters overwhelmingly passed an amendment to the city charter that created a Municipal Plans Commission. Funded by a quarter of a mill of all city taxes, it was to report no later than September 30, 1911, with "plans for the arrangement of the city with a view to such expansion as may meet future demands." Given the ways in which urban planning developed into a prolonged and complex process, it might seem that allowing the commission only eighteen months to prepare a plan for the city and environs meant that it could merely glance once or twice and have done. It was in fact a move of boldness and confidence and foresight, the height of the city's enthusiasm for parks, expositions, boulevards, regrades. City planning was then just coming into its own throughout the country, part of a nationwide move toward reform of municipal government, rising standards of health, and easier means of transportation. In an earlier age, to plan a city was a special act, with the intent of inaugurating or remaking a capitol; but now many American cities were seeking to emulate in their upper bourgeoisie what had hitherto been reserved for emperors and presidents.

The Municipal Plans Commission hired a civil engineer, Virgil Bogue, to draw up the plans. He had had an impressive career, working with Frederick Law Olmsted in designing Prospect Park in Brooklyn, building a trans-Andean railroad in Peru, discovering Stampede Pass in the Cascades, building railroad terminals in Baltimore and San Francisco. He had married a granddaughter of Arthur Denny, been consultant to the King County Board of Tideland Appraisers, and had formulated a strong plan for giving the city control of the tidelands that had been rejected because of the stubbornness and patience of Jim Hill. He had, thus, a national reputation as an engineer and planner, and a knowledge of the land of Seattle similar to what we have associated with Denny, Thomson, and Cotterill.

The document Bogue produced is most impressive, two volumes one can read today with envy and regret. The title was simply *Plan of Seattle*, published in a plain brown binding by Lowman and Hanford, but Bogue has gone only a little way in his introduction when he reveals the elegance and loftiness of his vision:

Paris, under the direction of the lawyer, Haussmann, Prefect of the Seine, not only prepared outlying areas for the extension of the city but cut great avenues through mazes of tangled streets and replaced noisome and congested districts with spacious squares. . . . London today is struggling to rid herself of wasteful confusion and evil congestion at a tremendous cost, a price which measures the surprising indifference and short-sightedness of her earlier citizens when, after the great fire of 1666, they turned deaf ears to the emphatic and earnest suggestions of Sir Christopher Wren, one of the grandest architects the metropolis has ever known.

Looking at the Paris of Haussmann and the London that rejected Wren, looking at the "breadth and dignity" of L'Enfant's Washington alongside the "noisome and congested" New York, we can see Bogue's bias and limitations. But they should not surprise us, since in 1911 and for a long time thereafter city planning meant to people giving a metropolis breadth and dignity: open spaces, boulevards, malls. Those who had hired the Olmsteds, those who had given land for parks, those who had built homes and neighborhoods of elegance were Bogue's natural constituents, and they had hired him to crown their present eminence with an appropriately grand future.

It is perhaps not surprising then that Bogue envisaged as the cornerstone of his plan a large and ambitious civic center. As he saw it, downtown Seattle had been given a great chance by the regrading of Denny Hill, because there was suddenly land available near downtown that was not yet prohibitive in price or fully developed. He also saw that since future residential development would be primarily north and east, so "the lines of main arterial highways" in the future would tend to "cross or approach each other near Fourth and Blanchard Streets, north of the city's principal business area." That was where he placed his civic center. He sketched in half a dozen buildings around a large square, with the largest building and the widest esplanade facing west, toward the Olympics. These were to house the official buildings of the city, county, state, and country. Although this center was for Bogue his showpiece, in fact it probably was the most derivative and ordinary part of his entire scheme, the part he made because he conceived of planning as he did and not because his civic center would necessarily be needed as he planned it.

But to serve his civic center, to make it be truly central in the city's life, Bogue imagined a transportation system with great care and poignant vision. His major ground arterial was Central Avenue, which was later built along a somewhat different route as Aurora Avenue; but Bogue had no way of knowing the future of the mass-produced automobile and so his greatest care was placed on his rail system. He planned, first, for a station at Lake Union that would be the terminal for all passenger trains—commuter, interurban, and long distance—which would leave the terminals on Jackson Street for commercial carrying only. He planned, second, tunnels under Lake Union and Lake Washington to connect existing and future residential areas with his downtown terminal. Since Bogue we have assumed that in cities so spread out as Seattle rapid transit could never handle commuter traffic as well as cars. Bogue saw how spread out the city would be, but thought that was an argument strongly in favor of rail transit. He looked at the hourglass shape of Seattle and the presence of large bodies of water nearby and said that this

> places the largest areas of present and future residence district development at an average of at least fifty percent further from the city's center than would be the case in a site of equal land area, unbroken by water areas, and generally rectangular in shape. From the outskirts of the present city, in any of its four quarters, it is six or seven miles to the central business section. The urban transportation problem is complicated by the varied topography resulting from both exterior and interior bodies of water. Hills, which in other vicinities would be dignified as mountains, rise with more or less abrupt slopes from the water's edge to elevations exceeding four hundred feet. Ridges obstruct routes to large valleys beyond. The water areas, with their irregular outlines, compel detours and circuits for transportation routes in every direction outward from the city center. These varied natural features are, however, a scenic asset and commercial opportunity of Seattle. They present an unrivaled combination of location and site.
>
> The city's growth will be retarded with a tendency to develop congested, undesirable and unhealthful districts unless rapid transit facilities are provided. Business men, and workers generally, cannot be served by a street railway system, over lines stretching out six or seven miles, with stops at every street crossing, consuming thirty minutes to an hour twice every day. And the more population increases in those suburban areas over which this city must expand, the more difficult the problem becomes.

Land and labor continuing to be the conditions precedent, Bogue's assessment continues to seem eloquent long after the automobile seemed to render it obsolete. He saw that the essential development of the city would be out rather than up, that urban development would be western, and so, by eastern standards, suburban in appearance. Knowing that such development would enhance the natural beauty of the city, he could see nothing less than rapid rail transit for moving the spread-out residents quickly to and from work downtown. The one thing he could not see was the practically perverse willingness of "business men, and workers generally" to spend "thirty minutes to an hour twice every day" getting to and from work, not by streetcar but by automobile. That, as we all know, has not solved Seattle's commuter transportation problems, and of course Bogue was absolutely right when he said that the problem becomes more difficult as the population increases. Failure to heed Bogue on this score can be claimed to be one of Seattle's great missed chances.

The insight into the need for rapid transit is perhaps Bogue's finest, though it was not the one he was proudest of or the one for which he is best known. The two other parts of his plan concern the two hundred miles of Seattle coastline, where he broods lovingly as a civil engineer, and the expansion of the Olmsted work in parks and boulevards. Perhaps the most striking thing about Bogue's understanding of the coastlines is his awareness of the diversity of uses to which they can, and indeed have been, put; and on this score, though there is always room for complaint and improvement, it must be said that the city did develop almost as well as Bogue imagined or was indeed possible. (Even more noteworthy, however, than Bogue's understanding of parks and boulevards is the city's almost total failure to follow his plans.) Actually he was only continuing Olmsted work, but, still, he did a very impressive job of it. There were 38,000 acres of land in Seattle in 1910, and just over 1,000 acres of parks and playgrounds. Since Bogue was asked to plan for a Seattle with an additional 57,000 acres, mostly in the city's north end, he simply set out to find 3,000 additional acres of park and play space. The city did expand by that much and more, and in the direction envisaged by Bogue, and since it did almost nothing with Bogue's suggestions, it might be fruitful to list his major sites, to see what might have been:

1. 235 acres just north of Richmond Beach, which includes a half mile of saltwater frontage
2. 475 acres on the hill behind Kenmore which overlooks the north end of Lake Washington, and 150 acres on the shores of Lake Ballinger (both well outside Seattle's limits, but Bogue had no difficulty imagining a city park outside city limits)
3. 28 acres on either side of a gulch, just outside the present city limits, near 3rd Avenue Northwest
4. 150 acres slightly west of the present site of the Jackson Park Golf Course, through which the freeway now runs
5. 100 acres above Lake Washington, just north of what is now Lake City, slightly south and east of Acacia Cemetery
6. 200 acres east of the lake, between Bothell and Juanita, now primarily the site of Saint Edward's Seminary
7. 65 acres encircling Bitter Lake

8. 60 acres north and west of Haller Lake, south of the present Jackson Park Golf Course

9. 50 acres between what is now Northgate and Lake City, including land along Thornton Creek

10. 400 acres along the sound, including some now occupied by Carkeek Park and running down from there to Golden Gardens, west of Ballard

11. 65 acres west of what is now 25th Avenue Northeast between Northeast 90th and Northeast 100th, along a ravine

12. 160 acres on the ridge about Kirkland, east of the lake, near the present path of Interstate 405

13. 22 acres on View Ridge, about Northeast 75th, the site of the Sand Point Country Club

14. 15 acres to enclose the reservoirs near 10th Avenue Northeast between Northeast 75th and Northeast 85th streets

15. 27 acres near Black River Junction, along the Duwamish, near the site of Southcenter

16. 16 acres on the south shore of Lake Burien

17. 100 acres, including some saltwater frontage, on Three Tree Point

The list can have little meaning to someone who has not seen what eventually happened to the land Bogue wanted set aside, and we must wait until we consider the development of the north end after World War II before looking carefully at the results. But a simple inventory is possible. Of the sixteen sites listed here, two came close to realization, at Carkeek Park and the Jackson Park Golf Course, and maybe three more can be said to have been developed privately in ways consonant with Bogue's plan. For the rest there has been despoiling by bad or mediocre home-building, by roads, by the way the roads were built nearby. Seattle's park development practically stopped with the Olmsteds, at least until very recently.

Finally, here is Bogue's summary of his fondest hope for a park: "It would indeed be a fitting climax to all park possibilities, and commensurate with the greatness of her opportunity and destiny, if Seattle should ultimately acquire Mercer Island and set aside this 4000 acres as an island park—a people's playground, worthy of the city of millions which will someday surround Lake Washington." In 1911 Mercer Island had almost no permanent residents, and the east side of the lake was sparsely settled. The city of millions was eventually built, but with no park, not Mercer Island or anything remotely comparable.

Bogue presented his plans to the mayor and city council in September 1911, and they in turn referred them to the voters for approval in the municipal election of March 1912, the election that brought George Cotterill and some other reformers to city hall. Probably not many people saw Bogue's two volumes, or knew or cared greatly what was in them. What they represented must have seemed caviar for the general run of the citizenry, who must have thought mostly that the realization of Bogue's plans would cost a lot of money. What we now think of as citizen participation in planning was unknown, and most likely few of Bogue's most avid supporters knew what he was planning until he submitted his volumes.

"To local capital falls the task to inaugurate, promote and push new enterprises," wrote the Board of Park Commissioners of Kansas City in 1893, and the board was only stating what most wealthy responsible citizens knew. They certainly had known it in Seattle, where local capital had been generated by land and labor and had in turn generated the boom. Some of this had been done directly, as with Thomson's regrades, and the new park land, while some had been done by the ballot box, as with the water and power supply and the Olmsted boulevard system. On the same ballot as Bogue's plan was a large bond issue for the development of Harbor Island at the mouth of the Duwamish, which was to become the heart of the city's port. In other words, local capital knew how to promote its interests among the general public, and had been remarkably successful in getting approval for at least some things that were not of great immediate benefit to the majority of the public. Here, with Bogue's plan, furthermore, there was no question of money, since all that was being asked was to approve the plan and to wait for further bond issues to gain authorization for its execution. There was no question whose responsibility it was to lead the campaign to get this approval: the same people who had spent the previous ten or twenty years securing their personal wealth and who were interested in finding new and decisive ways to make their city the place that could match their pretensions and dreams. How much it would have taken is anyone's guess.

The only organized opposition to Bogue's plan came not from middle- or working-class citizens but from the Civic Plans Investigation Committee, a group of downtown people afraid that Bogue's civic center would drive down property values on land they owned or managed: Charles Clise, representing the L. C. Smith heirs; C. E. Horton, part owner of the New York block on lower Second Avenue; T. N. Haller, who owned a corner at Second and Columbia; Ralph

Nichols, manager of the Chapelle properties which had holdings in lower downtown. In other words, the opposition was simply selfish and fearful. Yet from the beginning this Civic Plans Investigation Committee was allowed to take the offensive: "No more regrades," their advertisements shouted. "Their burdens are sufficient now without indulging the dreams of engineers and architects at the expense of the taxpayers." Former mayor and populist W. D. Wood echoed: "Let us have payrolls and health now—luxury and art as we can afford them."

Such voices were to be expected. But if luxury and art were all that could be found in Bogue's plan, then some way had to be found to show how what Bogue had imagined combined luxury and art with payrolls and health, the visionary and the eminently practical. Instead, after offering their support, the press for the wealthy, the *Post-Intelligencer* and the *Argus,* lavished their attention on a lukewarm candidate for mayor who didn't have a chance anyway. The Municipal League fought a defensive inept fight, placing ads in the working-class–oriented *Star* that sounded very much like a dentist telling a patient the drill won't hurt.

As a result, the high point of the campaign, such as it was, did not come on election day but the Saturday before, when the work of one "Richard E. Marwood, Taxpayer," appeared in the *Star:*

> Aye, tear the city inside out
> And turn her upside down
> We want a Civic Center
> In this good old Potlatch town
> We've won the wonder of the world
> With Thomson for our mentor
> But what's a world metropolis
> Without a Civic Center.
> We want arterial highways
> In our Civic Center Plan
> That radiate to everywhere
> Converging like a fan.
> When Bogue regrade assessments
> Their batteries unlimber
> They will give our population
> Short cuts to tallest timber.
> Seattle hasn't streets enough,
> She's hampered by her highways;
> She needs new angling avenues
> New slant arterial byways.
> Her old square corner thoroughfares
> Seattle has outgrown;
> She must have a star-like center,

Scintillation all her own.
Why hesitate that proud Queen Anne
Is standing in the way?
Did we not cut down Denny Hill
And drop it in the bay?
No, nothing shall deter us
Neither water, dales, nor hills
As long as our dear people
Don't refuse to pay the bills.
We are building for the future
"Building better than we know"
And in planning for that future
Prudence, common sense must go.
Come along then, Mr. Voter
Mark your ballot like a man;
Saddle on your children's children
This Bogue Civic Center Plan.
Aye, tear the city inside out
And turn her upside down
We want a Civic Center
In this good old Potlatch town.
We've stood for slides, for shattered dams
For regrades, for recall
Let's carry through the biggest
Baddest, boldest plan of all.

This poem of Marwood's is filled with innuendo and inaccuracy, and so some might well have found it pernicious. It is also, surely, rather charming. More than that, it can tell us, as few surviving documents can, something about a whole class of people in Seattle. Marwood is anti-Thomson, antiplan, antitaxes, anti-City Light (whose shattered dam at Cedar River is the one referred to near the end of the poem), antirecall, and presumably anti–progressive legislation in general. Marwood is hearty, in favor of the good old days, suspicious of the elegant and the grand. He sounds like a man in a tavern, among readers of the *Star* and the *Times,* middle-class, feeling "out" even though he is in among friends. He mistrusts the people who seem to run the city, and sees himself only as a taxpayer.

But responses like this one were to be expected, though it is surprising to find a know-nothing populist voice able to speak in such pleasant verse. Three days later, Bogue's plans were rejected, by a vote of 24,966 to 14,406, or almost two to one. The next day the *Post-Intelligencer* expressed brief sorrow, and consoled itself with the comfort that the city had the plans, after all, and so could adopt them piecemeal when and as it saw fit. Support for the plans never materialized, however, and after this one election they were soon forgotten.

The Seattle of Arthur Denny had ended. Denny began his life as a settler and ended it as a member of a class, and in the defeat of Virgil Bogue's plans we can see what happened to that class. Bogue himself was not Denny, but more a combination of R. H. Thomson and the Olmsteds. But Denny had in effect been transformed into that during the boom years, and Bogue had done his job well. It was his natural supporting constituency that had failed. It would be good if we knew better why they had, but the best that can be offered is more by image and analogy than anything like full-scale demonstration.

We saw in the office buildings and houses and parks and parkways of 1900–1910 an image of style and retirement being created, and in the defeat of the Bogue plan we can see how thoroughly that retirement had in fact taken place. It was the first instance in Seattle of a phenomenon that had been occurring, farther east and in Europe, for a long time. We now call it the flight to the suburbs. It was not the headlong flight of the years following World War II, and, as I understand it, "withdrawal" is a better term for what happened than "flight." The people who were moving to The Highlands, Washington Park, and Mount Baker, after all, were the same people who were building the new office blocks downtown and the new apartments nearby. They had not fled the city or lost faith in it in the way we usually associate with a move to the suburbs. But theirs was a City Beautiful way of thinking, and the way they had built their homes and neighborhoods shows their pride turning inward, away from street life and mixed residential neighborhoods, away from the streetcar lines, away from daily contact with others economically or socially different from themselves. Having done this, and in the first blush of feeling that what they had done was right, they relaxed. They could spend their weekend afternoons far from the watering places for the Employed, they could travel and send their children east to college. Their sin was not fear but complacence. Instead of seeing their land, as Arthur Denny had, as a way of seeing the city, they seem to have seen their land as a way of not having to see the city. They would not have quarreled with anything Virgil Bogue had planned, but they felt no urgent need for planning either, for more parks, or better public transportation, because they already had their parks and were not going to be riding trains to work.

There is nothing admirable in such withdrawing, and some of the long-range effects of it were damaging, but there is nothing particularly reprehensible about it, either. Perhaps it was the very modesty of their fortunes, as fortunes in America go, that produced the modesty of their aspirations. Their efforts to produce a High Society never worked very well, and their snobberies were never very strenuous. Within their own families and firms they established generational dynasties, but, with few exceptions, their children and grandchildren did not become and did not seek to become city shapers and movers of a later era. Their support of the arts and culture, like their support of Virgil Bogue, was and continued to be tepid. They were middle-class people, seldom aspiring to either the virtues or the vices of an aristocracy. Fortunate in having come to Seattle when it was enjoying its great flowering, they were successful enough never to have to ask why it had flowered, or what it needed to continue to do so. It is not at all surprising that the economy these people had helped to create began soon to slow down, and then to stagnate.

Between the first and second censuses of this century, the methods for obtaining manufacturing statistics were changed, so comparisons between decades are not easy. But if the failure of the Bogue plans was indicative in the way I have outlined, we could probably infer that Seattle's economy showed no obvious signs of distress (otherwise the retirement into comfort or seclusion or indifference about the future would not have been possible). But growth was slowing down, specialization was taking place, and new industries were not being developed. This was difficult to recognize at the time, however. The real blinder was the war, which boomed and expanded Seattle's economy phenomenally, but in false ways. The figures we have, conveniently broken up into the five-year periods of 1909–14 and 1914–19, show growth in the economy continuing in the first period, yet at a much slower rate than in the previous twenty years, while in the second comes the wartime boom.

	Number of Establishments	Employees	Cost of Materials	Value of Product
1909	753	11,523	$ 28,783,000	$ 50,814,000
1914	1,014	12,429	37,770,000	64,475,000
1919	1,229	40,843	149,650,000	274,431,000

If we did not have the 1914 figures, and if we did not know the war was responsible for most of the increase in the 1919 figures, we might see in the above a decade of unparalleled growth, analogous to the great booms earlier in the city's history. But the rate of growth between 1909 and 1914 is quite modest: the number of establishments increased in what seems a healthy way, but the ratio of the cost of manufacturing materials to the value of the manufactured product remains the same. Even this might be seen as a healthy sign if we could locate new but as yet inefficient industries coming into Seattle, but this is not the case. Here are the figures for "all other industries," which is often where new work is taking place:

	Number of Establishments	Employees	Cost of Materials	Value of Product
1909	282	4,326	$ 8,378,000	$ 16,831,000
1914	283	4,519	9,538,000	20,410,000
1919	371	26,776	69,200,000	145,319,000

There is almost no change between 1909 and 1914, and again, while there is a huge increase between 1914 and 1919, most of it represents the impact of inflated prices and business that will not be sustained after the war.

In a healthy economy the wartime boom might have offered opportunities for new and different kinds of manufacturing. The slowdown in the growth rate in the five years before the war, however, is a telltale sign that the opportunities would not be seized. Between 1909 and 1914 the only real growth was in the simpler industries like meat packing and flour milling, while foundry work and furniture manufacture fell off, and the usually indicative "all other industries" were barely expanding at all. In other words, Seattle's economy had really taken shape and had begun to rigidify within that shape by the time the war came. The new people coming to Seattle in this period did not create a significant change in import replacement as the new people of the two previous decades had done. In other words, people with money were not looking around for new work to do, new places in which to invest.

It should not be surprising, given the story of the Bogue plan failure, given the stiffening in the economy, that in the next generation there is less and less to be said about these newly arrived and soon withdrawn people. More and more we will be concerned with people of the middle and working classes, people for whom the development of industry and commerce and the acquisition of wealth were of little or no importance. To the various people and groups who were becoming prominent in Seattle in these and immediately subsequent years, the people of wealth, The Establishment, were just there, to be reviled or even occasionally courted, but mostly to be ignored. Seattle was becoming various Seattles, and, by and large, the Seattle of the wealthy just dropped away.

MORAL REFORM AND MIDDLE-CLASS PROSPERITY

George Cotterill was in fact a Prohibitionist, but his real enemy was not drink so much as liquor distillers and saloon keepers and the vices they spawned. Saloons were where men got drunk and spent money that should be spent on their families, places where the politicians of the Democratic party kept working-class people in fee. Allied with this feeling against drinking establishments were others: a fear of white slave trading and venereal disease, a desire to promote the rights of women, a fear that city life might eventually destroy middle-class values, a distrust of politicians. Others were more worried about some of these matters than Cotterill, but he is the best example we have of the Seattle moral reformer in the progressive era.

Cotterill was elected to the Washington State Senate in 1906, and while he continued to seek legislation that would curb the power of The Interests, he worked hard also on matters of moral reform, finding many in the Senate of his persuasion. Perhaps the most famous result of their work was Chapter 6 of Chapter 249 of the Criminal Code enacted by the legislature in 1909, "Crimes against Morality, Decency, etc." Certain sections of the law stand out: Section 204, defining "Crimes against Nature," carnal knowledge of animals, birds, the dead, plus sodomy; Section 205, "Adultery," a crime punishable by imprisonment for not more than two years; Section 206, "Lewdness," which includes cohabitation and indecent exposure; Section 207, a long, vague definition of the gross misdemeanor of selling, giving, or showing obscene literature to a minor; Section 208, the misdemeanor of selling or advertising contraceptives; Section 209, the misdemeanor of publishing material which gives "any detailed account of the commission or attempted commission of the crime of rape, carnal knowledge, seduction, adultery"; Section 210, the misdemeanor of advertising cures for venereal diseases; Section 211, the misdemeanor of publishing or advertising the means for obtaining a divorce; Section 242, the various misdemeanors resulting from disturbing "the first day of the week."

Since these laws were openly and secretly being broken every day, then and now, they must be judged bad laws, and it is a pity that George Cotterill and other good people were responsible for their being made. The intent was to legislate clean and upstanding communities as, a few years earlier, it had been to legislate clean water. People "emerging from the darkness of ages" by becoming hopeful homeowners for the first time wanted streets well and cheaply lighted, and wanted their children on those streets to be free from obscene literature, drunks, and the threat of white slavery. "We are suspicious and fearful," said the *Star* editorial, and one perhaps inevitable result was the Blue Laws. These were a middle-class equivalent of the idea of retirement we have noted among the wealthy, and both seek an abrogation of the essential urban idea of tolerance of variety in favor of the suburban commandment: be like me. People in Seattle who lived between the habitats of the wealthy were put in the position of emulating them, and the Blue Laws were the best they could do. Not having the money to retire, they could secure their streets and neighborhoods, or so they hoped. Similar laws were being passed at about this time throughout the country, and the fact that various strata of newly made middle-class people could live so close together in Seattle must have played a significant role in securing such legislation here. To walk almost anywhere within the city limits of what was then Seattle is to see sequences of houses and streets which make this fact evident, and eloquent.

Along with the "Crimes against Morality, Decency, etc." in 1909, Washington adopted a Public Accommodations Act which secured for minorities access to all public places, a law which has become honored by time. Also a local-option liquor law (cheek by jowl with the best public-spirited actions were the worst, or the least manageable), to which Seattle responded by voting to remain wet. In 1910 Hiram Gill, a wet Democrat, defeated the dry reform candidate, William Moore. But Gill was recalled in 1911, and in 1912 Cotterill beat off his attempt at re-election. In 1914 liquor reform escalated into Prohibition, and an initiative came on the ballot that would prevent the manufacture and sale of all liquor in the state except for druggists. It also allowed anyone to import liquor from outside the state for private use, which would thus keep the wealthy quiet while forcing everyone else to dry up. Seattle voted against the initiative, but it carried statewide.

For a majority of the people saloons and distillers and brewers were like The Interests, threats to the well-being of sober individuals. Norman Clark in *The Dry Years* summarizes the evidence this way: "Though it was filled with selfish economic motives, class tensions, maybe even with subconscious racial and sexual fears—with paranoias, stupidity, and greed—the prohibition movement also urged men and women to vote with their hearts and with their sometimes desperate hope that they could restore the lost purity of the great agrarian dream and make a better world." To have the whole populist movement boil down to this matter of Prohibition was unfortunate, but for Seattle it was worse than that. After the wealthy began their retirement, the major source of new energies here had to be the middle class, and the burden was being put on that class precisely when it was committing itself to a desperate hope that it could "restore the lost purity of the agrarian dream." Little good can be done when candidates for public office are saddled with epithets like "wet" and "dry," and it is especially sad that this happened to a person of consequence like George Cotterill.

Hiram Gill, who had let the town run wide open when elected mayor in 1910, announced in 1914 that he had reformed, and he was re-elected. Since brewing and distilling had been a sizable industry in pre-1914 Seattle, people expected the economy to slump when these manufacturers were banned. Instead, it seemed to pick up. Hiram Gill formed the Gill Dry Squad, which organized raids even on the respectable, but otherwise he kept to his promise to administer the new law unimpishly. The city, meanwhile, was inching toward full-scale Prohibition. In 1915 it voted dry in turning down two counterinitiatives by a margin almost as large as the one by which it had voted wet in 1914. Clearly moral reform had caught on; the numbers of the middle class were steadily increasing and using Prohibition as a means of declaring they had put their saloon days behind them.

One reason, perhaps the major immediate reason, for this trend was the wartime economy in a country still technically at peace. We looked earlier at the great spurts in Seattle's economy between 1914 and 1919, and while much of that took place after the nation entered the war, it began the moment the United States became the largest industrial power not at war. Norman Clark writes: "Workingmen and their families found in movies and automobiles—and, a little later, radios—a new ladder into the middle class, a ladder so sturdy and so smooth because of wartime prosperity that just about anyone could give it a try. Throughout Washington theatres were replacing saloons as centers of neighborhood entertainment; automobile registration between 1914 and 1918 increased over 300%." Prohibition, then, was only a sign of the times, and the times were marked by shifting social allegiances and habits. The bourgeois could ape the wealthy in the purchase of a home, could even outdo them in desire for clean, sober living. Because everyone was more prosperous, no one could note the deceleration of the economy before the war, or have reason to regret the loss of what had been best about the past. Arthur Denny, Mary Kenworthy, and John Keane had lived in a Seattle small enough for their personal visions to be visions of the common weal. In the next generation that vision had been transformed into urban populism, the city for the people. Now that, too, had gone, and public values evolved into a private vision of individual and family well being, and the possibility of politics as the expression of something more than personal desires was lost.

The Denny Hill regrade, about 1910, looking like an Egyptian desert because of those property owners who refused to have their land sluiced into Elliott Bay (courtesy of the Photography Collection, Suzzallo Library, University of Washington)

R. H. Thomson (courtesy of the Photography Collection, Suzzallo Library, University of Washington)

George Cotterill (courtesy of the Photography Collection, Suzzallo Library, University of Washington)

Colonel Alden Blethen of the Seattle *Times* (courtesy of the Photography Collection, Suzzallo Library, University of Washington)

Anna Louise Strong before she turned leftward in 1913 (courtesy of the Photography Collection, Suzzallo Library, University of Washington)

The Colonel and His Friends

A COMEDY IN THREE ACTS

By HULET M. WELLS

Dramatis Personae

COL. A. J. BLATHER.................Editor of The Seattle Crimes, BRUCE ROGERS
C. B. Blather....................Manager of The Seattle Crimes, Clarence Parks
Joseph Blather...................Vice-President Crimes Printing Co., George Armour
Miss Shortsight.................................Blather's Stenographer, Lallah Rogers
Jack Revere...James Miller
Erns Nordsk..A Detective Reporter, L. W. Buck
Judge Win-slow.........................."Conservative Socialist," R. H. Smith
Kate Sadler.................A Daughter of the "Social Revolution," Kate Sadler
Joseph Jarvis..A Socialist Lecturer, Joseph Jarvis
Fulton Walters...............................Blather's Attorney, Glen Hoover
S. Peele...............................A Deputy Prosecutor, Henry Wilbur
Mrs. Callender...Vera Minturn
Judge Humpty Dumpty..Millard Price
Janitor ....William H. Harris
Clerk of the Court.....................................William F. Johnson

News Boys.....................................⎰ Elsie Scherff
⎱ Agnes Scherff
Arthur Golden
Marion Parks
Sam Sadler

Stenographers, Newspaper Reporters, Bailiff, Office Boy,
Jurors, Newsboys and Spectators

ACT I. Scene, Blather's Office. Time, April 30, 1912.

NOTICE: At the conclusion of the first act the curtain will drop for a moment to indicate the passing of twelve hours. It will rise disclosing the Colonel asleep and having "A Red Nightmare."

ACT II. Scene, Street Corner by Crimes Building.

ACT III. Scene, Judge Humpty Dumpty's Court. Time, June 25, 1913.

LA GOURGUE'S ORCHESTRA

VICTOR BERGER Will speak in **DREAMLAND RINK, Sunday Aug. 3, 8 p. m.**
TICKETS TWENTY-FIVE CENTS. On sale in Lobby.

THE RED NEWS WAGON, Socialist Papers and Books, at Fourth and Pike. Open every Day in the Year.

TRUSTEE PRINTING CO.   SEATTLE, WASHINGTON

The program for Hulet Wells's farce about Colonel Blethen, issued just before Potlatch Days of 1913

Virgil Bogue (courtesy of the Photography Collection, Suzzallo Library, University of Washington)

Lake Washington Boulevard, looking south to Mount Baker Park and Mount Rainier (courtesy of the Photography Collection, Suzzallo Library, University of Washington)

The young Dave Beck (courtesy of the Photography Collection, Suzzallo Library, University of Washington)

ernon Louis Parrington (courtesy of e Photography Collection, Suzzallo ibrary, University of Washington)

Mark Tobey at the Pike Place Market (courtesy of the Seattle *Times*)

The Richard Fullers at home, with one of Tobey's murals behind them (courtesy of the Photography Collection, Suzzallo Library, University of Washington)

Rummage (1941), one of the great Market Tobeys; the medium is gouache, on masonite (by permission of the Seattle Art Museum)

Nellie Cornish in the 1920s (courtesy of the Photography Collection, Suzzallo Library, University of Washington)

Jesse Epstein in 1942, shortly after Yesler Terrace was completed (courtesy of the Seattle *Post-Intelligencer*)

COTTERILL, COLONEL BLETHEN, AND POTLATCH IN 1913

In 1913 the established newspaper in Seattle was, as it had always been, the *Post-Intelligencer*—conservative, respectable, honest, not a great paper but a consistently good one. Its biggest competitor for more than ten years was the *Times*, which, like the *P-I*, had a Sunday edition with separate sections on automobiles, real estate, fashion, and Society, but which, unlike the *P-I*, was generally a splashy and vulgar paper. Its owner and publisher, Colonel Blethen, had not been born to the purple, and his tone tended to be hectoring. The *Star* was a relatively new Scripps-Howard tabloid, designed for working-class and lower middle-class readers, politically liberal but often caught between supporting moral reform and moral tolerance. The *Sun*, a short-lived paper begun early in 1913, was politically more progressive than the *P-I* but otherwise very similar. The *Union-Record*, the lifelong dream of a man named Harry Ault for a daily that could truly reflect working-class interests, was just struggling into existence.

After George Cotterill was elected mayor in 1912, Colonel Blethen went into a tailspin. If the populist and reforming Cotterill could be mayor, and if the Socialist Wells could get almost as many votes as the Republican candidate, chaos had come again. Blethen began denouncing "red flag anarchists," "dynamiters," "I Won't Works," and he saved special scorn for Cotterill, who "tolerated" the "reds" and let them hold meetings and occupy street corners. Blethen announced that during a May Day parade in 1912 Hulet Wells was seen waving a "red Socialist flag" and defaming an American flag. Wells told his story to the prosecutor, who then got a grand jury to indict Blethen for criminal libel. The trial, in the autumn of 1912 in the court of John E. Humphries, a friend of Blethen's, was bizarre. The prosecutor did not want to be vigorous, so even after Blethen admitted that the story he printed about Wells came only from a rumor, nothing happened because the prosecutor made no effort to show Blethen's intent had been malicious.

Wells decided not to let the matter rest there, and wrote a "comedy in three acts" called *The Colonel and His Friends*, which consisted mostly of direct transcripts from the trial, with Blethen's name changed to Blather, the *Times* to the *Crimes*, and Judge Humphries to Humpty-Dumpty. He announced a production for July 27 at the Moore Theater in a handbill printed by The Red News Wagon ("Socialist Papers and Books, at Fourth and Pike. Open Every Day in the Year").

Wells himself was convinced that Blethen was so angry with the announcement of the play that he determined to create an incident. It may be simply that Blethen, edgy about all that was going wrong, needed no immediate excuse. In any event, before the first performance of *The Colonel and His Friends* came Potlatch Days, an annual Seattle occasion everyone loved, or was supposed to love. (Richard E. Marwood, Taxpayer, when he wanted to contrast the virtues of Seattle with the frills of Virgil Bogue's plans, called it a "good old Potlatch town.") The festivities included parades, speeches, auto races, boxing matches. The honored guest was Josephus Daniels, secretary of the navy, who came with a few thousand sailors to honor the Panama Canal, scheduled to open later in the year.

The *Times*'s lead story on Friday, July 18, began:

> Practically at the very moment a gang of red flag worshippers and anarchists were brutally beating two bluejackets and three soldiers who had dared protest against the insults heaped on the American flag at a soap box meeting on Washington Street last night, Secretary of the Navy Daniels, in the great banqueting hall of the Rainier Club, cheered on by the wildly enthusiastic and patriotic Americans present, flayed as a type the mayor of any city who permits red flag demonstrations in the community of which he is the head.

It may be the longest lead sentence, and the most loaded, in American journalism. A small incident of some kind had taken place the night before, near the I.W.W. office at Washington and Occidental. Secretary Daniels had given a speech at the Rainier Club. The rest was Blethen's fabrication, and Daniels spent the next week insisting that he had not meant to attack Seattle's mayor, about whom he knew nothing, and that indeed he had recently given the speech he gave in Seattle to an audience in Erie, Pennsylvania.

On Friday night there was a large demonstration in protest of whatever it was that had happened near the I.W.W. office. The group, mostly sailors when it first formed, sacked the Wobbly office, threw books and furniture onto the sidewalk, and set fire to the heap. It then moved north, picking up civilians on the way, looking for other leftist outposts. The Red News Wagon was demolished, Socialist offices in various downtown wards were attacked, and the Wobbly printing office was dismantled. There was much talk among the group about who was a "good Socialist," who a "bad Socialist," and who a Wobbly, and a meeting hall was spared when someone shouted that not Wobblies but Socialists gathered there. For all its wantonness the crowd was orderly, in control of itself, and it did only what it set out to do.

Mayor Cotterill was alarmed. He was convinced Blethen was dangerous and that he had caused the Friday night incident by the way he had reported Secretary Daniels' speech, which had been quietly covered in both the *P-I* and the *Star* as an ordinary event. Cotterill assumed charge of the police and ordered all saloons closed, all street meetings stopped, and the *Times* to stop printing until Potlatch Days were over. Blethen and the saloon owners quickly went to Judge Humphries and got Cotterill injoined from enforcing his order. Saturday night nothing happened or threatened to happen, the servicemen having been satisfied that they had avenged what had happened on Thursday. Whatever the danger, Cotterill clearly was responding personally to Blethen's assaults and allowing himself to play the game on Blethen's terms. It is a sign of the tenseness that could be created by the whole issue of the political left that it overtook someone normally as calm as Cotterill.

Having gotten permission to continue printing, Blethen was in his element. A huge American flag covered the front page of the Sunday *Times:* "Anarchy, the grizzly hydra-headed serpent which Seattle has been forced to nourish in its midst by a naturalized chief executive for eighteen months, was plucked from the city and wiped out in a blaze of patriotism." The *Times* also quoted Judge Humphries: "I want to tell everybody that the American born people are not going to permit a lot of irresponsible foreign born men and women to come here and ruin this country." A man named Abe Ransom, who had put up an American flag at I.W.W. headquarters, added: "I have respect for myself, for working men, and most of all for American women, and the IWW don't respect any of them." The stories went on and on: Cotterill is a foreign-born dictator, the Wobblies are cowards, the people have shown what they will and will not stand for.

Cotterill was, to be sure, born in England, just as, to be sure, the I.W.W. had no respect for Abe Ransom. Nor did Seattle have anything like the immigrant population of cities farther east, nor were the Wobblies particularly interested in women's rights. But Cotterill had been in Seattle as long as Blethen, and they had even been on the same side in the early days of the fights for municipal ownership of natural monopolies. Indeed, in his 1912 editorials against Cotterill, Blethen had expressed no great interest in the country of Cotterill's birth. It was only inside the pressure cooker of his own head, heated by the apparent rise of the Socialists and the Wobblies, that the super-patriot bigotry began to appear.

To understand Abe Ransom's remarks we have to find out what actually happened near the Wobbly office on Thursday night, and fortunately the *P-I*, conservative but honest, printed in its Sunday issue a story pieced together from affidavits taken by the police from people who were there. There had been a woman speaker, not a Wobbly at all but a suffragist. Three servicemen had appeared, a little drunk, and one of them denounced the woman and said all women had always been slaves. Someone grabbed her soapbox, and when she tried to get it back, one of the servicemen hit her. A well-dressed man wearing a diamond ring stepped in: "You'd hit a woman, would you?" he said, and hit one of the servicemen several times. After some scuffling the police arrived and arrested the servicemen.

No red flags, no anarchists, no Wobblies. Hulet Wells said later the Wobblies had earlier agreed, when asked by the mayor, not to hold street meetings during Potlatch Days. Blethen seems to have assumed that any speaker south of Yesler Way was in some way red, and to have assumed that an American serviceman could not do anything wrong. Cotterill seems to have recognized the kind of trouble Potlatch could provoke and then to have fallen victim to his own worst fears when he tried to halt publication of the *Times*. The Wobblies and the Socialists had their offices wrecked but got for their pains new proofs that patriotism can be the last refuge of scoundrels. It was shortly after this that the *Star* ran its editorial about the common people, fearful and suspicious, emerging from the darkness of ages. Blethen was fearful and Cotterill suspicious. On the one hand the rise of the Socialists and Wobblies, on the other the fifty thousand people who had joined in attacking their offices.

In dull times one can look back on an episode like the 1913 Potlatch and think how exciting and colorful it all was: how good to have a paper as excitable as the *Times*, a Socialist candidate for mayor turning dramatist, a Red News Wagon at Fourth and Pike, where nothing more exciting than a bus stop is now. Socialists Sam and Kate Sadler were on street corners and in meeting halls, and Kate was a rousing speaker. In the midst of the brothels and saloons in the Skid Road district a suffragist was bravely speaking for the rights of women. It all seems so open and active. If one thought the situation were fundamentally healthy, then the hysteria and violence could be seen as inevitable and not serious, as one might see the outbreaks at the end of the anti-Chinese episodes in 1886. If one thought the situation were fundamentally shaky or dangerous, however, then the hysteria and violence become ominous and oppressive. There was much that was powerful and healthy in the Seattle of 1913, but it was not, as we have seen, getting any healthier.

Super-patriotism is one response to an impending crisis, just as Prohibition is another, retirement or withdrawal a third. Social classes were sorting out, social allegiances were shifting, the economy was ostensibly strong but had lost its earlier inventive adventurousness. Perhaps the clearest sign of the dangers and opportunities of the time rests in the records of those people who were born to the middle or upper class but in these years felt themselves driven further and further left to find a political home.

On the Sunday after Potlatch the *P-I* ran a picture in its Society section with this caption: "Reverend Sydney Strong, pastor of Queen Anne Congregational Church, and his daughter, Anna Louise Strong, director of exhibits for the Child Welfare Society, New York, shown in the above cuts, are en route to Japan to study Japanese social and working conditions." They were indeed en route to Japan, but Anna Louise Strong, who had a Ph.D. from Pennsylvania and who was the author of *The Power of Prayer*, was also en route to the left. When she returned from Japan, she ran for the Seattle School Board in order to pick up the old fight against The Interests, and later still she became a leading voice in the General Strike of 1919. Likewise George Vanderveer, born to modest social eminence and wealth, in the same period was shifting from being Republican deputy prosecutor to attorney for the Wobblies charged with murder at the Everett Massacre of 1917.

Fortunately these and other stories have all been very well documented. Strong's autobiography, *I Change Worlds*, Vanderveer's biography, *Counsel for the Damned*, by Lowell Hawley and Ralph Potts, Hulet Wells's unpublished memoir, "I Wanted to Work," and Harvey O'Connor's reminiscence, *Revolution in Seattle*, all tell stories of educated bourgeois people turning to the left in the years just before and during the first world war. All are good, furthermore, and as a result this group is as well chronicled as the pioneers. The outline of each story is the same: an idealism and enthusiasm for Seattle and for America feeling itself forced left in the face of the freezing of the economic power of the wealthy and the fragmentation of middle-class urban populist politics into moral zealots, patriots, and quietism. For all these people, at least for a little while, radicalism gave them a sense of purpose and community and strength.

Of all the people on the left in those days, it was these refugees from the middle and upper classes who were most feared and most reviled. The immigrants and others in the working class might be expected to be dissatisfied, and it was generally believed that the saloons made them victims, kept them in bondage, prevented them from becoming part of bourgeois America. But people like Anna Louise Strong and George Vanderveer had been born in that America, had enjoyed its benefits and then rejected them. That was betrayal, or, if one likes, it was blowing the whistle to remind everyone that the bourgeois America of the early twentieth century was a country that had lost its way.

In older cities the move to the left took on the aspect of missionary work when people born to some comfort saw the conditions under which the poor, especially the immigrant poor, had to live. There is a huge literature on the filth, corruption, disease, and vice in American cities during the period, of which perhaps the best known today is Lincoln Steffens' *The Shame of the Cities*, and it was common for educated people to see in that shame the failure of America. "There is a large class," a New York judge said in 1888, "I was about to say a majority—of the population of New York and Brooklyn, who just live, and to whom the rearing of two or more children means inevitably a boy for the penitentiary, and a girl for the brothel." Chronicles of bossism and slums were written about every major eastern and midwestern American city.

The recourses most obvious in those days were a flight farther west or an attempt at reforming the politics and the living conditions. We have seen reflections of these in Seattle almost from its beginning; it was one of the places to which people could come on their flight west, especially after the opening of the transcontinental railroads, and it too quickly inherited a need for an urban politics to attempt to gain or keep control of the city in the hands of its citizens. But as the flight west gradually ceased being a flight to anything different, and as the efforts at reform found themselves either modestly successful or thwarted, other recourses had to be found. For many this meant labor unions, though labor unions became established in this period mostly among the skilled or artisan lower middle class. For others this meant a further turn left, to anarchism, socialism, the Industrial Workers of the World. "Let us know the modern city in its weakness and wickedness," wrote Jane Addams of Hull House, "and then seek to rectify and purify it until it shall be free." But if that impulse to rectify and purify had led only to Prohibition, then someone with the same fire as Jane Addams could easily feel forced to find refuge in the idealism of the left.

Within the city of Seattle the inducement to the left seems to have had less to do with actual living conditions than it did farther east.

Within the downtown area living conditions often were not very good, but Seattle had little resembling the rows of tenement houses that bred rats, disease, and crime. On the slopes leading out into Rainier Valley to the south and around the sawmills in Ballard were shacks and small houses, but even these could hardly qualify as slums. This lack of slums encouraged people opposed to the left to argue that conditions here were better than elsewhere, which could in turn be a license to indifference or neglect.

It was not the presence of slums, though, that pushed people politically leftward in Seattle. The records they have left indicate that it was a purer idealism, less tangible but no less passionate. They were spurred by a sense of injustice, of the arrogance of The Interests as much as their actual oppression, of the indifference of the middle-class moral reformers to the interests of working-class people. People turned left precisely because what they were objecting to was not something that could be easily rectified by simple political reform, which had never been needed much here since city government had never been boss-ridden. What Socialists and the I.W.W. and other industrial unions were interested in was the fulfillment of Jeffersonian democracy tempered by the knowledge that America was irrevocably urban and that the industrial, commercial, and financial forces Jefferson had feared had gained vastly more power in the intervening century than Jefferson himself could have dreamed of.

This idealism of the radicalized middle-class person is perhaps the most distinctive strain of the left in Seattle, but of course it is not the only one. Here, and throughout the west, were longshoremen; here, and throughout the west, were loggers; here, during World War I, was a great boom in shipbuilding and logging that required hundreds of unskilled workers. In other words, Seattle was a haven or home for thousands of single men on the move, many of whom had experienced the awful living conditions of logging camps, freighters, migrant farm camps, and waterfront flophouses. Radicalism was just about the only alternative these men had to assimilation in the middle class. In Seattle itself there were countless buffers and gradations in class and income between these people and the lumber barons. But the men had worked where these buffers did not exist, and so Seattle was where they came, to relax, to organize, to gain news of other radical and labor movements and of friends in arms in other cities.

Perhaps the strength and character of the Seattle left is seen most clearly in Harry Ault and James Duncan. Ault was the man whose dream of publishing a labor daily newspaper materialized in the

Union-Record, which gained a larger and larger circulation through-out the decade. Duncan was president of the Seattle Central Labor Council. Neither was a Wobbly, nor in the strict sense a radical. Both believed passionately in what they thought of as the rights of the working man, and both saw industrial unionism as the bulwark of their hope. The *Union-Record* was the only daily labor paper in the country. Duncan twice cast the only dissenting votes against the re-election of Samuel Gompers at national A.F. of L. conventions. Wobblies and others more radical in Seattle thought of Ault and Duncan as acceptable people but too stodgy. Compared to the rest of American labor, however, they were flame throwers on the left.

Perhaps it can be understood why Seattle was becoming simulta-neously more radical and more bourgeois during these years, or, if not more bourgeois in character, more populated by middle-class people. The power of The Interests, especially outside Seattle itself; the presence of large numbers of angry dissatisfied men on the move; the relative decency of living conditions in Seattle which kept the middle-class radicals going further and further left to find a home for their idealism—all this put a special stamp on the Seattle left and explains why it could grow so strong in a city so essentially assimila-tive and bourgeois.

THE WAR

It has been clear for a long time that World War I was a disaster unequaled in Europe's long history, and many historians now recog-nize that in a different way it was a disaster for the United States as well. "What the Spanish War began the World War accomplished," wrote Anna Louise Strong in 1935. "America became the world's banker, and ceased to be the world's pioneer."

Between 1914 and 1917 America was hesitantly, reluctantly, but inexorably drawn into the European war. In 1914 President Wilson wanted nothing so much as to be able to concentrate on progressive politics and reform. The country as a whole, including recent im-migrants from Europe, felt it was a sign of the superiority of The American Way that the United States was not involved. What no one, here or in Europe, understood was what a century of increased technological skill would do to warfare. When it began to dawn on the British and French how much they had committed themselves to in the way of men and munitions, they turned to the United States for money and supplies because they could not finance or arm them-selves sufficiently. Secretary of State William Jennings Bryan, the old warhorse populist, reflected the mood of middle and far westerners when he resisted loans to the Allies by eastern banks; he was out of place in Washington, however, where Wilson, Colonel House, and Bryan's undersecretary, Robert Lansing, all were convinced that the loans could be made without the country's forfeiting its neutrality.

The American aid gave the Allies the confidence they needed and, late in 1916, they told the Germans the only peace to which they would agree was one in which the Germans admitted they had been the aggressors. The Germans, refusing to accept what would be tantamount to surrender, decided to undertake full-scale submarine warfare. They knew this could draw America into the war, since American ships would be sunk, but the Germans could see little difference between a United States at war with Germany and a United States supplying money and materials to the Allies. Thus Wilson, who had been re-elected in 1916 because "he kept us out of war," found himself almost immediately thereafter driven by his own policies and the German U-boats into asking Congress for a declaration of war.

Wilson's difficulty was that his reason for advocating entry into the war could not be the German attacks upon our ships, because that would raise the question of why they were in the war zone at all. Instead he had to find reasons as high-minded as those he had used in keeping us out. If we were superior to the Europeans because we were at peace, we also had to be superior while going to war. The United States would fight the "war to end war," which meant the Europeans would be put in their place once and for all; we would fight "to make the world safe for democracy," which meant the United States would become powerful enough to dictate what political systems they could and could not have. It was a fearful burden Wilson put on himself, on the language he used to justify the war, and on the people.

At the outset Seattle people were markedly neutral about the war, but they had grown prosperous between 1914 and 1917, so it was difficult to be against it, too. Leaps in productivity dwarfed all Seattle's previous growth: 12,429 manufacturing employees in 1914, 40,843 in 1919; a total of $64,475,000 in manufactured products in 1914, $274,431,000 in 1919. Few were excited about America's entrance into the war, but to attack it was to rock the boat. It was a precarious position to be in, and we can see this most clearly in the transformation of the Seattle *Star* during the war years.

The *Star* was the "third" paper in Seattle, class-conscious, generally progressive. During the war it became increasingly successful despite having no Sunday edition and making no effort to curry the favor of the wealthy. From a sheet of eight pages filled with features from the Scripps-Howard chain it grew to a paper of as many as twenty pages, written mostly in Seattle, and became the largest-selling paper in the city. It had been for municipal ownership of natural monopolies, for Prohibition, pro-labor without being strongly antibusiness. It had supported Cotterill for mayor against Hiram Gill, but was not strongly against Gill, either. By 1917 Gill, who really just enjoyed holding public office, was back, claiming to be a reform mayor. The *Star* didn't believe him or his Dry Squad, suspected he still favored liquor, and denounced everything Gill did.

Early in 1917 the *Star*'s banners moved back and forth between the trial of Mayor Gill for conspiring with bootleggers and exhortations to get ready for the noble and just war about to be declared against Germany. But it still kept some of its head. Amidst headlines that shouted "Stand by the President" and "Prepare" it denounced as super-patriotism legislation making flag ceremonies mandatory at all public gatherings in Seattle. It also assiduously reported the trial of the Wobblies charged with murder in the Everett Massacre. During March, then, it had the two trials, of Gill and the Wobblies, and the war preparations to account for, which was more than a small newspaper that fed on sensation could handle, since one big story at a time was obviously best. It decided to play down the Everett Massacre trial, and to try to mediate between liquor scandals and the war.

The trial of Hiram Gill was the kind of farce that is inevitable when a mania like Prohibition hits the people. A bootlegger named Logan Billingsley spent a week bathing himself in confessions of what a wicked man he had been: he had been wanted for murder, he said, back in Oklahoma, he was indeed a bootlegger, and he had bribed Gill and the police chief to gain protection for his local operations. Gill, who never claimed to be an angel, seemed really caught this time, and the *Star* ate it up. It even widened the terms of the scandal by pointing out more than once that Billingsley's regular attorney was George Vanderveer who, at that moment, was in another court defending the Wobblies charged with murder. Much to the chagrin of the *Star*, Gill's lawyers quickly toppled the whole story: Billingsley was trying to frame Gill; he was trying to bribe witnesses; he was even giving one thousand dollars to the rabid Prohibitionist, the Reverend Mark Mathews of the First Presbyterian Church, so Mathews could open a vice campaign against Gill. The jury took only a few hours to acquit Gill, and the *Star* found itself in the position often occupied by Colonel Blethen of having to extricate itself from overenthusiastic support of a losing and lying side. It followed

Blethen's method: drop the case, act as if it had never happened, switch subjects from liquor to war, and raise the decibel level.

Fortunately for the *Star*, the verdict in the Gill case came only two days before Wilson asked Congress to declare war, and it took the occasion to announce, in its very enthusiasm for war, that others did not agree with them: "Today, in this land of ours, there are only two classes of people. One class consists of Americans. These will stand solidly behind President Wilson. All others are TRAITORS." It was a terrible thing to feel compelled to do. Six months after Wilson was re-elected for having kept America out of war, all those who continued to want America neutral were traitors.

On the same day, April 6, George Vanderveer opened his defense of Tom Tracy, the first Wobbly to be tried in the Everett case. The *Star* was protected by the onset of war from making the same mistake with this case it had made with Gill's, and it could conveniently put its stories of the trial on back pages and devote itself to whooping it up for the war and Wilson. The Wobbly trial was the longest criminal trial in the history of King County, and also one of the most exciting, but its unfolding seems to have gone almost unnoticed in the city. The other papers didn't even do as much with it as did the *Star*, and the best contemporary accounts were the ones Anna Louise Strong wrote for the New York *Evening Post*. Yet it was the high point for radical labor in Seattle. The I.W.W. had grown in strength by leaps and bounds as the European war produced American prosperity, and Seattle was the headquarters for Wobblies all over the northwest. The legendary Joe Hill had slept on Seattle's waterfront; two radically minded men in John Dos Passos' *The 42nd Parallel* sit in a logging camp in Minnesota and one urges the other to come west, to Seattle, where, he has been told, they have great free night schools. These people did not "stand behind President Wilson," and did not pretend to, and so, if for no other reason, they became marked, doomed. In the eyes of those who feared them they were not just "outside agitators" or "red flag anarchists" (which they were) but "traitors" (which many of them, at least, were not).

The Everett Massacre is treated best and most thoroughly by Norman Clark in *Mill Town*, and the details need not concern us here. But the trial was important for Seattle because it was held here and concerned many Seattle people who were among those charged with murder. Unlike the Gill trial, it was not a simple frame-up; but, like the Gill trial, it became apparent as the defense proceeded that the defendants would be acquitted, and this was a bitter pill for all who were frightened of the I.W.W. and were determined to destroy it.

The *Star* reported as George Vanderveer mounted his defense that there were many witnesses to the massacre, some standing on the dock with Everett's five hundred armed deputies, some standing on the *Verona* with the Wobblies as they attempted to land, and the witnesses testified that the deputies had been responsible for a good deal of the bloodshed. Though Snohomish County Sheriff Donald McCrae insisted he was only defending Everett against the incursions of an outside mob, his men had shot a number of unarmed men who had fallen into the water. But the *Star* apparently drew the line at reporting some of the testimony, as, for example, when the prosecutor tried to shake a defense witness and to make him admit there were cartridges on the deck of the *Verona* after it had returned to Seattle:

> *Prosecutor H. D. Cooley:* Didn't you pick up anything at all from the deck?
> *Witness:* I picked up an eye. A man's eye.

Although it could never be settled who or what side had fired first, it could be shown that there were many more deputies than Wobblies, that many of the Wobblies were unarmed, that at least two of the deputies were killed by shots from the dock and not the boat. None of this did the *Star* want to believe, or have to print. When Tom Tracy and then the rest of the Wobblies were acquitted, the paper once again had to forget the case had ever happened. This left the paper with only the war to wrestle with.

The *Star* could begin by saying that support for the war was so strong that there was no need for a conscription law; then, when that proved palpably false, it had to turn around and denounce Hulet Wells and Sam Sadler as seditionists when they opposed the draft law. It said that Seattle's business people were for conscripting profits as well as men, but it had to report the business community's solid opposition to an excess profits tax. It said that most of labor was solidly behind the war effort, but then it had to report strike after strike, in lumber camps, in shipyards, in packing plants, in the offices of the telephone company. It announced that Wells and Sadler were guilty before their trial began, but had to report that the judge himself threw out three of the five charges against them and that the jury was hung on the other two. It printed a page of a textbook called *Im Vaterland* that was used in the public schools and insisted that it be withdrawn, but then reported that members of the school board found it harmless, though they did agree to withdraw it in the interests of "tranquillity"—which, as board member Anna Louise Strong said, meant "pacifying the *Star.*" So here was a paper, strong in bourgeois working-class roots, capable of that fine editorial back in 1913 which eloquently described the fears of common people about The Interests and democracy, gradually turning into a sorry spectacle, a paper constantly forced into contradicting itself because the war had in effect put it and its readers in a hopelessly contradictory position. Unable to locate any real enthusiasm for the war itself—beyond the enthusiasm for increased wages and profits—the *Star* increasingly had to take on as its true enemies those who opposed the war.

It tried to locate these, first, among its old enemies, Hiram Gill and the Wobblies. When Major General H. A. Greene at Camp Lewis, south of Tacoma, declared Seattle's toleration of vice might lead him to declare the city off limits to soldiers, the *Star* spent two weeks denouncing Mayor Gill and hinting that the "vice ring" in Seattle was supported by "German" or "pro-German" money. Thus the first news of the Bolshevik Revolution in Russia passed almost unnoticed in the *Star,* as did the first major shipyard strike in Seattle, as the paper fired away at Gill in stories and editorials. Gill was used to such things by this time, and seemed to convince the *Star* and General Greene that vice had been abolished in Seattle because he had secured the resignation of the chief of police. In November, fourteen Wobblies were arrested in a bunkhouse at Camp Lewis, and the *Star* blared: "Bare German Plot at Camp Lewis." It turned out that "officials here have been working for months to connect German spies with vice conditions in Seattle . . . and secret service agents have spent weeks gathering evidence to show that the IWW is inspired by German capital." Whatever the secret service agents had been doing, they had delighted the *Star* by connecting Germany, vice in Seattle, and the Wobblies; unfortunately, there was nothing resembling a case. A month later a lawyer who needed one of the fourteen Wobblies arrested in another case found the man in jail and asked with what he had been charged. With nothing, it turned out; the men were simply being incarcerated. The lawyer got all fourteen released on a habeas corpus writ, but it had been only chance that had led him to them at all. This kind of hysteria, on the part of newspapers and government officials, was not, of course, restricted to Seattle, and had the *Times* rather than the *Star* been behaving this way, one would not have been surprised. But the *Star* had been cool when Colonel Blethen got hot about Cotterill and Hulet Wells, and now it was given over to his kind of thinking and tactics.

Finally, there was Anna Louise Strong, the daughter of the Congregational minister, young, vigorous, respectable, and progressive, who had come back from her trip to Japan and become a member of the school board. That job proved mostly onerous, since she could never find out if The Interests she had pledged to attack were being served by the endless contracts for rewiring or new playgrounds. After the war began she got into the fight to keep the United States neutral; after that fight was lost, she fought against the conscription laws. She testified in the trials of Sam Sadler and Hulet Wells; she sat beside a self-confessed anarchist, Louise Olivereau, who was being tried and convicted for distributing anticonscription literature; she began writing under the name of Gale for the brief-lived leftist paper, the *Daily Call.* Hers was the most notorious of the journeys made by thoughtful middle-class people toward the political left. Predictably, petitions began circulating for her recall from the school board. As Strong herself tells it:

> Yet at first they got so few signatures that the recall languished and almost died. A friend of mine was passing the recall headquarters on a prominent thoroughfare and was asked by a woman who stopped to observe the placards: "What are they recalling her for? What has she done?" . . . "She's against the war," said my friend. . . . "My God, who isn't?" grunted the woman, and moved on.

Yet after she appeared with Olivereau, after the *Im Vaterland* incident (though Strong had finally voted to withdraw the book), the petitions began filling up, and late in 1917 enough had been collected for the recall to be voted on in the regular municipal elections in March 1918.

All Strong's old supporters, the women's clubs, temperance leagues, the PTA, and the Municipal League, who had admired her so much when she worked for the Child Welfare Society, had deserted her. The three major papers were against her: "It is sufficient for loyal Americans," said the *Star,* "to know that she is an unyielding pacifist" and "her place as a public official is inconsistent with American aims and purposes." The *Union-Record* very helpfully printed the names and addresses of those people who circulated petitions for Strong's recall, and it should not be surprising to learn that most came from new, outlying residential areas, *Star* readers, old-line working class or newly arrived middle class: 2804 Alki, 4751 19th Northeast, 2258 North 57th, 4222 Evanston, 3828 Fremont, 3533 South Ferdinand, 4024 5th Southwest, 8438 Rainier Avenue South. Such were the people who were most incited by the shouts of the *Star,* the people who had most recently settled into their new homes and new status, people who could be against Anna Louise Strong both because she was a pacifist and the daughter of a Queen Anne minister.

Just before the election the *Star* went all out: "Treason cannot be tolerated, and if we in Seattle are truly American, it will not be. Let not seditionists and NEAR-SEDITIONISTS gain the least foothold." It was worse, you see, to be Anna Louise Strong, who insisted she loved America and was fighting to save the country from mania, than Louise Olivereau, who was not at all interested in proclaiming her loyalty, and who, incidentally, became totally embittered and disillusioned by her experience, as Strong did not. Strong was not a bum, a deportable foreigner, a bomb thrower, a member of the I.W.W; but by that very fact, in the eyes of the *Star*, she was really worse than those who were these things: "The Real Issue Is AMERICANISM" read the banner on election day.

Ole Hanson, a real estate developer also running for mayor on the Americanist platform, won easily, and so by all rights Strong should have been recalled by a large margin. But no. Strong herself reports it this way:

> But, though no word of our side was printed for three months by any newspaper except the Seattle *Daily Call*, yet when the votes were counted the good citizens who had expected a ten to one victory over "a handful of traitors" won by only two thousand votes in a total of eighty-five thousand. They actually lost the city council to the "reds" who had intelligently prepared a whole slate, while the patriots had emotionally concentrated on the recall and the mayor. The patriots were momentarily crushed into silence; they were actually worried. We celebrated our "victorious defeat" in the Central Labor Council.

Strong is embroidering here: 85,000 was the total number of registered voters, not the number of ballots cast, and the actual count was 27,157 to 21,824 against her. Still, she was right in believing the election showed splits in the citizenry which could not be resolved by appeals to Americanism. World War I never had the popular support "enjoyed" by World War II, and so the prosperity it created had to have a kind of moral falsity to it, as well as an economic hollowness. In a city of Seattle's youth and vigor, this falsity could put the people under a strain that might not have been felt as strongly elsewhere, and under that strain powerful people became almost habitually committed to lying and deceit in an effort to galvanize a spirit, to make a people unanimous about something concerning which they almost had to have divided feelings. Anne Louise Strong was no traitor, but the whole habit of moral reform, pressurized into excitement by the war, had led the *Star* and a majority of those voting to believe she at least was that hated thing, a near-traitor.

They hadn't carried the day by so much that they could feel very comfortable in their victory over her. Strong herself puts it this way: "Instead of the time honored division between 'progressives' and the 'interests,' in which the progressives won most of the offices while the interests remained unscathed in the industries, a bitter battle ensued between 'good citizens' and 'reds.' " Seattle was, to repeat, becoming both more bourgeois and more radical at the same time, more divided into a feeling that each group as it gained its power had "natural" enemies. Partly, the war brought feelings to the surface, exacerbating what might otherwise have lain dormant and been forgotten; mostly, however, it gave all groups a sense of power that they did not in fact have, a power that made them not only more belligerent but more blind, and everyone seemed to get more of all these things as the war went on.

The shipbuilders and the lumber capitalists were in a hurry because they knew the huge profits could not last forever. In different ways, both the Everett Massacre and the Seattle General Strike were caused by that awareness on the part of owners and managers. The Prohibitionists were in a hurry because suddenly the whole country seemed on the verge of going dry, a prospect only a few had even hoped for ten years earlier. The patriots were in a hurry because now was the time to mobilize the country and to make the world safe for democracy. The unions were in a hurry because wartime employment and demand gave them bargaining powers they had never known before, and the Wobblies felt, especially after news came from Russia that the Bolsheviks had overthrown Kerensky, that worldwide revolution might be at hand. Under the excitement of this hurrying, people reached out for all they could and became more heedless of others, more careless of facts, more frightened that someone else might step in and block their headlong rush to their dreams. When the Wobblies took the verdict in the Everett Massacre trial or the news from Russia as a sign that Seattle was ready for revolution, they were as loony as the *Star* was in imagining the people were solidly behind their sloganeering.

Seattle was, in one sense, too young to resist the various hysterias of wartime. It had come to its affluence and power not only just during the previous generation, but to a lot of it after the war began. Almost everyone in the city was a newcomer, a stranger, and very much in need, were they able to admit it, of guides and signposts. In an older city many more people went on as they had always had and so provided a stability unknown in Seattle. But in another sense Seattle was too old to resist the hysterias of the war. There had begun a stiffening of the economic joints, not a cutdown in efficiency and productivity but a settling in, a developing of what was obviously there to be developed, in lumber, shipbuilding, railroad and port traffic, real estate. We have noticed this settling in more in the private and domestic lives of the wealthy than in their businesses, but we will have a good chance to examine its results when we look at the paralysis of the economy that set in after the war. It seems as though there was more openness, more economic adventurousness, more attentiveness to true local conditions and possibilities before the turn of the century than after.

So too with the political behavior of the middle class. Strong was under the impression that the progressives had always held the political offices and The Interests had held the real power, because that was true in her first years here just before the war. But that had not always been the case, and the failure of progressive politics lies in the failure of reformers to realize the chances they had right after the turn of the century to build a political base that would indeed be strong enough to fight the interests. By the time the war came, Seattle had, for this phase of its life, passed its peak, and was too old to resist.

The two perspectives thus offered us—Seattle was too young, Seattle was too old—are not really contradictory, and each can tell us something important. Anyone who knows anything of the older cities of the world would be inclined to think that "of course" Seattle was just young and so more susceptible to strife and grabbiness and hysteria than older cities; it always takes longer than a generation, does it not, for anything final to happen in a city. Don't The Interests always dominate the economy of a city? Aren't hotbeds of radicalism likely to be found where youthfulness and amorphousness create the hopes and despairs that radicalism is made of? Of course, one says. But the local historian, attuned as much as possible to changes year-by-year as well as era-by-era, sees the withdrawal of the wealthy, the veering of the middle class into Prohibition and patriotism, the leggy and not always intelligent growth of the left, and says that Seattle was less well equipped to face the pressures of an ill-conceived and foully fought war than it would have been in 1907, or 1897, or even 1887. After the demise of the *Star*, and the withdrawal of the *Post-Intelligencer* into complacence, Seattle has never had better than pretty good newspapers. More than that, between 1917 and 1967 Seattle underwent no fundamental economic changes. It had, without apparently realizing it, assumed its essential economic shape, and the war only heightened, simplified, and rigidified that shape. People were making money, hand over fist, but in a way that almost guaranteed that when the temporary external stimulus of the war was taken away, they would not go on doing so, and would not know what to do about it.

THE GENERAL STRIKE

In the fall of 1918 Seattle and the country were hit hard by an influenza epidemic, and by rumors of many kinds. As the first sizable American casualties were reported, so too came stories of "German atrocities." There were rumors of an impending armistice, rumors that the United States might go to war with Russia after defeating Germany. As part of a propaganda effort there were rumors of labor uprisings in Germany, but it also was said that the "Bolshevik horde" were looming in England, France, Italy, China, the United States. The war was almost over, the American presence in France had been decisive, but everywhere people seemed bitter and weary rather than buoyed or excited.

There was wild cheering when the armistice news arrived in Seattle, but it brought no peace, or harmony. The fight between the "good citizens" and the "reds" was not over; indeed, it had not truly been joined yet. The labor unions, "red" and otherwise, saw that they needed to work immediately to consolidate some wartime gains. The war gave impetus to Wobblies in many unions to try to revolutionize the A.F. of L. craft union system into their One Big Union, and it also enabled many working-class people to begin to adopt the habits of the bourgeois. The leaders of the Seattle Central Labor Council reflected both impulses. They were home-owning and God-fearing people, sober and Prohibitionist. But while they were not Wobblies themselves, they were generally sympathetic to them, even though the Wobblies in Seattle tended to be close to what in the revolutionary efforts of the 1960s were student groups: young, idealistic, transient, short-lived rather than longtime labor people. Ault, Duncan, and many Seattle labor people believed in industrial unionism and disagreed with the Wobblies only over how it was to be achieved. Their hope and strength lay not in the national A.F. of L. but in a strong local organization that could bring together all Seattle labor as a united front against any employer or group of employers.

The great weakness of the unions, which they seemed only partly to realize at the time, was that most of their great horde of new members worked in the shipyards, and shipbuilding was almost entirely a wartime activity. Since most yards built steel-hulled ships, the Metal Trades Council was the labor power in the yards. Throughout the war there had been dickering between the shipbuilders, especially Skinner and Eddy, and the Metal Trades Council, and various governmental boards. In order to insure a steady labor supply, Skinner and Eddy was willing to pay very high wages, and when wages were consequently driven up in other yards, the government became alarmed. Charles Piez of the federal Emergency Fleet Corporation finally agreed to the inflated wages after the Metal Trades Council guaranteed that there would be no further strikes in the shipyards in wartime. The moment the war ended, the unions were free to strike to try to get guarantees about peacetime wages. But at that point the government and the shipbuilders might welcome a strike as the best means of getting lots of suddenly unwanted workers off the payroll.

The incident that set the conflict in motion began with a misdelivered telegram. Charles Piez sent a wire to the shipbuilders' employer group, the Metal Trades Association, telling them that if they gave in to union demands, the government would cancel their steel allotment. But instead of going to the Metal Trades Association the telegram went to the Metal Trades Council, and so the unions learned that Piez had doublecrossed them by outwardly granting a free hand to negotiate after the armistice, then threatening employers who negotiated. One version of the story says that the shipbuilders deliberately had the telegram misdelivered so that the unions would vent their anger on Piez and not on them. Another is that the smaller Seattle shipbuilders got Piez to send the telegram because they could not afford new contracts while Skinner and Eddy could. Another is that Piez was frightened of the power of Seattle's unions. Another claims that the shipbuilders had the telegram misdelivered to get the unions to break the government's hold on the shipbuilding industry. Parts of all these explanations could well be true, and all are plausible under the circumstances. In any event, the shipyards were struck on January 21, 1919, when about thirty-five thousand workers walked off the job.

Thus far, with or without the misdelivered telegram, the story, of economic squeeze and labor unrest, seems a familiar one. But something happened, not just in the Metal Trades Council, not just among those workers we associate with the left. It was in its way so extraordinary that if we could understand it, we would understand a good deal about Seattle. At the beginning no one thought of a general strike, and no more than a few people had ever heard the phrase. The idea at first was to strike in sympathy with the shipyard workers because a show of force and solidarity like that surely would be good and helpful. The more the workers became convinced that the government, or the shipbuilders, or the newspapers, or Mayor Ole Hanson, or all employers were out to crush the power of labor, the more the idea of a general strike seemed attractive. Conversely, the more anyone tried to say just what would be gained by such a strike, the more confused and apprehensive many workers got.

So, when David Skinner, who had been thought friendly to labor because of his high wages, wired Piez in Washington that the strike was the work of "radical leaders whose real desire is to disrupt the whole organization of society," he provided the workers with just the target they needed. When the local and national press insisted the rank and file did not want to strike, they too offered themselves as a target. When the largest local union in the world, the Boilermakers' Local 104, voted unanimously in favor of the shipyard strike, they gave great impetus to a union of all Seattle labor in a more general strike. That vote was taken on January 26, and the next day union leaders met to sound out opinion and discovered that many unions, including some of the more conservative ones—the roofers, the cooks, the hotel maids—had already indicated sympathy with the idea of a general strike. Despite protests from some unions that any breach of an authorized contract violated the principles on which the unions were based, it was agreed that if a majority of the unions voted to have a general strike, then on February 2 a mass meeting would be held to decide what to do next.

In *The Seattle General Strike* Robert Friedheim describes some of the ensuing events:

> Even before the committees could effectively organize themselves, five more Seattle unions reported their members had voted to strike: the structural iron workers, the newsboys, the engineers in the gas plant and the public schools, Carpenters' Local 1335, and Barbers' Local 195. . . . Night after night, as locals held their meetings, votes for a general strike continued to roll in. Electrical Workers' Local 77, Milkman's Local 338, Leather Workers' Local 40, Hotel Maids' Local 528, and the jewelry workers' local all certified officially that their members were willing to strike.

The names of these unions show that this was not in the usual sense a class matter. Some of these unions had been in existence as long as the A.F. of L., and members of the skilled crafts and the small local service unions had no reason to ally themselves with large unions like the Boilermakers, to say nothing of the I.W.W. Of those reporting by January 29, only the gas workers and the federal employees were against the strike. Of course, all members of all unions were not in favor, but it is surprising that 99 out of 101 unions had majorities in favor. By the time of the February 2 mass meeting the point to be discussed no longer was whether there would be a strike, but how it would take place.

What had happened to produce this great show of sympathy and antagonism? Had there been a referendum on the war sometime in 1918, a considerable majority would have said they were for it, since not to be for the war was to be unpatriotic, disloyal, a traitor. But there was, very obviously, a strong feeling against people in government and especially in industry who seemed to be reaping huge profits in money and power from the war. There is good evidence that in all the Allied countries, including the United States, many people fought and worked willingly in the war effort though they distrusted and even hated their leaders. The common people, emerging from the darkness of ages, were suspicious and fearful of people with money and power and, at this point, no moral legislation and no sudden access to the bourgeois class could allay those feelings, and no assurances offered by newspapers or governments or employers could either. We know, furthermore, that what was happening in Seattle was not happening elsewhere, and from that we can draw at least two conclusions. First, working people in Seattle had not become completely settled or completely cynical and had retained some of the idealism, be it bourgeois or radical, on which so much of the westward expansion of the country had been based. Second, moneyed people in Seattle had lost or had hidden whatever idealism *they* had, so they seemed to the workers only to be the enemy.

Anna Louise Strong's is the best account of the meetings of February 2 and after:

> The General Strike Committee, composed of more than three hundred delegates from one hundred and ten unions, met all day Sunday, February 2, 1919. They faced and disregarded the national officers of craft unions, who were telegraphing orders from the East. They met the threats of the Seattle Health Department to jail drivers of garbage wagons if garbage was not removed, by agreeing to permit the collection of "wet garbage only" on special permit under the strikers' control. They rejected as strike slogan the motto "We have nothing to lose but our chains and a whole world to win" in favor of "Together We Win." For they reasoned that they had a good deal to lose—jobs at good wages with which they were buying silk shirts, pianos, and homes. They wanted solidarity but not class war. Then so little did they realize the problems before them that they fixed the strike for the following Thursday at 10 A.M. and adjourned to meet on Thursday evening after the strike should have started, meantime referring any new problems that might arise to a rather hastily elected "Committee of Fifteen."

Strong's jibes at the lunchpail unions with their pianos and silk shirts perhaps shows a little too clearly that she had had such things and had rejected them. It also shows that the strikers were neither transients nor radical nor rabble, and that she shared the enthusiasm, however naïve, of the others.

She wrote in an editorial in the *Union-Record* two days before the strike: "We are undertaking the most tremendous move ever made by labor in this country, a move that will lead—No One Knows Where! We do not need hysteria! We need the iron march of labor!" She and many others saw that the strikers could stay united only if they did not try to say where they were heading:

> Later when I was arrested, this editorial was one of the counts against me. Its very vagueness saved me. "No one knows where"—the prosecution claimed this threatened anarchy. The defense retorted that it merely admitted the fact that the future is unknown. Neither gave the real essence of those words. They appealed to the faith of the pioneer in inevitable progress; they stirred the passion of the march to the undiscovered West. Yet they carefully avoided battle.

Is the idea of a march to the undiscovered West in 1919 preposterous? Eight years later George Cotterill was still saying the northwest was "the world's outpost of outlook and opportunity, the place of vision and achievement." Thirty, forty, and fifty years after 1919 people still came west, many feeling and saying something very close to what Strong says here.

The strike happened. At 10:00 A.M. Thursday, February 6, the city stopped. No work was done, except for the setting up of food lines, the delivery of drugs to hospitals and milk to babies, the maintenance of electric power—all at the direction of the Committee of Fifteen. No one seems to have expected that the result would be the usual result of inactivity: silence. Workers had been urged to stay home, and so they did. The streets were occupied only by children and dogs, and it was hard even for them to do much when everything else was silent. There were squabbles about control of the City Light plant, and many outside the labor movement were nervous about what might happen next; but as an initial show of peaceful force, the strike was a total success.

That was as far as anyone had planned. Revolutionaries wanted working people to assume control of the city's manufacture, government, and services; more conservative people felt one show of strength was enough and quickly wanted to get back to work; most seemed simply unclear. They may have thought the employers and the city officials would surrender, though no one planned what to do if they did. The Committee of Fifteen, with the power of the city in their hands, kept things running smoothly but made no plans, and the *Union-Record* was not full of ideas about the future. So when the other side moved, the strikers could do little beyond saying they would or would not cooperate.

Anna Louise Strong's editorial gained wide national circulation and was widely interpreted as a revolutionary document, in which case the strike had to be broken. Mayor Ole Hanson began to see himself as a patriotic strikebreaker. The National Guard was called out, and Hanson said their presence began the stemming of the revolutionary tide. He then said he would declare martial law. As the labor leaders told him, Hanson's moves were fraudulent, designed to interpret the situation falsely to the rest of the country, because the troops were not needed, martial law was not needed, and the number of arrests on February 6 and 7 was two-thirds the normal number. Hanson, though, felt he had to do something to indicate he was a real tiger, and so on Friday evening he sent this notice to the Committee of Fifteen: "I hereby notify you that unless the sympathy strike is called off by 8 o'clock tomorrow morning, February 8, 1919, I will take advantage of the protection offered this city by the national government and operate all the essential services." This may have gained Hanson the support of business people in Seattle and of Good Citizens elsewhere, but the strikers were not about to be forced into anything, and they refused.

On Saturday afternoon the Committee of Fifteen gave the parent General Strike Committee a resolution denouncing Charles Piez and Ole Hanson, declaring the strike a success, and urging everyone back to work after midnight that night. The leaders seemed inclined to support the resolution, but their rank and file opposed it, and the resolution was rejected that night. No one worked the following day, Sunday, and by Monday enough cracks had appeared in the solid front to convince the Committee of Fifteen that continuation of the strike could only lead to factions within the movement. On that afternoon it urged everyone to walk off on Monday but to go back to work Tuesday noon. Most of those working on Monday stayed on the job, and by Tuesday all but a few went back to work. The strike was over.

It was hard not to see the strike as a failure. The men had gotten nothing, really, and Ole Hanson had gotten himself onto the lecture circuit as an expert on crushing red revolutions. Strong offers this analysis:

Shall one blame the yellow leaders who sabotaged the strike and wished to end it? Such a charge is easy to make—and true. But it is more to the point to ask why it happened that as soon as any worker was made a leader he wanted to end that strike. A score of times in those five days I saw it happen. Workers in the ranks felt the thrill of massed power which they trusted their leaders to carry to victory. But as soon as one of these workers was put on a responsible committee, he also wished to stop "before there is riot and blood." The strike could produce no leaders willing to keep it going. All of us were red in the ranks and yellow as leaders. For we lacked all intention of real battle; we expected to drift into power. We loved the emotion of a better world coming, but all of our leaders and not a few of the rank and file had much to lose in the old world. The general strike put into our hands the organized life of the city—all except the guns. We could last only until they started shooting; we were one gigantic bluff. That expert in bluffing, Ole Hanson, saw this on the second day of the struggle.

Strong's instincts surely are the right ones. The strike didn't go on because the leaders did not know where to take it and began to fear the outcome. Ole Hanson could prove that "Together We Win" and "No One Knows Where" were shams as political gestures simply by waiting the strikers out, bluffing on his part, and watching the strike collapse.

It is important for us, however, not simply to see Strong's analysis as the last word or the slogans as political gestures. When Strong says the workers were red in the ranks but yellow as leaders, she is only saying that people like Harry Ault and James Duncan did not feel in need of revolution. They had a stake in the labor movement, but they also had a stake in Seattle, which was their home as well as where they had come to power and had seen labor become stronger than anywhere else in the country. That did not abate their rage against Ole Hanson or David Skinner or Charles Piez, but it had to shape their vision of what they had, what they might lose. Many of labor's best leaders had come to power under the unreal conditions of the war. Harry Ault had in 1917 achieved his long-time dream of editing a labor daily mostly because the great increase in the labor force had inflated his circulation. But the achievement of the dream itself had to make him cautious. The war had produced villains for many workers in the form of their employers making huge profits, but it had also given the workers themselves power to fight. The more the worker won, the more he had to lose; the more that Seattle was his home, the more cautious he became when made a leader. Nothing shows the way Seattle became simultaneously radical and bourgeois more clearly than the success and failure of the General Strike.

For it was a success. Compared to the outcries of the newspapers, the hysteria of many Good Citizens, and the opportunism of Ole

Hanson, the strikers were wonderful: practical, decent, idealistic, scrupulously democratic, able for a moment at least to harmonize the huge energies of a great variety of people. In that moment the natural pettiness to which flesh is heir, the self-seeking that a fragmented craft union system builds into itself, the anger and disillusion that were exacerbated by the war were abrogated. But it was a local success, and was short-lived because the very ingredients that went into making it happen in the first place contributed to its demise the moment it became clear that very few people wanted a revolution. Too many had too much to lose in the old Seattle, and they got into more than they had really bargained for. It was a show of hope and desire, not the first step in a revolution, and the conditions that had made the hope possible were already passing as they became articulated in the strike.

So it was a failure too. A year later, Lincoln Steffens came to Seattle, and Anna Louise Strong told him of all the disasters that had overtaken the strikers:

> "It's been getting worse for months," I answered. "The Central Labor Council meetings that used to have such fine speeches from workers all over the world have turned into nasty wrangles between carpenters and plumbers for control of little jobs. I think it began when the shipyards closed and the metal trades workers began to leave. Those workers' enterprises of which we were so proud began to go to pieces. And everyone who took part in them got blamed. Now some of the members of our staff are attacking Harry Ault, our editor, most horribly; one of them said that if I didn't join the attack, they would 'rub my name in the dirt.' It was a man I used to like who threatened me."
> "So you are siding with Harry?" Steffens asked.
> "Well, no, I can't exactly side with Harry." Under the questions I began to analyze. "I think it's terrible the way our paper is going. We are beginning to be bossed by advertisers. When the labor movement was united business firms had to advertise in our paper. But now they come creeping up on us and make us soften our tone. Harry is between the devil and the deep sea. I think he's not bold enough; he ought to defy those advertisers even if we have to have a smaller paper. But the paper is his child; he dreamed of it when he used to work as a small boy in a printing office and sleep on the table at night. He gave his best years to make this paper; I hate to see these upstarts call him traitor. But I can't agree with Harry either; he's begun to say the workers are ungrateful. One can't say that."

Under circumstances as sad and crushing as that, Steffens told Strong, she had no choice but to leave, to go to Moscow. Which she did, launched on a strange and grand career that would end with her being one of the few westerners to gain and keep the admiration of Mao Tse-tung.

But for Harry Ault, and for thousands of others like him, leaving was not what they wanted. Seattle was where they lived, where they had achieved at least a small measure of their dreams, where they had to stay and watch those dreams crumble. Robert Friedheim in *The Seattle General Strike* concludes that "in the days ahead they were to learn that it was worse than a failure—it was a disaster." Clearly, for many, it was that. But Friedheim implies that the strike might have been a different kind of success from the success it was, and that the subsequent fragmentation of the labor movement would not have happened had the strike never taken place. The implications are false. The war gave the radicals and the labor movement as a whole some rather unreal hopes, and it also gave many of them a home. Strong loved it when people coming in from outside made great speeches to the Central Labor Council. But those making the speeches either went or stayed, and if they stayed, the less revolutionary they became, just as, when the wartime boom was over, the less powerful they became. Both the radicals and the whole labor movement had to begin to find out all over again what their resources were, and had to live with the bitter knowledge that they were fewer than they had thought.

For the opportunity, the real opportunity, had been mostly lost well before the end of the war, and the strike was really only a sign that some were able to respond to the resultant dangers bravely, if briefly. There was talk in some of the newspapers near the end of the war about a postwar boom in shipbuilding, but that turned out to be overoptimistic. The coming of the war had delayed the arrival of the diminished and more rigid Seattle economy, but when the war was over, the trouble was rudely exposed for everyone to see. Whatever might have happened after the strike, the fact of a general economic slump speeded up the time when the carpenters would quarrel with the plumbers for control of the little jobs, because Seattle was suffering from a national slump very much as Tacoma did from the 1893 panic, and it was in 1919 powerless, as Tacoma had been then.

As for the radicals, many of them left. Quite interestingly, those who stayed did not become restless again as their bitterness increased, but they stayed as if to savor the taste of that bitterness. Harvey O'Connor in *Revolution in Seattle* describes, though unfortunately not in great detail, the later lives of people who had been here during the heyday of Socialist and radical thought and work, who saw the strike, the collapse of labor, the rise of Dave Beck, and the coming of the New Deal, which they saw as a mere palliative. They neither left, like Anna Louise Strong, nor became assimilated into the bourgeois working class; over fifty years later, they could keep the old dream alive, hating the Boeing Company with the same passion as they hated Skinner or Weyerhaeuser or Stone and Webster in the old days. How many there are is impossible to determine, though enough so that most long-time natives of Seattle know one or two or many. Whatever we write of the history of Seattle after this first crisis, we must try to account for the curious fact that so many who seem to hate it so much do not leave.

In 1919 one famous man visited Seattle, and another who had not yet achieved his fame returned home to it after his wartime hitch in the navy. The visitor was Woodrow Wilson making his whirlwind tour in an effort to gain support for the League of Nations, coming to Seattle shortly after his paralyzing stroke. John Dos Passos fantasizes a small picture of the reception Wilson received:

> In Seattle the wobblies whose leaders were in jail, in Seattle the wobblies whose leaders had been lynched, who'd been shot down like dogs, in Seattle the wobblies lined four blocks and when Wilson passed, stood silent with their arms folded, staring at the great liberal as he was hurried past in his car, huddled in his overcoat, haggard with fatigue, one side of his face twitching. The men in overalls, the workingstiffs let him pass in silence after all the other blocks of handclapping and patriotic cheers.

Resolute, righteous, in some respects right, faces turned to the past, the Wobblies died, crushed as much by the ensuing peace as by the previous war. That was one Seattle in 1919, a city that had lost more than the Wobblies ever realized.

The other Seattle was the one seen by Dave Beck when he came home and observed what Wilson had seen: anarchy, idealism, disillusion. Murray Morgan writes: "Beck thought the strike had been wrong, criminally wrong; it had been impetuous, it had been pointless; it brought disrepute to Labor and had won nothing. He was disgusted with the idealists who had dreamed it up. He would no longer answer when the Wobblies greeted him as a 'fellow worker.' " Resolute, righteous, in some respects right, face turned to the future, Beck went back to driving truck, soliciting business for his boss, organizing the laundry teamsters. That was another Seattle in 1919. Its crisis past, it could not tolerate the Wobblies, and was ready for the ministrations of Dave Beck.

V

Seattle between the Wars

THE first phase of our story is over. The Seattle General Strike was the swan song of the generations of growth and hope, and it may also have been the last event which involved or directly affected everyone in the city. With it the war came to an end, the boom to an end, and the stiffening of economic joints began to be apparent to everyone. Battered, withdrawn, greatly reduced in optimism and vigor, blessed and cursed with a simple and generally honest inactive city government, Seattle settled in as a provincial commercial city, content to live off its past achievements and its continuing role as processor and shipper of northwest raw materials—lumber, wheat, fish. The railroads were in their heyday, the Alaska trade was good. Whereas in earlier times of financial panic in the country, in 1873 and 1893 and 1907, Seattle had been strong enough to withstand blows that crippled other cities, during the twenties each minor recession was felt hard in Seattle, and the Depression of the thirties laid the city as low as any in the country.

People obviously did not know what had hit them. Many developed theories about how that which had happened was inevitable; some did not even know they had been hit. In the spring of 1929, for instance, the Municipal Reference Division of the Seattle Public Library issued a document called *The Population of Seattle*. Between 1910 and 1920, the last decade for which there were census figures, the population had grown from 237,194 to 315,685, about 25 percent. No one noticed, or was bothered by, the fact that this growth had been much less than in the three previous decades, since some leveling off, presumably, had to be expected.

The library also took a whole series of indices—percentage in-

136

creases and arithmetical progressions, the Skagit Engineering Commission figures compiled for Seattle City Light, the school censuses, the telephone company estimates—and projected Seattle's population in 1930 at about 425,000. Extending their projection, the library offered as a conservative guess a population of a half million by 1940, of between 600,000 and a million by 1950, and between 800,000 and 1,300,000 by 1960. These estimates were not the result of a speculator's early 1929 euphoria, but of projecting from the figures of the past without asking what created them. If, as people were coming to believe, Seattle grew because of lumber and the Alaska trade, and if these industries remained strong, then such estimates surely had to prove right. Since, however, that was not how Seattle had grown, the theory was wrong and the projections way off. The 1930 census showed Seattle grew by fewer than 50,000 in the previous decade, or half the most conservative guess; between 1930 and 1940, the population growth was under 3,000, or practically none at all. Lest one think that Seattle's experience was just the reflection of national experience, during the same twenty years Los Angeles doubled its size, Houston and San Diego almost tripled theirs; even the state of Washington grew by 10 percent during the thirties, and the already stagnant Tacoma and Spokane gained more in population than did Seattle during that decade.

The manufacturing figures are even starker, though it should be kept in mind that the 1919 figures are inflated by wartime boom:

	Number of Establishments	Number of Wage Earners	Materials	Value Added by Manufacture
1919	1,229	40,843	$149,650,000	$125,219,000
1929	1,219	23,003	199,810,000	97,322,000
1939	1,083	20,352	152,748,000	70,000,000

Once the boom busted in 1919–20, Seattle never recovered during the next generation of peace. There were fewer wage earners in the entire Seattle-Tacoma industrial area in 1940 than there had been inside Seattle in 1920. The most revealing figure is the significant "value added by manufacturing," which reflects what the city is actually doing as opposed to the value of the raw material, and in absolute and percentage terms the figure steadily declined throughout the period. The lumber and wheat and meat and fish were still there, worth whatever they were worth, but Seattle had become only a way station in their transport. The lumber companies could go on making profits, but employed fewer and fewer people, and the value added through manufacture diminished. This had the added effect of making people more dependent on the few ongoing industries whose market could go up and down rather unpredictably. What Seattle made in 1920 in major quantity it made in major quantity in 1940. Some new work was added in small industries, but the only one of these that put itself in a position to offer genuinely new economic possibilities was The Boeing Company.

Bleakest of all, perhaps, is the picture offered by a group called the Study of Population Distribution, which was asked by J. S. Lansill, director of the Land Program of the federal Resettlement Administration, to identify those areas in the country that showed enough opportunities in future employment to justify the government's coming in and building new homes through what was to become the Federal Housing Authority. The study designated thirty-three areas "industrial" and ranked them; Seattle-Tacoma was thirty-third, right at the bottom with perennially depressed Springfield-Holyoke, Massachusetts, showing "declines in every factor chosen for consideration." This was 1935, the depth of the Depression, but that of course does not explain why Seattle was hit so much harder and had so little recovery power. The study also included a group of revealing maps to show migratory trends. In the period between 1900 and 1910, the period of Seattle's greatest growth, there are two large arrows dominating the map, one going out of the central midwest to California, the other going out of the upper midwest to the Pacific Northwest, mostly to Puget Sound. But in the next two decades the arrow going from the midwest to California grows larger and the arrow west to Washington practically disappears, to be replaced by another showing migration out of this state and toward California.

To explain all this, to live with it, even to try to be happy with it, people in Seattle had to develop a myth about the original growth of Seattle that could explain why it stopped growing. It then developed stories and jokes that showed this stagnation was really a good thing. The myth that grew up says that it is not people but nature that makes a city, that Seattle was founded and grew because of lumber, because of the Alaska Gold Rush, because of a good harbor. And if nature was responsible for Seattle, then nature could be held responsible for Seattle's failure to continue growing: the supply and demand for lumber are limited, Seattle is off at the corner of the country and too far from large markets, Seattle had reached its "natural" level or size and then stayed there, as though there were something ordained about a number approximating 350,000 for Seattle's population.

But even the simplest promoters of this myth could see that was not enough, because all the time it was being formed, California to the south was growing by leaps and bounds, California with its great arid stretches and its long distance from large national markets. Nature had made California The Golden State, so the myth said, it was "inevitable" for it to grow: it had a great climate, rich agricultural potentialities, wonderful scenery. Of course, none of the statements made by the mythologizers is false, but they all are inadequate as explanations for growth. There are, after all, other facts. For just under half the year California except along the coast is so hot as to be almost uninhabitable, while during the same period Seattle's climate is just about the finest in the country. All the time California was growing, San Francisco was not growing. The state of Washington is only slightly less rich in agricultural potentialities and is richer in scenery and possesses in notable and gatherable abundance a water supply that is much greater than California's.

The argument which seeks to explain city growth as a result of natural advantages can always be made, can always be seen to cut in two or three different ways, and is never adequate. Venice was built on a swamp, but became one of the great cities of the world. London has a dreadful climate and is in a country poor in natural resources, yet became one of the great cities of the world. Cities of course always take advantage of their naturally created opportunities; even bad cities can do that. But what nature proposes as possible, people create decisively, in one place and not in another, often seemingly in defiance of great natural limitations. It was not inevitable that Seattle was ever founded, it was not inevitable that it grew so strongly and healthily, and it was not inevitable that it stopped growing, that its economy became lethargic. But faced with the obvious fact in the twenties and thirties that it did stop growing, that its economy became lethargic, then the myth had to be created that made it inevitable, due to "natural" causes. There even grew up, especially among journalists, the idea that it is *right* that Seattle grew no more—send out stories about how bad the climate is, how few the opportunities are, so people will not come and those who are here can be freer to enjoy it. What do you do in Seattle in the summer? Well, if it comes on Sunday we go for a picnic. Mark Twain is supposed to have said that one of the nicest winters he ever spent was the summer he had on Puget Sound.

But there is behind these one-line jokes more than a sheepish desire for self-protection or a genuine desire to keep others away. Actually, most people in Seattle are chauvinistic about it, and there is a reason for this that tells us a good deal about Seattle between the wars. I have spoken to a great many people born in Seattle between about 1910 and about 1930 and I have yet to meet one who does not say that Seattle in the twenties and thirties was a wonderful place in which to grow up. One can reply to this, if one feels obliged to, by saying Seattle has always been a good place in which to grow up, and one discounts a great deal for nostalgia. The verdict is still unanimous, and the evidence adduced is strikingly coherent, so one gets a clear picture from people raised in quite different parts of the city and in quite different social and economic states. It may seem contradictory to describe a stagnant city as a wonderful place in which to grow up, but the explanation of that contradiction is not difficult, and it is important.

We can begin with two observations which confirm the idea that the city had in many significant ways been a much more vital place in the years before World War I. The first is that a great many of the people who delight in describing how Seattle was wonderful for them as children also admit that their parents' experience was very different, much less happy, often embittered, often with specific local villains taking the blame: Stone and Webster, David Skinner, Jim Hill, Frederick Weyerhaeuser, R. H. Thomson—in other words, the dominant figures in the previous, the decisive generation, people who left the parents of the young with a sense that their life was marginal, or less than it might have been. Money was tight and capricious, promises were broken—familiar stories anywhere, surely, remarkable here perhaps for the persistence of the sense of bitterness and lapse.

The second observation to make is that a great deal that the older, the decisive generation built seemed good and right to the children who grow up nearby. The expensive and settled neighborhoods, the parks and boulevards, became part of the inheritance of people growing up a generation later, and not the inheritance of something bygone—like the grand old houses in Port Townsend—but an inheritance that could be enjoyed by the living as part of their life. Children who grew up on top of Queen Anne Hill knew children who lived in big houses on the south and west slopes, children who grew up in the Empire Way Valley knew children who lived in Washington Park or Denny Blaine. Except for downtown and in the south end, the parks were everywhere, and of course gradually they ceased being the retirement areas of the rich and became the playgrounds of almost everyone.

I intuit that for those growing up between the wars the most outstanding feature was the city's lack of change, which provided a kind of solidity and possibility that could be simultaneously reassuring and exciting. The child begins by hearing of other places in the city, by knowing that other people go off here or there to work or play or live. Growing up, he or she discovers these places for himself or herself, still in existence eight or ten years later. The street life, the neighborhood life, the city life changes as the mood or the cast of characters changes, but the landscape remains the same: the stream that was in the back yard, the playground down the street, the streetcar lines and the streets, the downtown buildings, all to be found out about in due time. Because it was not dawn, it might not have been bliss to be alive around Green Lake, but to have been young there and then might well have been very heaven. Small and modest houses, most quite new, piled up on the slopes around the lake, which was in itself of perfect size and disposition for the young boater or fisher. To the southwest side were the playfields and tennis courts which still are a great magnet for play and for watching others play; to the west was Woodland Park and the zoo; meandering off to the east was Ravenna Boulevard, which leads to Cowen and Ravenna parks. It is what suburbs sometimes try to be, but never achieve because they cannot stand things so jammed together, and all for a family whose income could be well under two thousand dollars a year.

Fixity of landscape leads to fixity of neighborhood, and these were the great years of Seattle's high schools. Broadway and Garfield were in the middle, with Queen Anne and West Seattle to the west, Franklin and Cleveland to the south, and Ballard, Lincoln, and Roosevelt to the north, none of the buildings older than the century. All the ingredients one can imagine as necessary to great high school life were here. Seattle was a young bourgeois city, where a majority of the adult population seeks, as one mark of its "civilization," to give their children a better education than the one they received. Almost as important, a majority of the population could not seriously imagine college for themselves or their children, so that high school was as far as most would go. In addition, the topographical basis of boundaries for a fairly large number of these schools tended to offer a minor sense of identity while including within almost every high school area a mixture of wealthy, middle-, and working-class people, producing a strong sense that democracy was working here much more than it was in adult life. Also, the resulting blend of racial and ethnic minorities allowed a predominantly white, Anglo-Saxon populace to feel proud of its tolerance, yet remain aware of "the Swedes" in Ballard, or "the Italians" in Rainier Valley, or "the colored people" and "the Japanese" in the central area and the international district because, except in the case of Ballard, none of these minorities was close to being a majority within any given high school.

The result was a very good school system. After the second world war, the possibility of a good high school became increasingly obsolete as the high schools themselves became stations on the road to college for 40 to 80 percent of their graduates, but before this, energies were poured into high school education that later were dissipated as they were spread out over a much longer span of years. Many of the schools had rather strong vocational programs, but the strength at almost all was in the standard academic subjects. In the postwar years, anyone taking two to four years of Latin, four years of math, two to four years of science, in addition to the regular English and history, would be preparing for college. Not so in the twenties and thirties, when many took all that, and did well at a good deal of it, on the way to becoming part of the family business or an employee at Frederick's or a local insurance agency. They received a classic liberal education, far beyond the demands of career and income.

In other words, high school was taken seriously by teachers and by students, and the rewards, whatever else they might be, included a sense of neighborhood community that extended well beyond the immediate neighborhood but that was nonetheless clearly felt by most individuals within it as shared experience. The lad who grew up on 30th Avenue South, say, on a street of modest houses for middle-class people of modest means, not only "knew about" but "knew" the "rich kids" from Mount Baker and the "Italians" from "the valley" and "Japs" from the slopes of Beacon Hill. He knew these people perhaps not as friends but as people in his community, part of his shared experience. The experience was worth something to him intrinsically because Franklin High School was important to him, and worth more because he knew as part of his community experience others raised differently from him, people he knew better than his parents. The pride of graduates from the "integrated" schools, Franklin or Garfield or Broadway, is a naïve pride, because the nonwhite minorities were there in small and undisturbing numbers. It is a real and understandable pride, too, because life in high school was on a scale that offered challenges that could be met. Over and over, people talk about "the feeling" at their school, a feeling that sophisticated people today, thirty and forty years later, are not the least ashamed of. The sentences one hears can vary from "Let me tell you about growing up as a hood in West Seattle in the thirties" to

"I received a better education at Garfield than I did later at the University of Washington or Yale," to "a whole bunch of us from Queen Anne would walk down to the old Opera House on Friday nights and hear a good classical music concert for a quarter." It may be true that human beings never come closer to getting blood from a stone than when deriving nostalgia and lore from bleak experiences, but my sense of growing up in these high schools in the twenties and thirties is not that at all. One might even say that these schools were most possible because the city was static, because the adults had to entrust many of their aspirations to their children.

Of the many potential benefits from good high schools, one that may not stand out is of considerable significance in our history; namely the possibility to derive from such schools a strong sense of the city as a whole. On the one hand, of course, the first strength is more local, of a neighborhood and of a high school serving as a mold for a conglomeration of smaller neighborhoods. But on the other there is the relation among these high schools, their awareness of each other, their lore and mythology about each other, perhaps most often and obviously felt with athletics, but capable of being expressed in many other ways as well.

Here is a city of houses, a population of 350,000, covering therefore a very large area; here are people without cars, but with the ability of young people cheerfully to travel long distances by streetcar or even on foot. The act of going from Roosevelt High School, and of feeling a strong identification with that school, to a game, or a play or a concert or a beach or a fireworks display in the Garfield or the Ballard area is to expand one's world in what must seem a small but potentially significant way. If the child growing up in a static city knows that the downtown buildings and the roads and streetcar lines are all there to be found out about at age twelve just as he or she has heard of them since age five, so too are the other neighborhoods which become places to be explored as soon as one gains the badge of identification offered by one's own school. In a city of houses, in a city where a good deal of neighborhood life is sorted out by income level, this exploring and mixing is a great deal of how one finds out about the city one lives in, and, thereby, about the world one is going to inhabit. The process that begins when the lad on 30th Avenue South finds out about the rich Mount Baker kids continues when he meets the Jewish Garfield kids at Madrona Beach or the Queen Anne crowd at the concert at the old Opera House, which is in Queen Anne territory. No one speaks of city life, under such circumstances, as being anonymous, crushing, alienating. One hears of prejudices aplenty, and snobberies; but the prejudice, about Jews and Italians, was that of parents, and the snobberies, about people with little or less money, seem at least no more marked in Seattle than anywhere else.

One listens to people talk about "the old days" and begins to understand why so many natives of these years between the wars never wanted to leave, or, if forced to do so, they so often found their way back. These people express an ease that is not at all a quality of their personal lives, an ease one associates more with the natives of a small town than those of a good-sized city. It seems the result of having been able to grow outwardly in the right way in their first twenty years, so that the result is not so much complacence (though there is that, to be sure) as urban competence. They learned the city not as an act but as a part of the air they breathe. We will see some of the results of this in the next chapter when we can see what this growing up matured into, what heritage these people claimed.

DAVE BECK

In Murray Morgan's *Skid Road* Seattle between the wars is, simply, "The World of Dave Beck." Morgan was writing in 1951, when Beck was at the height of his power—national Teamster executive vice-president, a preferred customer of the Seattle-First National Bank, regent of the University of Washington—and when nothing in Seattle seemed not his for the asking. Morgan was right, for Beck was the dominant figure of those years, because of what he and Seattle had been in the twenties and thirties.

Immediately following World War I neither labor nor business had any essential strength. The unions were weak, business was hardly thriving except in the basic extractive industries, and one major residue of the General Strike was a profound mistrust of all labor by business. All this was meat and drink for Dave Beck, because he knew that as far as he was concerned labor and business could be partners, if only each would learn to do things his way. After he got out of the navy in 1919, Beck drove laundry truck for a while; by 1920 he was business agent for the local, by 1924 he was secretary. He had caught the eye of San Francisco Teamster boss Mike Casey and national president Dan Tobin, and in 1925 he was hired by the union as a full-time organizer.

Organization was Beck's genius and passion. He cared about wages, hours, and working conditions, not politics or justice or social reform. He wore business suits and denounced communism and really believed in the American Way. Since he never graduated from high school and his manners were a little rough and his determination ruthless, business people took years to realize that he was essentially one of them. He did not want to tell business people how to run their affairs unless it was to show them how to be more efficient and profitable; it was not business he wanted to control, but labor.

It was all home-grown stuff, and probably Beck could never have succeeded as well elsewhere as in Seattle. The old A.F. of L. craft unions were geared to getting and keeping contracts, and Beck agreed with them in denouncing strikes as a losing proposition for both business and labor. He was also interested in organizing whole industries, as the Wobblies had been earlier, as the Committee of Industrial Organizations was to be later, but Beck hated both the I.W.W. and the C.I.O. for their fundamentally antagonistic stance toward business. He wanted to use the Teamsters as a wedge, first to take over, or manage, or at least partially control related unions, like retail clerks and warehousemen, and then to turn to business and industry with full power to make a deal that he could claim was best for both sides. He was certainly not hindered by the fact that trucks were hauling increasing amounts of the country's goods, and by the depressed local economic circumstances that made many union people grateful that Beck could get them steady jobs and many business people happy that, once the deals were struck, they need fear nothing from Beck's unions. Beck always kept his word and his contracts.

The reason Beck came to be thought of as a dictator was not just that his tactics were often brutal or that he controlled a powerful union. His way of doing business meant he began to control business as well and to let everyone else pay. Beck was a good friend of Emil Sick, who brewed Rainier beer and ale, and with whom he bailed out Saint Mark's Episcopal Cathedral when the building was half-finished and the established fortunes had spent all they were going to. One cannot know all the deals Beck and Sick made, but one can note some results: after Prohibition beer in Washington State became by law low in alcoholic content no matter where it was brewed; for all the years Beck was running the Western Conference of Teamsters it was almost impossible for truckers from the east and midwest to haul in beer brewed in their areas; to this day one can buy the full-strength Rainier ale only in Oregon or, at a very high price, in Washington liquor stores, while everywhere else one buys a diluted product. These dilutions and boycotts meant more money for Sick, more loads for Beck's teamsters, and more pulls of the tap in local taverns, whose bartenders Beck also organized.

Or, in a less complicated way, Beck would find ways to fix prices in an entire industry. Gifted with a passion for research and a good business head, he would decide how many filling stations there should be in Seattle, or how many clerks a department store needed, or if there were enough restaurants in a given area. He would then make his deal for just that many gas stations or clerks or restaurants. If someone tried to move in, or to undersell the others, or to lay off clerks, Beck would simply refuse to let trucks go there, and, as a result, soon the industry was what Beck called "stabilized." No labor leader before Beck thought of such things, or got them done if he did.

Nothing did more to gain Beck the support, or at least the grudging respect, of Seattle business people than his fight in the mid-thirties with Harry Bridges and the longshoremen. In 1936 he had backed the Newspaper Guild in a fight against the *Post-Intelligencer*, by then a Hearst paper and slowly losing its long battle for supremacy with the *Times*. That had gotten Beck at least temporary support from housewives, ministers, faculty and students, all of whom supported the guild's pickets. But he had always had a reputation for ruthlessness, and when he moved in and settled the *P-I* strike in favor of the guild, business people were edgy. What were the limits of his power?

Harry Bridges made the answer to that question irrelevant. He was trying to move his power inland from the docks just as Beck was trying to organize everything that depended in any way on trucks. The actual dispute involved nothing more than the warehouses of five drug companies located near the waterfront. Bridges' people got there first, but Beck was not about to honor another union's contracts or pickets if he didn't want to. He tried to organize the whole warehouse as teamsters. The A.F. of L. came in on one side, the C.I.O. on the other, and it was all thrown at the new National Labor Relations Board, which took just long enough to hear and decide the case to give Beck the time he needed. By the time the NLRB said there had to be an election, Beck had gained majority support in most of the warehouses, which was all he needed to gain a Teamster closed shop and to blunt Bridges' power. Beck's methods earned him the anger and hatred of many in other labor unions, but Harry Bridges was "a foreigner," a "Communist," devoted to the struggle against capital and management, and so the Chamber of Commerce began seeing things Beck's way. He was American, a businessman, devoted to the cooperation of labor and management. What really scared business people, it turned out, was that Beck was not only like them but better than they were at what they thought they were good at.

Beck's was a naked grasping of power, and as a cover he kept insisting on all the good he was doing for the teamsters, for business people. Slowly and tirelessly strengthening himself, within the Teamsters throughout the west, within related unions, within the Seattle business establishment, Beck became the most powerful figure in the city and, up to that time, the best-known Seattleite on the national scene. But had power been all there was to it, then when the Internal Revenue Service and the United States Justice Department clipped Dave Beck's wings in the late fifties, that power might have slipped away and left no trace. Instead, his effects can be felt everywhere still, twenty years after he was first indicted, because he was symptomatic of a need as much as being a singular personal force.

By the time Beck effectively left the Teamsters, Seattle was one of the most highly unionized cities in the country and Washington one of the most highly unionized states. Most of this unionization was due to Beck. Labor became powerful by becoming bourgeois and politically conservative if politically anything. What he showed was what many have gone on refusing to believe: Seattle never really had been a great radical labor town. It had been, to be sure, a place where radical labor had met, a place where some radical labor people went on living, but that was more because of the radicals in the lumber camps, the militant progressives in the farm granges, the maverick power of Harry Bridges among west coast longshoremen than because of anything inherently radical in Seattle itself. Seattle business people, generally an unreconstructed lot, were inclined to look at any noise from any union as a sign of incipient revolution; in fact, labor in Seattle might be strong but it was not about to be revolutionary. Most good labor people, and all the liberals who sympathized with labor, hated Beck for selling out the labor movement by making it a business establishment. But Beck knew better than they the age-old appeal of Seattle: get a job, a house, a family, settle down, move to the suburbs, buy a trailer, have good vacations. He was anything but a middle-class reformer, but he was effective because he continued or completed the mission on which middle-class reformers had embarked when they turned their backs on populism, embraced moral reform, and settled in. Beck tamed labor by making it strong, homeowning, content. Here is a voice of such content. It happens to be that of Ralph Potts, a business lawyer, but its purr is Beck-like, Seattle-like:

But out of the Battle of Seattle has arisen a new social structure. There are more working men who own their own homes in Seattle than in any city of equal size in the nation. Seattle is one of the cities that has a record number of automobiles and one of the top metropolises for the number and size of its insurance policies. Savings bank deposits are at a maximum peak. Seattle has become the city of the "little millionaires."

It is the boosterism of Welford Beaton and Judge Burke all over again, this time in the name of Dave Beck.

He was, and is, an ordinary man, for all his huge energies and business acumen, and he sought to make others ordinary. His success was dependent on Seattle itself being more ordinary than it had been. If he did not feel contempt for the average teamster, he unquestionably patronized him, had nothing personally to do with him, told him what he wanted, got him what he said he would. The ground he was working was fertile and the Seattle he exposed was closer to being his than most people would like to admit. James Farley, postmaster-general under President Roosevelt, has often been quoted as saying there were forty-seven states and the Soviet of Washington. He was dead wrong, looking only at the fringes. Seattle was Beck's town, and, in many ways, Washington was Beck's state. The radicals and Communists lived here, but on sufferance, as it were. Beck knew that, and worked hard to make it true.

But if at the very time Beck was coming to power Seattle was a great city in which to grow up, and if it had originally been a city built well, we should be careful not to let Dave Beck become another name for Seattle. In 1957 Constance McL. Green said about the Seattle Beck had seemed to make:

> Family life looms large. People outside the inner circle scarcely matter. Most householders own their own homes [and] are more likely to concern themselves with their rosebeds than with impersonal civic affairs, and with buying new cars than with examining the meaning of Seattle's labor history. Their pride in their city strikes the outlander as uncritical.

What Ralph Potts, himself being in something like the "inner circle," saw and loved was exactly what Green saw and disliked. Both knew Dave Beck was responsible.

But he was in fact only expressing a strain that had been strong in the city all along. If the new rich of the early decades of the century had gained their fortunes and retired, Beck was only finding ways to extend a similar offer and largesse to union people. If he shared with Arthur Denny or R. H. Thomson such qualities as strength of will, belief in capitalism and the sanctity of property, rootedness in the local landscape, he lacked their ability to make, in Green's terms, a care for rosebeds and a care for impersonal civic affairs part of the same concern. Yet the line between them is a narrow one, and it can be drawn and made effective only if we see that it is. Those who say they love Seattle and hate Dave Beck—and there are many of these—are more at war with themselves than they tend to realize. In a city that had lapsed, Beck did what could still be done to extend the terms or the franchise of Seattle's original dream.

Still, cities that have been successful, no matter how lapsed, are more mysterious places than the likes of Dave Beck can possibly know, and we must not fall into the trap of equating the city with its most powerful citizen. Fortunately we have other stories to tell besides his, of others coming of age in Seattle between the wars. Their cases are individual, not collective like Beck's, but they are as revealing as he is of the city in which he thrived.

FIVE PORTRAITS

In 1941 Sir Thomas Beecham accepted a post as director of what he then regarded as only an embryonic musical organization, the Seattle Symphony. He was to remain almost until the end of the war, but perhaps his most famous contribution to the history of Seattle was a remark he made to an audience at the Washington Athletic Club on November 14, 1941: "If I were a member of this community, really I should get weary of being looked on as a sort of aesthetic dust-bin." Beecham did not say just who regarded Seattle as an "aesthetic dust-bin," and he went on to say that he would be quite willing to help in any efforts the city might make to improve matters. But the remark has stuck, probably because it had some merit.

A city that is not growing or maintaining its economy well, a city of good high schools (one can imagine Beecham's response to the very idea), a city whose leading figure is Dave Beck, is not one likely to impress England's greatest conductor with its peaks of cultural achievement. By the most obvious measurements of high culture, Seattle was in those days impoverished, and not just when compared with London but with some other provincial cities in America. It had no showcase, no Cleveland Symphony, no San Francisco Opera, and it did not have the philanthropists of unbounded wealth that might have supported such a showcase. "Give us art and luxury as we can afford them," W. D. Wood had said when opposing Virgil Bogue's plan.

But Wood and perhaps Beecham were conceiving the matter of culture too narrowly. Unquestionably a great cultural showcase can do much to create an atmosphere in which related arts and activities will be benefited and from which the citizenry can gain its bearings. The amateur and the aspiring young often need a fine orchestra or opera company or ballet troupe to give shape to their dreams. Mary McCarthy, Merce Cunningham, Robert Joffrey all had been raised in Seattle, and all had to move away to become the significant figures that they were destined to be. Whatever else sent them on their way, it is hard to imagine what in Seattle's cultural centers could have held them.

The achievements were there nonetheless, though most did not have a great deal to do with high culture conceived primarily as a matter of the performing arts. Most were individual and isolated rather than collective. It is not easy to imagine them happening either earlier or later than they did, either in the burgeoning turn-of-the-century Seattle or in the more affluent Seattle of the Boeing years. They belong distinctively to this period. Richard Fuller, Vernon Parrington, Nellie Cornish, Jesse Epstein, Mark Tobey—each is worth more attention than they can be given here, each is an outsider who could not have done what he or she did where they came from (or perhaps anywhere else), each shows us distinctive and important things about the city between the wars that we could not otherwise see.

Richard Fuller came to Seattle in his mid-twenties because his father, for reasons that are not totally clear, moved here to practice surgery. Fuller himself immediately adopted the place as his home. He had received a B.A. from Yale in 1921, but entered the University of Washington to study geology in 1923, got a second B.A., an M.S., and a Ph.D. The Fuller family, part of the famous New England Fullers, had plenty of money, and Richard Fuller could not have done what he did without it. Behind Fuller's spending, however, there was always a sense that money existed to be spent with care, dedication, and taste. Quiet, shy, forceful, he did almost everything as though he were inwardly so secure and serene that he never left a personal mark of any kind. In 1930 he was elected president of the Art Institute of Seattle, and in the same year he came into his full inheritance when his father died. The result was the Seattle Art Museum, situated in Volunteer Park and owned by the city, but built and paid for by Fuller with his legacy.

That was more than most other local people of means had done or would dream of doing, but for Fuller it was only the beginning. He became director of the museum without pay, a post he held for almost forty years. He donated to the museum a great deal that is now its permanent collection. He made its taste a constant expression of his own, as though the museum itself were a work of art that would take a lifetime to complete. He and the museum came along when it was no longer possible for someone, even someone many times wealthier than Fuller, to go and ransack Europe of its treasures. Had he tried, as Norton Simon did, he could only have picked up what others had left, and while the Simon collection is far from inconsiderable, it is also very much like the collections of others who started buying earlier. Or Fuller might have spent everything on one hugely expensive painting and then tried to call that a museum.

Instead Fuller turned where the collectors of European art had not been—to the Near East, to India, to China and Japan—and to the northwest. He did it slowly, carefully, returning from each of his numerous trips with a scroll or a screen or a vase or a metal or a wooden case, making note of what he would like one day to return and buy. A quiet person, he purchased quiet things. A hurried trip through the museum's collection is a waste of time. One can dash through the Samuel Kress Collection quickly enough, because that is a latter-day gathering of inferior European paintings that the museum uses as its conventional base. But the rest is all unassertive, a lot of it physically small and easily missed, undistinctive to the first or the second glance. When one tries to define Fuller's taste, it seems absurdly easy because so much of what he has acquired is so unassertive. But then it seems impossible because within that huge category there is only variety, with no clear preference made for the work of any country or era or medium. Fuller seems to recognize things of a spirit kindred to his, and then to adapt his admiration to whatever is distinctive about each individual work. As a result, though the museum is clearly the achievement of a single person, beyond certain obvious characteristics, the person is a presence rather than a personality.

So, too, with his patronage of Seattle and northwest painters. Having made his original decision to have the museum be a patron, Fuller seemed to impose no ideas, no dogma, no preferences among the quite large variety of good regional artists. Fuller began by offering regional annual exhibitions, then by giving group and one-man shows; and while he can hardly get or is interested in claiming credit for discovering Mark Tobey, Kenneth Callahan, Morris Graves, Leo Kenney, or Richard Gilkey, he gave them encouragement, in some cases employment, and a showcase for their work. Consequently, a tradition has grown up, not around a particular artist or a particular kind of work, but around the idea that there is, should be, and should continue to be northwest art, some regional in outlook, some not, some quite derivative, some distinctively original.

What Fuller has made in the Seattle Art Museum is not anything that exists to compete favorably or unfavorably with other small museums and collecting. It is in many ways more like the Victoria and Albert Museum in London than like most galleries of paintings, yet where the profusion of the Victoria and Albert bespeaks the great ransacking expeditions of the British within their empire, the Seattle museum bespeaks a single person, quietly alert to what he can do, buy, bring back, show. It is a perfect expression of this kind of quiet and elegant taste that when, late in life, Fuller married, he and his wife bought the Baillargeon house on East Prospect in Washington Park, where the music room is decorated by a series of wonderful Mark Tobey murals, themselves unlike much of Tobey's work at the time but just like Richard Fuller, pastels of quiet elegance that seem at once still and in motion. They were not, but nonetheless they seem, made for Fuller.

Vernon Parrington could not have had a more different background than Richard Fuller's. Fuller's ancestry was Boston, intellectual, wealthy, as aristocratic as all but a few families in America; Parrington's was poor and bleak, from what he taught a whole generation to call the Middle Border. Fuller went to Yale, Parrington to Emporia College in Kansas. Yet not only did both settle and achieve their measure of greatness in Seattle, but both were quiet, shy, forceful, formal people, finding here precisely the surroundings they needed.

Parrington was a generation older than Fuller, and his life was ending when most of Fuller's was just beginning. His roots lie in a populist time of the sort that Fuller would never have known. After leaving Emporia College he went to Harvard and he hated and feared it in ways that shaped him as much as his home had done. He went back to Emporia, taught for three years, then moved to the University of Oklahoma, where he was the English department and football coach. He was fired in 1908 because, apparently, Parrington had been to Harvard, and those who fired him hated and feared it as much as he did. It is hard to think where he could have gone, since he had had enough of eastern pretensions and midwest know-nothings, other than the odd, quiet school in Seattle, the University of Washington. It was barely a college then, and decidedly not the university it was later to become. In 1908 Seattle was still populist enough to give Parrington a sense that he knew where he was, but it was a city too, though unlike the behemoths of power that had put him off in the east.

From all accounts, the University of Washington in Parrington's time was a pleasant, benign, and undemanding place. College was still possible only for a quite small number of students, the faculty tended to be badly underpaid, and most departments consisted of one or two professors and a large number of young instructors. One probably should not inquire into how good the university was, though it is clear that a few faculty and a few students were very good indeed. The children of the wealthy did not go to the University of Washington, but to Stanford or the east, yet there were enough who came from more modest or more intellectually ambitious families to keep the university growing until the middle-class high schools began feeding students there as a matter of course.

It was perfect for Parrington. He had plenty of privacy and time to work on his own, he had enough good and demanding students, he had an intellectual atmosphere, insofar as it existed at all, that was liberal, radical, progressive—the words are never accurate when lifted from their normal political moorings and placed down on a college campus. Parrington taught carefully and quietly but in ways students found exciting, filled with the conviction that the students had been raised in a tradition wider and deeper than they knew: Jefferson above all, but Jackson and Lincoln and John Ruskin and William Morris as well. It was the kind of teaching that implicitly flatters as it fosters questions and engagement and respect for the past. It was partisan teaching, because Parrington could not but convey his contempt for the powerful, the eastern, the Federalist. But his kind of partisanship could instill a desire to know the great patterns of a culture, the good and the bad, in order to enforce the partisanship with warmth, learning, taste, humanity. The result was not just a generation of adoring students—Edmond Meany had had that just by being narrowly chauvinistic about the northwest—but *Main Currents in American Thought*, written over Parrington's years in Seattle, three volumes published between 1927 and 1930, just before and after he died, and still the best book to come out of this city.

It happened that the publication of Parrington's book coincided with the arrival of the liberal intellectuals of the thirties, so that it gained a quick and powerful popularity throughout the country. "His book now stands at the center of our thought about America" wrote Lionel Trilling in a very critical assessment in 1940. As often happens, however, the book that stands in one decade at the center of thought stands in succeeding decades very much in the shadows. *Main Currents in American Thought* will never again be read as it was by the eager liberal young throughout America in the thirties, but it is a vastly better work than its subsequent detractors have tried to realize, one that people who share none of Parrington's bias can read with admiration and pleasure.

Bias it has: Jeffersonian, rural, democratic, French, as opposed to Hamiltonian, city, federalist, English. But no one reads the three volumes of this capacious survey of America looking just for Parrington's bias, which is only his way of shaping, not his sense of what we must see. The whole work is done in portraits and, when Parrington is at his best, in groups of portraits that for him make up the "mind" of a region in a given period. Here, for instance, is part of the portrait of Jefferson Davis:

> Jefferson Davis was cut out from the same tough oak that fashioned John C. Calhoun. Hard and unyielding, tenacious of opinion, dictatorial, somewhat inclined to arrogance, he might break, but he would not bend. The Scotch-Irish stock was rarely genial or tolerant, and Davis possessed none of the seeming pliability of Lincoln that yielded the non-essentials to secure the essentials. Utterly lacking in humor and easy-going good nature, he offended by his very virtues. Profoundly Puritan, he was narrow and rigid, a legalist in temperament, proud and jealous of authority. Meticulously honest, he could not get on well with men, he quarreled with his generals and wore himself out trying to do everything himself. . . . At bottom he was a Jeffersonian and to the end of his life he was faithful to the principles of his party. Kindly and humane, he treated his dependents with singular consideration. He set up a curious little democracy amongst the slaves of his plantation, and his negroes were devoted to him with rare loyalty. There was in his nature not the slightest trace of the exploiter; he was a patriarchal master after the old Virginia ideal, with no hint of the speculator or the middleman. The background of his thought was agrarian and he shared with Jefferson a dislike for capitalistic industrialism. The President of the Confederacy may have been an unfortunate civil leader, but the slanders that so long clung to his name are only worthy of the gutter. The sin that he was led into was not counted sin in his southern decalogue; it was the sin, not of secession, but of imperialism—a sin common to all America in those drunken times when the great West invited exploitation.

The bias is clearly "there." We understand that "Jeffersonian" and "agrarian" are good, that "speculator" and "capitalistic industrialism" and "exploiter" are bad. But the portrait that Parrington builds is much more complicated than this idea of his preferences can possibly indicate. We are asked to see how "hard and unyielding," "lacking in humor," "proud and jealous of authority," "kindly and humane," "patriarchal master," and "no hint of the speculator" all belong to one man driven pathetically beyond his limits because of "those drunken times" when the country was exploiting the frontier. Parrington keeps asking his reader to be nimble, to jump, not to relax, to see virtue in unlikely places, to extend sympathy because circumstances can crush, to make the act of judging both stern and a gesture of the heart.

From this one can see that Parrington is best when he does not have a full-fledged hero or villain to deal with, when he himself cannot let his bias control everything, as with his portrait gallery of Abolitionists: William Lloyd Garrison, John Greenleaf Whittier, Harriet Beecher Stowe. The common beliefs of these three highlighted rather than muted their individuality, so that for twenty-five pages the writing turns and turns again, and we feel a sense of great human density and variety derived from just three members of a militant minority, and Parrington is warm in approval, clear in judgment, complex in vision. Abolitionism is a particular strain of a Yankee puritanism that Parrington is apt to dislike, yet here it is put in the service of a noble cause, Garrison giving it a needed stridency, Whittier a needed gentleness, Stowe a needed unconscious literary power. So too with the series of portraits that ends Parrington's section on New York, which fell victim to bossism as Hamilton had feared, which bloated itself with commercial triumph, which drove James Fenimore Cooper to strange and misunderstood political positions, which shaped Bryant, Greeley, and Melville, all New York, all very different from each other, all bound by a common experience which Parrington uses as a glue to bring them together.

Most of what is best in this full and polished way of Parrington's is in his second volume. The first, dealing with colonial America, comes too close to Parrington's prejudices and covers a period he did not know enough about, while the third, dealing with America after the Civil War, is sadly unfinished, though often superb in places, as in the section on the Great Barbeque that ends with a typical excellent gallery of folk heroes: Ulysses S. Grant, Jay Cooke, and Charles A. Dana. Later, after the decade of the thirties when Parrington was adored, critics began complaining that he had slighted the "literature" of America because he was vitally engaged in political and social issues. Thus, it was often alleged, he gives only two pages to Poe and a dozen to William Gilmore Simms, a minor and almost totally unread literary figure in pre–Civil War Charleston. Parrington did this not because he thought Simms was six times better than Poe, but because Simms can tell us more about the ante-bellum South; put Simms together with Alexander Stephens and John C. Calhoun and we see the "mind of the South" moving from Virginia to South Carolina at a time when Charleston could hold sway only briefly over the more rapacious spirits that were turning the gulf states into the Black Belt. When Parrington has the feel of a period in his fingertips, then every trait of every individual portrait, every event, every ironic play can be both an individual characteristic and a generalization for a whole period and region. This may lead to a slighting of Poe, but Poe is in no serious danger of being ignored anyway, and what is gained in exchange is much more valuable, really, than another portrait of Poe could be. For thirty and forty pages at a stretch Parrington gathers and folds a variety of figures and groups in a way that is both clarifying and grand. Parrington's own aloof and somewhat stubbornly naïve temperament is expressed in a prose that is always American in its idiom and English neoclassic— like Gibbon or Johnson—in its structure. His critics have not produced anything as good to take its place, and the work that has replaced it as the central book about American literature, D. H. Lawrence's *Studies in Classic American Literature,* may be a better book in some important ways than *Main Currents in American Thought,* but is so different from Parrington's as not to begin to supersede it.

Parrington believed in the frontier as strongly as any populist, but he was under no illusions about the pinching and narrowing meanness of frontier life. As early as 1903 he wrote an essay for *House Beautiful* called "On the Lack of Privacy in American Village Homes," and because of this insight, of all the portraits in *Main Currents,* the one that rings deepest and truest is the lonely section on Hamlin Garland, stuck off amidst chapters that were only outlined or partially written in the third volume. Reading it, we can see most clearly the forces that shaped not only Garland but Parrington himself, and also begin to see why Seattle did so much for Parrington, why he might not have been able to do anything as good had he not come here. Garland was also a son of the Middle Border, only ten years older than Parrington, so as we read about the feelings of the one we are really reading about the feelings of the other:

> The blight laid upon men and women and children by the drab pioneer life was a familiar fact to him. The Garlands and the McClintocks had suffered from it as their neighbors suffered, and a rebellious wrath filled his heart as he contemplated the Middle Border—the barnyards where tired men did the evening chores, the ungainly houses where tired women stood over hot stoves, the fertile acres that produced more than the markets consumed. It was a life without grace or beauty or homely charm—a treadmill existence that got nowhere. If this were the Valley of Democracy then the democracy was a mean thing and helpless, and having himself escaped from it he would do what he could to help others escape. . . . And yet in the light of his total work one hesitates to call Garland a realist.

Perhaps more justly he might be called a thwarted romantic, and his early rebellious realism be traced to its source in a passionate refusal to be denied the beauty that should be a portion of any rational way of living.

For Parrington to go from the mean and hopeless Valley of Democracy to Harvard was all wrong, because the frontier student was too proud to treat himself or to let himself be treated as a hick, however bright. But clearly the return, to Emporia and Oklahoma, was all wrong too. So he came west, to where the frontier was completely in city life, and it made all the difference.

Seattle in the years of Parrington's maturity still had its own populist tradition, a thwarted one to be sure, but more vital than it could still be farther east. Seattle was not mean and drab, but lush, green, quiet, filled with beautiful houses and invitations to formality and seclusion. That it was static may have been part of its appeal. Here he could settle, and feel both the thwarted romanticism of his frontier populist belief and the quiet formality of his temperament gain strength, direction, flexible life. He lived on 19th Avenue Northeast, in a comfortable house a few blocks from the university, where he worked on his garden and in his greenhouse and on his great book all in the same spirit, quietly and slowly. He did not need what Seattle could not have given him: the abrasiveness or constant challenge of one's peers, the visible signs of an older culture. But from here he could look backward into American history and find more than a buttress for his own thwarted populism, though he could find that too.

Although the third volume of *Main Currents* is only a torso and some fragments, it shows what the years in Seattle had done for Parrington's sense of American history and destiny. As he comes down closer to the present, he gains confidence from his having conceived and written this huge book, as he also becomes more troubled and dubious because there is so much to be angry about, so much to persuade him that the American enterprise had never truly found itself. Parrington was not Hamlin Garland because he had come to Seattle, where he could find ways of matching his own delight in portaiture and architecture with the grandness of the sweep of American history, where he could match his own angry, thwarted frontier romanticism with a sense that our history would make a thwarted and angry romantic out of anyone. There is no evidence that Parrington was in any sense a city person, but only a city like this one could have provided what he then needed. He did not enter into the populist arena as did his friend and colleague J. Allen Smith, but he needed the sense that such an arena might still exist. He did not need a city of high culture because he was both too shy and too much a frontier man to be susceptible to that kind of thing. Grand, formal, quiet, stubborn, naïve—it seems an odd combination of qualities, but they express, at least in part, both Parrington and the Seattle he found a home in. Had he been born or come to Seattle earlier, the city undoubtedly would have been too crude and bustling; had he been born or come much later, the city undoubtedly would have seemed too much the creature of capitalistic industrialism. But in the static period in between, Parrington came and found himself, and quietly wrote his book.

In the fall of 1914 Nellie Cornish was thirty-eight, a single woman living in Salt Lake City. She had just been frustrated in her desire to study music in Europe by the outbreak of the war. She felt she was coming to the end of whatever life she had known, which had been spent teaching music, mostly in Seattle, according to methods she had picked up from a Boston woman named Fletcher-Copp, herself a follower of Maria Montessori, and from a California man named Calvin Cady, who gave lectures up and down the coast on "The Education of the Individual through the Realm of Music and Allied Arts." Nellie Cornish had had at least moderate success as a teacher, but something about it had not satisfied her. She had ideas, but clearly felt she had missed something by never having had a formal music education, by having picked up what she knew from here and there. From Salt Lake she wrote Mrs. Fletcher-Copp in Boston to inquire about the possibility of establishing a music school for children in Boston; Mrs. Fletcher-Copp replied that she had neither knowledge nor experience enough. Apparently this convinced Miss Cornish only to give up going to Boston, for she returned to Seattle, which she had left only six months earlier with the intention of never going back, and opened The Cornish School, in the Booth Building, on the corner of Broadway and East Pine Street, across from Broadway High School. The school became Seattle's pride and joy; that it never quite became what it could have been is one of its great shames.

The Cornish School was successful from the beginning, mostly because Miss Cornish insisted that it be. During her critical months in Salt Lake, she had read and been steadied by reading Mary Baker Eddy, who gave Miss Cornish none of the trappings of Christian Science but, instead, a central confidence in human will. Her idea was not to teach instruments, though most of her first pupils were simply taking piano lessons, but to teach music, and music in relation to all the other arts. It was one of the many ideas we now associate with progressive education, though Miss Cornish knew no such name and might have disapproved if she had. The emphasis was on neither knowledge nor technique, but on understanding, and its aim was not virtuosi but expressive and capable people. One of the first things she did after obtaining enough pupils and teachers to get established was to hire Calvin Cady, who had given her the idea in the first place and was for thirteen years The Cornish School's central intellectual force. They were both lucky in finding each other. Most people who toured the west lecturing on culture were either frauds or harmless drudges, but Cady was solid and serious as well as compelling, a good man with a strong mind. Miss Cornish gave him what he could not otherwise have found, a school built by her will and energy, dedicated to music and untainted by a *Heart Songs* mentality, able to attract a loyal regular faculty and a distinguished group of visitors.

The school thrived. After piano came singing and stringed instruments, and then a dance school and a theater; later came puppetry and eurythmics and drawing and painting. The summer school was able to attract faculty and students who could not come full-time during the year, and that gave the operation as a whole a confidence and a prestige that sustained it during the winter. If one tries to imagine a school with a steady, competent, and reliable faculty, made up mostly of local people, invaded by a steady stream of mercurial outsiders of great talent and appeal, one imagines trouble. A regular teacher gets along on a small salary and under cramped working conditions, then sees a visitor come in, at a greater salary, who demands and gets a new studio, or a stage, or new costumes or lighting. Clearly there was trouble, and, equally clearly, it was overcome by Miss Cornish's insistence that it had to be. It was an insistence that the goal was not a style or a format but a school, an integrated education and life for the students, who needed both the steady competence of the permanent people and the splash and talent of the eastern or foreign visitors. The most promising violinist in the school was expected not just to learn solfège and to play in chamber groups, but to play for dance and ballet recitals and for musical theater and marionette shows, perhaps to take part in the dancing and theatrical productions as well. No one had his or her own way about these matters; this was serious business, a school.

Miss Cornish, in her autobiography, *Miss Aunt Nellie*, calls the years between 1924 and 1927 Cornish's golden years. In 1921 the school moved out of the Booth Building into a new one built just for the school and to Miss Cornish's specifications. After the war it became increasingly possible for her to hire a very distinguished series of Europeans, especially White Russians, and for a few years the whole operation seemed to be what she and Cady had dreamed it could become. In 1928 Cady died, and, Miss Cornish said, "after he left us, the School never seemed to me quite as important as before." So it was the mid-twenties that were golden, and a look at the program for the summer school of 1925 will show us in outline what it was like during its heyday. There were twelve piano teachers, headed by Berthe Poncy; three violin teachers, headed by Peter Merenblum; one harp, three voice, two eurhythmics, two drama, three dance, and four art teachers, including Mark Tobey. In addition, students could take courses in public school music, phonetics, weaving, French, and German. There were about 150 full-time students and about 250 part-time students. The daily schedule for full-time students was six hours of regular classes plus as many more for private lessons and practicing. A typical program for a piano student beyond the beginning stage, for instance, consisted of an hour of advanced solfège and an hour of the science of music, two hours of harmony, and two hours of eurhythmics; students beyond that stage took more harmony, more eurhythmics, and two hours of ensemble. How much private work the student took depended both on the student's talent and ability to pay. The school placed great emphasis on classroom work, because Miss Cornish felt the students were there not just to perform but to become a certain type of person. The school was intended to fill the lives of students and faculty completely; when they were not in classes or private lessons, they were in practice and rehearsal. There is a note in the 1925 catalogue that reads: "The Director does not approve of students living in rooms and apartments without board. However, when the economic necessity demands arrangements may be made for students to live in approved apartments." That may seem mostly like a moral statement, but it was meant also as a pedagogical one. To be a student at Cornish left no time for buying groceries and keeping house.

Given this emphasis, one cannot assess the achievement of The Cornish School by listing the distinguished faculty it once attracted, or the famous names among its graduates. It might be important in public relations to say that Martha Graham taught there for a while before she became famous, or that Chet Huntley studied radio at Cornish during the thirties, but beyond that purpose such lists do not matter. The idea was absorption not in one's talent but in one's ability to grow in a life in the arts. Obviously, "having talent" mattered, because even rudimentary performing can be frustrating without it. The point about the talent, however, was not that it should be exploited into virtuosity but that it should be used as a means to understanding, creation, expression. On the other hand, there was never any nonsense about creativity with Miss Cornish; to do anything took work and discipline, to do any one thing well, furthermore, took work and discipline in more than one thing. It is an idea or ideal that is at once lofty and democratic, similar in that way to Parrington's *Main Currents* and to Richard Fuller's establishment of his personal collection as a public art museum.

Unlike Fuller, however, Nellie Cornish had no private fortune, and, unlike Parrington, she needed a good deal of money to do her work well. She was constantly plagued with financial problems, constantly convinced that the school was ahead of its time in Seattle. She may have been right, and by the time that at least some money for the arts became available in Seattle, The Cornish School no longer had Miss Cornish, and so has continued to suffer as she did. In the early years the school's leading benefactor was Axel Soelberg, a banker and personal friend of Miss Cornish who kept the beginning school going with gifts and loans. Later, the wives of two lumber barons, Mrs. A. H. Anderson and Mrs. C. H. Stimson, gave generously and worked hard at getting others to give. Still later, the daughter of another lumberman, Olive Kerry, helped a great deal.

But a handful of benefactors could never be enough, especially since Miss Cornish insisted on being generous with scholarships. To the people who knew the school, it was remarkable how much got done without extravagance, but to the reasonably wealthy citizens of Seattle it was a luxury, an "Art School," to them worse and not better because Miss Cornish insisted that money was secondary to excellence. Mrs. Anderson might at a moment's notice write the school a check for seventy-five hundred dollars, and Mrs. Stimson might persuade a local banker not to be stingy, but that only meant the school could stay open, as it always did and has done, and it also meant that it could never gain the endowment it needed to survive lean years, and to continue without the constant energy and genius of Miss Cornish herself. When Calvin Cady died in 1928, some of Miss Cornish's enthusiasm went with him; when she herself left in 1939, the school was on the one hand a famous institution in Seattle and, on the other, doomed to decline. We have seen the habits of mind of the wealthy being formed in the years shortly after the turn of the century, so it should not be surprising that there was little recognition from them of what Miss Cornish had achieved and of what she needed from those who would have to sustain that achievement.

Still, The Cornish School is a striking instance of the best kind of institution for a provincial city to have, one that draws heavily upon and enriches local talent as it enlivens and broadens itself by bringing in fresh, talented people from outside. As I was looking into the history of The Cornish School I talked to two people who had been there during its golden years and who in their strikingly different ways expressed a common love and understanding of Miss Cornish and the school. Ellen Wood Murphy, who was with Miss Cornish even before there was a Cornish School, was born and raised in the Puget Sound area, and is as plainly and splendidly straightforward American as can be. She taught a number of musical subjects, primarily solfège, so that she worked with beginning students. When she talked about Cornish what shone through were patience and warmth and an almost tireless devotion to the simple and beautiful fact of people learning. She is precisely the sort of person one wants so much and so seldom finds in a beginning teacher.

Let Ellen Murphy represent the home-grown side of Miss Cornish and her school, and then put beside her Berthe Poncy Jacobson, a Swiss woman who had been educated at the Schola Cantorum in Paris and who, while teaching eurhythmics at the Dalcroze School in Geneva, had met and married an American student, Wallace Dow. Miss Cornish brought them both to Seattle and then discovered that Berthe Poncy was an excellent pianist and an excellent piano teacher. What struck Poncy about The Cornish School, and what endeared it to her, was its great difference from the European schools she had known: its emphasis on education, its refusal to nurture the single desire for virtuosity. Berthe Poncy became one of the school's leading performers as part of the Cornish Trio, which for years was the highlight of all Cornish recitals, but she loved the school for the same reasons Miss Cornish and Ellen Murphy did. Elegant, cultured, filled with opinions and charm, where Ellen Murphy is plain and warm and full of humor, she represents the European and the fully developed artist at The Cornish School. What was striking in talking to these two people was, first, how different they seemed, and, second, how they told the same story.

Almost any building in the world can make someone or other nostalgic because the memory is quite capable of making the plain seem lovely and the ugly seem quaint. The remarkable quality about The Cornish School building is that it can invoke nostalgia in someone who has never studied or taught there. When first built, the school was in a quiet residential neighborhood, just off the streetcar line on Broadway. The neighbors had protested when the Century Club raised its building on East Roy, and they grumbled some more when

Miss Cornish moved in. All that has changed. The apartments are now a mixture of new and old; the Century Club has been turned into a movie theater, the Harvard Exit; the Russian Samovar restaurant is all that remains of Miss Cornish's Russians, Peter Merenblum, Elena Miramova, Alexander Koiransky. Nearby are the severely colonial D.A.R. building and the enchanting Loveless Block, stores and apartments of an elegance that Arthur Loveless alone among traditional Seattle architects seemed to have. It is one of the finest sequences of buildings on a street in Seattle, and, as one walks past the others and comes on The Cornish School, one sees that for all the changes that have taken place since 1920, the essence of the neighborhood is still there, the site for the school still right, Miss Cornish correct in thinking her school would not destroy the residential quality. The building itself is good enough: stucco, solid, not remarkable. Both outside and inside one finds the same combination of taste and functional plainness that marks Miss Cornish and the school in every respect. "The Cornish School: Dance, Drama, Music," says the lettering on the façade, in a way that is firm, precise, but not intimidating. The halls inside are bare, and the wooden floors are perfect at making one feel that work is being done here; there is no fakery, no showiness. Yet at night, when a concert or a performance is about to go on, bustle, laughter, and elegance can transform the place into a celebration.

The 1930s were the bleakest of all Seattle's years, as they were for many American cities, and if the young could personally feel the Depression mostly as a fact in the lives of their parents, the parents could feel it straight, hard, crushing. The dedication of the New Deal of Franklin Roosevelt led to the appearance of the federal government in Seattle in a way that was new to the city, exciting to some, poison to others. Its two most visible legacies were Harborview Hospital on First Hill and the Public Health Hospital on Beacon Hill, and neither is a joy to the eye; the Public Health Hospital is indeed like the Depression itself, hard and crushing in appearance. But in between these two buildings is the Yesler Terrace housing project, a shining New Deal achievement, and the major work of Jesse Epstein, a man almost totally unknown in Seattle, then or now, a man whose story is in outline like that of many others, but whose intelligence, perseverance, decency, and quiet vision deserve special memorial as one of the clearest instances of what one person and a government can do, if the one person is the right person.

Epstein came to Seattle from a small town in Montana to go to the University of Washington, from which he graduated in 1931 as a political science major. He went to law school to study constitutional and administrative law to prepare himself for some kind of government career; in his own mind he was a staunch and unradical liberal, one of many his age who were excited by the idea of governmental action as a means of extricating the country from the grasp of the Depression. He took a job with the Washington State Research Council, which at the time included the Associated Cities of Washington, and he kept cities informed of the impact and benefits of New Deal legislation. Thus, when the National Housing Authority was formed in 1937, Epstein went to the mayor of Seattle, Arthur Langlie, and told him how Seattle could get federal money to begin slum clearance projects. Langlie, a progressive downtown Republican, was lukewarm, but told Epstein to form a committee to secure state enabling legislation so the city could have a housing authority. The committee was mostly Epstein himself, and he successfully lobbied the legislature, and then the Seattle City Council, in 1939. Epstein became chairman of the board of the Seattle Housing Authority and then, when the federal government appeared with three million dollars, Epstein resigned that post to become executive director of the SHA.

He had what was in those days a great deal of money to spend, which of course gave him entrée to all the people he wanted to see, but the reception he got was mixed: people were mostly curious, some friendly, some hostile. The whole idea of slum clearance and federal housing was not only new but likely to rub Seattle people the wrong way. In a sprawling city of houses, lots of people never see slums and do not like to call what they do see by that name. There was no housing shortage, but a generation of stagnation and neglect and a legacy of overspeculation in real estate left the city with many empty houses and apartments and many people living in shacks, especially in the area known as Hooverville, down in the tideflats. In a number of residential areas near downtown the situation was bad enough so that no one would have lost much money had the houses been torn down, but the fear of lost profits in the future was enough to alarm many real estate people. The area Epstein chose for the first SHA development, at the south end of First Hill, at the top of the old Yesler Skid Road, was replete with abandoned houses and apartments partly occupied, and its major retail business was prostitution. Undoubtedly, if that area had simply disappeared from the earth, few in Seattle would know or care. But still, the idea of "the government going into competition with private enterprise" was alarming, and so Epstein had to go out, over and over again, and sell his project to businesses and civic groups. Small in stature, mild in manner, soft in speech, quietly and even confidently assured in purpose, Epstein presented himself as he saw himself, as a bureaucrat more than a revolutionary. His task was, first, to calm ruffled feathers; second, to assemble all the people he would need to build the best project he could imagine; third, to get it built; and, fourth, to get people to come live there. There were obstacles at each stage.

The site Epstein chose was suitable not just because it was a slum: it was close to shopping, schools, and Harborview Hospital, it was accessible to downtown and to the industrial area by streetcar, and it commanded a fine 180-degree view of the west and south, so that the people who lived there could feel a pride of place and those who did not could see it easily. Epstein chose five architects rather than one, partly because it was a lucrative contract and deserving of being divided, but mostly because Epstein felt he had spotted different people in different firms who were best suited to different parts of the project. George Stoddard, Lister Holmes, and John T. Jacobson did the designs, William Aitken did the administering, William Bain did design specification and procurement. Nothing visible in Epstein's background shows a genius for such picking of the right people to do jobs in fields in which he himself was not expert. He not only got the right people, but he got some prestigious people, too, whose names were useful in silencing Epstein's critics. The result was Yesler Terrace, completed in 1941 and fully occupied almost right away.

Yesler Terrace looked good when first completed, and looks even better now, because it was built to last, because the trees have grown up around it, because we have had so much experience in the interim to see how bad such housing projects can be. The great curse of low-cost housing is the sameness that seems to try to demean each person into being like every other, with the added curse that if the housing is for the poor, the poor then become set apart and identified. Though Yesler Terrace works with the same colors and materials throughout, it constantly shows these from different angles and stances, so that the houses seldom seem to be repeating each other. The topography of the hillside is used to force the eye to be aware of differences, and both new and previously existing streets are employed to avoid the sense that the whole thing is just dropped down from the sky. The number of houses in a row, the distances between rows, the different heights of the dwellings, the distribution of lawn and street space—all these are varied in interesting and unarbitrary ways. Given this, what was good and plain when the project opened could be transformed into something accommodating and beautiful, as the trees grew, the wood weathered, as the residents built their gardens. Once a housing project feels like a demeaning place to live, its residents will gradually let it fall apart through carelessness and then bored wantonness. That happened in most other projects in the city and country which were more quickly and sloppily built, and that has never happened in Yesler Terrace, which today has the look of an old, settled neighborhood. If it was not built for the ages, it was built to have a long and good life.

Jesse Epstein did more than choose the people who designed and built the project. He also insisted from the beginning that Yesler Terrace was going to be racially integrated, which was almost unheard of at the time and disturbed many potential residents of all races. The NHA and FHA policy was not to rock whatever boat was floating locally; Epstein's policy was not to have a policy that people could argue about, but quietly to go about making a project that did not deny the obvious fact that people of all races were poor. Epstein says he had not intended when he first chose the Yesler site to pick a place near where minorities were already living, but the site happened to be such a place, and that had the effect of convincing both blacks and Asians that they were not unwanted. The blacks were the most wary; even after they applied to live in Yesler Terrace, they seemed to want to have their own separate section, which they got, though to as small an extent as Epstein could wangle. So here was a small, quiet Jew from Montana, forming and blending an integration of urban whites, blacks, and Asians, an idea that was no one's but his own, and it was only after Epstein had done it that others could see he had created a project that in this and every other respect was a model of its kind.

Epstein continued as director of the SHA all through the war and supervised the construction of four more permanent projects: Rainier Vista on Empire Way, Holly Park at the south end of Beacon Hill, Highpoint in West Seattle, Sand Point near the naval air station on Lake Washington. None was or could later be made to be what Yesler Terrace is, mostly because wartime shortages made it difficult to get the right materials and because their sites were chosen in somewhat remote areas that could be obtained with little negotiation and litigation. None is bad, but none has thrived either, and one reason for this must be that integrated projects in these remote areas tend to stick out, to be alien from the surrounding urban ecology, to stand as incitements to racism rather than replies to its follies. More than one person has pointed out that Yesler Terrace is better than most middle-income, privately developed complexes, in Seattle and else-where; it is only at rare moments that anyone can feel inspired to say that about any of the other four, though this was no fault of Ep-stein's.

During its heyday the Seattle Housing Authority consisted of one office with space enough for Epstein, an assistant, and a secretary. Given the way it and other bureaucracies have proliferated since, this original set-up is an invitation to envy, and nostalgia. But the New Deal spawned lots of such offices, and few that left anything like Jesse Epstein's legacy of Yesler Terrace. Epstein's way of work-ing was different entirely from Vernon Parrington's or Nellie Cor-nish's; it was the configuration of a single person, working with quiet intensity and full integrity, taking advantage of what the static city could offer to produce something unique, is still there. As it is with the last figure in our gallery, Mark Tobey.

Tobey was a midwest painter struggling to make ends meet as a magazine illustrator in New York when a friend of his, George Brown, persuaded him to come west to Seattle where, Brown was sure, Miss Nellie Cornish could find something for him to do. He came, thirty-two and single, and Miss Cornish hired him to teach, even though he had never taught before. He seems to have done superbly from the beginning: "For children, Tobey's advice to anx-ious parents was: 'Just give them materials and be interested in art yourself.' Older students were told to 'start with the imagination,' and then to 'go out and look at things, to study them, and that will stimulate your retentive memory and your retentive memory will bring it back in your imagination again.' " The imagination, the memory, "go out and look at things"—it is an ideal that appeals to curiosity and intellect as well as to eye and imagination; it is a way of insisting that each person makes his and her own discoveries, but in a way that makes no appeal to the ego of the discoverer.

As his students questioned him, and because he had no formal training to fall back on, he studied other painters on his own to see what answers they offered to such questions. That, in turn, led to his characteristic "personal discovery of cubism":

> One night at the Cornish School he pictured himself, in his mind, working in a small, centrally illuminated room. Within this compartment a portrait on an easel before him formed a smaller compartment of space. Next he imagined a fly moving freely around him and the objects in the room. It was able to move up or down, and in any other direction, to light on the artist's back, head, or hand, on the ceiling, wall or floor, and then to take off in another direction. As the path of movement crossed and recrossed

around the central axis, it generated a complex of line, and by its many crossings, imaginary planes and shapes. Although related to the objects in the room, this secondary matrix of form was independent of them, and was entirely the product of movement.

As one might well imagine, Tobey never became a cubist painter in the manner of Picasso or Braque; it is not really cubism that he discovered here, although because he thought it was, he painted some rather obvious cubist works shortly thereafter. The discovery is space in motion, what would become the white light of his work ten years later, and what still is close to being his signature. That the discovery occurred ten years before its implementation is not surprising either. Since Tobey's learning was all personal, trusting of the imagination (as a guide, not as some primal romantic force), the learning was slow and might even have seemed haphazard, since it was pointing toward not a "style" so much as an ability to do all the things he wanted to do.

Tobey liked Seattle very much, but he was too restless to stay for long. By 1925 he was in Paris, then back in this country for a while, then in England between 1931 and 1938. Had World War II not happened, he might never have come back, since it was only when he realized that he was going to have to live in this country that he then decided he would rather be in Seattle than anywhere else. He was here from 1938 to 1960, the years of his later maturity, the years in which he became a painter of regional, then national, then international importance. It might seem that a discussion of him does not belong in this chapter, "between the wars," but, as we will see, Tobey's sense of Seattle and his work here can tell us a good deal about the changes that did and did not take place when World War II came.

There had been a breakthrough in Tobey's painting before he returned to Seattle; it occurred in 1935, in England, with *Broadway Norm, Broadway,* and *Welcome Hero.* Here the fly he had imagined back in his room at Cornish becomes a fine white brush moving against a darker background, and the surface is both used as a surface and set in motion by the white line that keeps the eye moving "into" or "beyond" the surface. Tobey was interested in and had learned from too many things to cry "Eureka" and go on to more of the same. But while he painted in many different media and with many different styles that developed many different ways of being "realistic" and "abstract," he did, after 1935, have a method that was distinctly his and that could be used in everything he did. Lots of other things enter in: Oriental influences, both Chinese and Japanese; the Baha'i faith to which Tobey had long adhered, and Zen; traces of what seems like the influence of Klee and Kandinsky. None of these, especially taken separately, is of much importance compared to the assurance that the Broadway paintings gave. Now whatever he turned to he could do, so that everything he saw or imagined could be explored as if for its own sake and still be distinctively his.

As the Broadway paintings show, Tobey felt most of the familiar twentieth-century fears about the largeness and inhumanity of big American cities, and he loved Seattle for the many ways it was not like Chicago or New York. Of course, Seattle never has been very much like those cities, but in the late thirties its pace must have been leisurely, its demeanor pacific and unthreatening, a depressed area economically, but with great natural beauty and acquired charm. Tobey would continue to love it as long as it stayed that way. He lived on Brooklyn Avenue Northeast, near the still small and unhurried university, he had his studio on University Way, which was still only a residential shopping district and not an emporium and haunt for students. The houses, apartments, stores, and schools had almost all been built in the years right after the university moved out of downtown and the streetcar line was put in over University Bridge, and thirty and forty years later gave a sense of being weathered and settled.

When Tobey returned to Seattle in 1938 he did the murals for the Baillargeon house in Washington Park in which the Fullers later lived, he worked for a WPA Federal Arts project, he won first prize in the annual Exhibit of Northwest Artists with *Modal Tides,* a very modest and lovely work that caused consternation among the flatly conventional painters of Mount Rainier and sunsets. His relation to Seattle was best expressed, however, in his sketches and paintings of the Pike Place Market, and what he left thereby is the finest monument to the city that it has, or is likely to have for a long time.

For many people the Public Market *is* Seattle, its one great city achievement, the place they love most, the place they take visitors first. It was begun back in 1907, during the boom years, as a place where farmers could sell their produce and thereby circumvent the grasp of middlemen. Gradually it became a fish and meat market, and an emporium for produce from eastern Washington and California; it acquired a few taverns and cafes, a bakery or two, an Italian grocery; in recent years the young have begun selling jewelry, leatherwork, pottery, and health foods. So it has not been strictly a farmer's market for years, but it has been able to keep its essential tone, which is of a place where no one is more or less welcome than anyone else, where the honky-tonk and derelict air of First Avenue meets the salt air and everyone else in the area. The smell of food and the sounds of its being sold dominate, work has purpose, and buying something can make people happy. Always afraid of encroaching "progress," always an individual set against the herd instinct, Tobey loved the Market as an expression of all that was best and possible in Seattle and city life:

> Gathered in small groups like islands in the constant stream of people are the men for whom the Market is more than a place of gathering, almost a home. They live in furnished rooms and rundown hotels, some of them habitués of the Skid Road at night and the Market in the day. From the many faces I picked out one man as someone I would like to know. He had looked at me with his friendly eyes—I felt he knew me, so why not speak? "What is your lineage?" But I did not expect the answer I got. "Adam and Eve, just like you, my son."

And Tobey begins here, not with a technique or a theory, but with something outside him, a person, that he must see, and capture with pencil or brush. Day after day he returned to the Market, to sketch and paint: a single man in a long coat, walking away, hands thrust disconsolately into his pockets; two men on a railing, lounging, interested in what they see; three figures who seem to emerge from the crates they are unpacking; an old man with a white beard and a cane, perhaps rich, perhaps poor, happy or sad, needing no external signs to proclaim his dignity. Sometimes they look like sketches for *New Yorker* covers, sometimes like a Dufy, or a Daumier, or a more somber Picasso. Tobey was too absorbed to have artistic problems, to be looking for artistic solutions.

But these daily sketches of market people were not enough for him, and at least half a dozen times he went back to the studio to do something more ambitious and composed, to transform the sketches into something distilled and final. There is one in oil, *Time Off;* one in tempera, *E Pluribus Unum;* and four in gouache, painted on board, *Farmer's Market, Rummage, Point Five—Vertical, Working Man.* One need not claim these are Tobey's best work in order to claim they are the essence of his way of seeing and loving Seattle. There is considerable stylistic variety in the group, since Tobey always let style evolve from subject. *Time Off* is as much Tobey's homage to Cézanne as to the lounging workers; *Point Five—Vertical* works with figures placed in motion by a series of rectangular planes that show what Tobey had learned from cubism; *Working Man* is a straightforward realistic painting where the white writing contains and enfolds the figure rather than sets the composition in motion; *E Pluribus Unum* is a descendant of the Broadway paintings, a crowd and a jumble of decorations.

Best of all, for me, is *Rummage,* one of the really great Tobeys, grander and more elusive than the others. The background, as usual, is very dark, and, as usual, the white line sets it in motion; but here the white line is itself in the background so that the objects emerge from it and are connected by it, and the motion of the Market is a network in which the objects are fixed. The eye is kept moving, but is allowed to dwell on the objects: on the chair tilted at an odd angle—it is being discarded and will be sold soon; on the bust of a woman modeling a brassiere, on her feathered hat; on the cowboy next to her, who could be looking at her, but perhaps his eye is like ours and is going down an alley to a sign with letters that may be Japanese, or up to a stark hunched figure brooding at a bar counter. After watching the painting move and be still for a while, one becomes overwhelmed by it, as though it were a world one could explore forever, as though the world to be explored were one's own. Everything in the picture may be rummage, but they all have a fixedness and therefore an individuality and dignity. There may be social or political commentary here, or a message as in Tobey's allegories, but one feels clumsy trying to say what it is. Look for a moment at the large four-sided figure in the upper middle. It is just there, perhaps the largest single object in the painting; it may be a newspaper, or at least there is a man behind it who may be reading it. The eye is drawn to and away from it constantly, yet mostly it is just there, maybe a joke, maybe not, but surely defeating efforts to put this marvelous painting "together" into some point or message.

In *Rummage,* and in the whole Market series, one has Tobey's Seattle, and, for all the loneliness and pain to be found there, it is a city one would have liked to have lived in. If there were few new buildings, the old ones could become thoroughly lived in; if there was little to do, there were more time and moods for watching plants and trees grow and other people move and a fence becoming dilapidated and a street becoming pock-marked. To someone like Tobey, who needed a few friends and subjects for his paintings and a soft diffuse light much more than he needed money or new things to do, Seattle was ideal, static and in motion at the same time. Needing the quiet of its apparent stagnation, he became increasingly nervous about Seattle in the fifteen years after World War II when he continued to live here. Had the changes brought about by the war been sudden and decisive, he probably would have left long before he did; but the changes came slowly and were not to be fully felt until the 1960s. He could see it coming long before that, for when he left to travel in 1950 he said: "This house is better suited to the operation of a hit-and-miss cleaning shop, or a drive in boiler-factory, than it is to the artist. . . . It would make an ideal rendezvous for the stone deaf. The only thing worse than moving is staying where you are."

With that, with Tobey's sense that Seattle after World War II was no longer what it had been, we can properly conclude this chapter. There are many other things to discuss: Carl Gould's elegant quadrangle at the university; Emil Sick's ball park at Rainier Avenue South and Empire Way that helped make Seattle one of the finest minor league baseball towns at a time when that term meant something; the later expressions of the turn of the century feeling, like the Skinner and the Exchange buildings, Frederick and Nelson's and the Bon Marche; the progressive Cincinnatus Club of the thirties that tried to make the Republican party active again and was the major force behind Arthur Langlie, as mayor and governor; Joe Gottstein's Longacres Race Track out near Renton, which began with the whirlwind building of its grandstand with designs by B. Marcus Priteca and has become in more recent years one of the most elegant minor tracks anywhere; the other work of Priteca, especially in downtown movie theaters. The list could be extended a long time without exhausting the interesting and distinguished legacies of the period. In most of these, however, we find expressed something close to what we have already seen, a city that had failed its earlier vision and gone quiet, a city that therefore became a great place in which to grow up, a city for individuals who already knew what they wanted to do and needed only a modest opportunity to do it.

It was a bad time in many ways—bitter, depressed, a time of myths that told no truths. Yet the Seattle that had grown by the end of World War I had a fineness and fullness to it that made even some of its worst parts yield their compensations. It was not the Venice of the new Mediterranean, but it was not Scranton or Butte, either.

VI

The Boeing Years

ANNA Louise Strong had said that after World War I America ceased to be the world's pioneer, and she and many other Americans went to the Finland station and beyond to watch and be part of the Russian Revolution that they assumed was now the beacon to the future. They were wrong, because the Russian Revolution was Russian, industrial, and cruel, seeking a state based on the kind of technological power the other European nations and the United States had already achieved. As for the other European combatants in the first war, they had not stopped fighting, as D. H. Lawrence said in 1919, but had only stopped to catch their breath. Japan became a major industrial power and, rebuffed during the twenties in its effort to grow in concert with the United States, it began to build its own Asian empire, which it might have done successfully had not its own hand felt as heavy as the European hands it sought to replace. The United States simply withdrew into a shell of isolation and Prohibition, seeking to be ignorant or heedless of the fact that this was the American century, and that every move every other country made after 1918 only helped to secure that role for it. Had Hitler only been a fascist, he might not have driven some of his finest scientists to this country. But he was a fanatic as well, and so the United States, throughout the war the only industrial power free from the threat of enemy attack, could also build the bombs and then the rockets which decided the latter stages of the war and shaped the American empire that engineered the peace.

The bellicosity of Germany and Japan meant that Americans came into World War II much more eagerly than they had World War I. Whatever Roosevelt or this country had or had not done, whatever misgivings an alliance with Russia might bring, there was a job to be done, and, for many at least, the responsibility was not just patriotic. More obviously, the war was the country's way out of the Depression, the invitation to cast off fear, to realize the power it had. It was the revolution, the tunnel into which the country moved to pass through to a different world on the other side. The experience of Americans became a national experience. There was a huge burgeoning of federal power, far beyond the now seemingly modest programs of the New Deal, and a corresponding decline in state power and regional feeling. On the other side of the way lay television, the interstate highway system, and the jet airplane to complete the task of making the country one.

When the national experience is both powerful and binding, it is often hard to separate out the particular experience of a relatively small unit like the city of Seattle. The two wartime events we will look at, the evacuation of the Japanese Americans and the Boeing boom, were both created by decisions made in Washington, D.C., and Seattle's postwar experience often seems a replica of the experience of all postwar American cities. It continues to be true, however, that what Seattle became in these years cannot be explained simply by reference to a national situation; it emerged from the city it had been.

JAPANESE AMERICANS

Within the memories of people now living in Seattle there is nothing more shameful than the awful fate of the Japanese Americans, who were captured like criminals, hauled away to concentration camps, and made to bear collectively a guilt that in fact was not even the responsibility of a single one, since no one in Seattle was ever charged with collaboration with the government of Japan. There must be many reasons why so few protested or did anything to help when this happened, but one reason almost certainly was the ability of people in Seattle to be ethnically naïve. The Chinese had been driven away in 1885–86 and had drifted back only slowly, the Japanese had migrated slowly and many had left in consequence of alien land laws that had been passed in the early 1920s. Seattle had only a small black community, though it was to begin to grow during the war years. Except for the Scandinavians in Ballard, it had no sizable ethnic Caucasian neighborhood. As a result, the central experience of many other American cities—the influx of major immigrant populations and the consequent clashes and enrichments—had never really happened here. There were quite a few foreign language newspapers at one time or another, but few of consequence, and in most areas of the city one could grow up without ever hearing a language other than English being spoken. As a result, Seattle in this regard was not unlike most of America in the early years of World War I, feeling somehow superior without ever having been given a challenge: *they* have these problems, *we* don't. So Seattle fell victim to a wartime hysteria, and, perhaps because it was a wartime experience, seemed to learn almost nothing from it. Its naïveté was almost intact when the blacks appeared in force in the fifties and sixties.

Perhaps the most revealing evidence offered by Seattle's newspapers concerning the capture and incarceration of Seattle's Japanese is the matter-of-factness with which the whole affair was reported. Between December 1941 and May 1942, various plans were proposed, locally and nationally, and some were finally enforced, so that the city had almost no Japanese Americans six months after the war began. The news was reported with something close to blandness, neither played up nor hidden. There were few vitriolic racist letters to the editor, fewer cries of protest. There were pictures of some uprooted families and stories of farewells told with wan acceptance. It is as though it were an event taking place somewhere else.

For this reason if for no other, the best testimony comes from the Japanese themselves, and, luckily, three have left stories that can be assembled to form a before-during-after triptych symbolic of the whole experience: Monica Sone, author of *Nisei Daughter;* Gordon Hirabayashi, who forced his defiance of American madness as high as the United States Supreme Court; John Okada, author of *No-No Boy.*

Monica Sone was born Kazuko Itoi in 1919, the third child of the owner and manager of the Carrollton Hotel, a clean, well-lighted flophouse in the Skid Road area. The opening chapters of her book show very clearly how it was great to grow up in Seattle between the wars. Like most Japanese American families, Kazuko Itoi's was bicultural. Her parents spoke mostly Japanese, while she and the other children spoke mostly English. Her parents felt they were aliens here and were proud of their heritage, while Kazuko was unalterably American and had to be reminded constantly that she was considered Japanese by her parents and by whites. She went to school at Bailey Gatzert, up regraded Jackson Street from home, and at first she was mystified: "There were some pale-looking children who spoke a strange dialect of English, rapidly like gunfire. Matsuko told me they were '*hagu-jins,*' white people. Then there were children who looked very much like me with their black hair and black eyes, but they spoke in high, musical singing voices. Matsuko whispered to me that they were Chinese." All this was exciting to Kazuko and she came to love school. What she hated was having to go to Japanese school in the afternoons, where she was made to be stiff, quiet, obedient, a stranger to herself. Being American was easy, being Japanese was hard.

The Japanese were the largest nonwhite group in Seattle, and Seattle had the second largest Japanese population on the coast. They still numbered under 7,000 in a city of over 350,000, though, so for most whites they were invisible. They lived in the Skid Road, on Jackson Street, and had begun to move onto the south side of First Hill, into Rainier Valley, and up onto Beacon Hill. It was the oldest residential area of the city and the houses were getting shabby, the apartments rundown. Commerce and light industry operated next to and into the same buildings as the residences. A part of this area was the site of Jesse Epstein's Yesler Terrace housing project. Since most whites shunned this area, they learned of the Japanese of Kazuko Itoi's generation only in high school, if they went to Broadway or Garfield, or in college, if they went to a local business school or the university. The first generation, the Issei, stayed close to home, and the Nisei were beginning to break that pattern.

On December 7, the day the Japanese attacked Pearl Harbor, the FBI arrested and held without charge or bail between fifty and one hundred important Japanese Americans in Seattle. Obviously, the FBI had been prepared, and the Japanese themselves were not. Kazuko Itei's father refused to believe the news of the arrests until he heard it in Japanese on the short-wave radio. Kazuko herself felt betrayed:

I felt as if I were on fire. "Mama, they never should have done it," I cried. "Why did they do it? Why? Why?"

Mother's face turned paper white. "What do you know about it? Right or wrong, the Japanese have been chafing with resentment for years. It was bound to happen, one time or another. You're young, Ka-chan, you know very little about the ways of nations. It's not as simple as you think, but this is hardly the time to be quarreling about it, is it?"

"No, it's too late, too late," and I let the tears pour down my face.

Kazuko's "great place to grow up in" had, overnight, become a nightmare of betrayal and lost innocence. Like her, most of the Nisei were adolescents or in their early twenties in 1941, and they were totally unprepared for what was happening. Kathleen Sonoda, a housegirl for a Japanese launderer, thought, "How could they do this, knowing what effect it will have on us?" Most of those arrested were Issei with some obvious tie to Japan, and while not one was ever charged with or convicted of being a saboteur or an enemy agent, they could temper their bitterness with a suspicious wisdom that told them never to expect much more than that from white Americans. Their children, the Nisei, had no such wisdom, and Kazuko Itoi was one among many who could only reply by going dumb, blocking out the pain.

After the first arrests, there was a period of quiet, during which most voices that were raised loud enough to be heard attested to the loyalty of west coast Japanese Americans. But the super-patriots were soon at work, and the federal government and most white Americans just did not want to fight. Since it was not demonstrable that the Japanese Americans posed any kind of threat to American security, an argument had to be constructed to make it plausible that they might be a threat. It seemed to go like this: because the Japanese were all hard-working, quiet, taxpaying, they were inscrutable and it was difficult to tell the loyal ones from the traitors. Because the Issei were proud of their heritage and still spoke Japanese, they were obviously not American; because they diligently sent their children to school and worked hard to send them to college, they obviously meant to take over the country. Blacks were lazy and shiftless and obviously inferior, Japanese were industrious and law-abiding and therefore dangerous.

It was a feeling and an argument that was almost as dangerous in its innocence as hysteria or malice. President Roosevelt signed Executive Order 9066, bowing mostly to political pressure from California, authorizing the secretary of war to designate military areas and to exclude any or all people from them. For some reason the Japanese on Bainbridge Island, across the Sound from Seattle, were ordered to leave for Mazanar, in California, on March 29, 1942. Others in the area were told later to be ready to go by May 1, when they were shipped to a temporary camp at the state fairgrounds in Puyallup and then to various "permanent" camps inland, mostly in Idaho.

Kazuko Itoi and her family went, not knowing how to fight, and Kazuko's father was lucky enough to get someone to manage the Carrollton Hotel for him for the duration. Most others fared worse, losing land, or house, or belongings, or else being forced to sell them for practically nothing. Gordon Hirabayashi decided to fight. Born in the same year as Kazuko Itoi, of Quaker parents, in 1942 he was a senior at the University of Washington, vice-president of the University YMCA, and a conscientious objector. He refused to register to be evacuated, he refused to obey the army's curfew. Two weeks after most Japanese in Seattle had been carted off to Puyallup, he turned himself in, arguing that any compliance with the army's regulations "would be giving hopeless consent to the denial of practically all of the things which give me incentive to live." He was tried in federal court and sentenced to three months in prison. He appealed, first to the Ninth Circuit, then to the United States Supreme Court, where in June 1943, his conviction was upheld. What is most implicating about the court's decision is that it upheld the conviction without facing the major issue of collective guilt, and then it turned around and used the Hirabayashi decision as support in *Korematsu* v. *U.S.* a few months later. In that decision, which involved a California truck farmer, it was argued that wartime considerations could force the government to suspend a citizen's liberties. At that time young liberal Justice William O. Douglas went out of his way to say the matter did not involve racial discrimination or collective guilt, which it obviously did, as was pointed out in a fine and justly famous dissent by Justice Robert Jackson.

Hirabayashi served his three months, then another nine "in detention" in the King County jail. When he was released, he went to work for the American Friends Service Committee in Spokane, and, undaunted, refused to fill out the questionnaire given to all Japanese Americans to test their loyalty. Most of the protesting about the questionnaire concerned questions 28 and 29, which asked the Japanese to forswear all loyalty and allegiance to the emperor of Japan; those who answered in the negative and refused to forswear were called No-No people. Hirabayashi refused to have anything to do with this or to report for his pre-induction physical examination, and thereby got another year in federal prison.

After the war, his sentence completed, he returned to Seattle and finished his B.A. at the university. He then went on to graduate school, and, tellingly, his two theses were "A Sociomatric Study of University of Washington Students of Japanese Ancestry" and "The Russian Doukhabors of British Columbia: A Study of Social Adjustment and Conflict." The Doukhabors were a religious sect who lived as isolated as possible and were the victims of relentless persecution, and it says much for Hirabayashi that he was able to see ways to extend his interest and sympathy to other groups who, though very different, had suffered as he had.

Kazuko Itoi, out of pain, went dumb; Gordon Hirabayashi, out of courage, became a hero. Saddest of all, perhaps, is the story John Okada tells, presumably about himself, in his 1957 novel, *No-No Boy*. It is by no means a great work, but it should be required reading nonetheless for all white people in Seattle, and the country. Since it was not published for a dozen years after the war, one might expect a work dispassionate and wise and healed by time; instead, it is a passionate cry of pain and anger and inarticulate desire to know what to make of a broken life.

The novel is about the first months home after the war, a time when for many victory seems empty and life out of focus, the gap between those who went and those who stayed seemingly unbridgeable. The difference is that Okada's hero, Ichiro Yamada, had refused to answer questions 28 and 29 of the government's questionnaire and so became a "No-No Boy" and an inmate of a federal prison for two years. After he is released, Ichiro comes home, gets off a bus at Second Avenue and Main Street, and begins the walk up Jackson Street. He meets an old friend, Eto Minato, who is all openness and laughter until he finds out that Ichiro has been in prison:

> "Rotten bastard. Shit on you." Eto coughed up a mouthful of sputum and rolled his words around in it: "Rotten, no-good bastard."
>
> Surprisingly Ichiro felt relieved. Eto's anger seemed to serve as a release to his own naked tensions. As he stooped to lift the suitcase a wet wad splattered over his hand and dripped onto the black leather. The legs of his accuser were in front of him. God in a pair of green fatigues, U.S. Army style. They were the legs of the jury that had passed sentence on him.

Ichiro hurries up Jackson Street, where "everything looked older and dirtier and shabbier." He meets a group of blacks in front of a pool hall, and one of them shouts "persecution in the drawl of the persecuted": "Go back to Tokyo, boy!"

Home is worse. From the beginning Ichiro's mother had believed in the power and glory of Japan, had insisted Japan would win the war, and had extracted Ichiro's "No-No" as a badge of her faith. Now she refuses to believe Japan has lost, and Ichiro sees that his loyalty, which has been to her rather than to Japan, has no object beyond faded and fantastic dreams. His father, sad and defeated by it all, beginning to drink, can help no one; his brother, thinking Ichiro a fool, plans to join the navy, and one night he lures Ichiro into a parking lot where some toughs beat him up. His one friendship is with a veteran, Kenji Kanno, who was wounded in Italy, had a leg amputated, and whose life is totally uncertain because the infection from the wound spreads and the doctors can only cut off a little more of him at a time. Kenji sees his pain as a way of understanding Ichiro's, and they insistently ask who is the worse off.

The action of the novel is the reeling of Ichiro and Kenji among other Japanese Americans reeling in different directions: a girl whose husband signs on for another army hitch in Europe so he won't have to face the shame of having a No-No boy for his brother; a waiter in a cafe in Portland who wears his veteran's button to show he is not really Japanese; a white contractor who offers Ichiro a job even after he learns about his prison stint; another No-No boy who works as a painter on a church-organized boondoggle. Kenji dies in a veteran's hospital, Ichiro's mother dies in a final withdrawal from the truth. Ichiro is neither dead nor alive, and he doesn't even know what he hopes for besides a totally different world. In the end Ichiro is left, and there is no territory ahead for which he might strike out.

Twelve years after the war was over, the bitterness was still pure in John Okada's heart, and, almost twenty years later, it is still just as pure for many who had their lives stunted and misshapen, by betrayal, the camps, prison, a home that was no longer there upon return. It was the most sordid American act of the entire war, and the number of non-Japanese of Seattle who can feel anything but ashamed at their part in it is very few indeed. In law, guilt is not collective, and the failure of American courts to heed that in the case of the Japanese Americans is not in itself excuse to argue the collective guilt of whites in Seattle, the coast, or the country. The saddest part of the whole experience, to repeat, was that people learned so little from it.

BOEING

When the war broke out in 1939, the Boeing Airplane Company was an enterprising firm with the one customer airplane builders had in those days, the federal government. Employing about four thousand people, with sales just under ten million dollars a year, it was a good if unspectacular business for Seattle. William Boeing had begun the company in 1916, on the shore of Lake Union, but by 1939 Boeing himself had left and the company was situated on the Duwamish a few miles below Harbor Island.

William Boeing was a person of wealth who liked to fly planes and who realized that the backbone of an airplane firm was its engineers. In 1916 he had hired three engineers off the University of Washington campus, and in 1939 two of them, Philip Johnson and Claire Egtvedt, were Boeing president and chairman of the board. They understood technical problems, they built planes, and that was their genius and their mentality. Having only one customer meant there was little need for marketing and public relations experts. There were commercial airlines, but most flew adaptations of planes built for the air force. In the late thirties even the air force wasn't much of a customer. Boeing had developed some planes that were admired, but in September 1939 the company was building planes subcontracted to them from the Douglas Company in California.

One of Boeing's planes of the thirties was called the Flying Fortress, and after the fall of France and the German blitz of England in 1940, the Royal Air Force decided that Boeing's version of the B-17 was just what they needed to strike back at the Germans. Suddenly the demand was immense, more than the company could handle. The 4,000 employees of 1939 swelled to 10,000 by July 1941, to 20,000 that September, to 30,000 when the United States officially entered the war. No company in the northwest, and few entire industries, had ever had so large a payroll.

The real demand had only begun. In 1942 President Roosevelt said the country would build fifty thousand planes a year, which was more than had been built in the entire history of aviation. No one saw how it could be done, since airplanes had never been mass-produced. Working on a cost-plus-fixed-fee basis and with capital given it by the government, Boeing built buildings larger than anyone had ever fathomed before, each with long rows of planes being assembled, each plane larger than any previous man-made machine. Boeing developed a larger and longer-range plane, the B-29, which became operational in 1943. By 1944, the peak war year, Boeing employment was up to 50,000 in Seattle, and its total sales were over 600 million dollars. All Seattle manufacturing in 1939 amounted to 70 million dollars, or about one-eighth of Boeing's 1944 figure, and the total manufacturing business in the state of Washington in 1939 was only slightly more than what Boeing alone was doing five years later.

Boeing was like a gigantic baby dropped into Seattle's lap. Wartime procurement can always wreak havoc on a local economy, especially one as frail as Seattle's had been. If a company has only one customer and a city only one company, then any fluctuation in the customer's demand greatly affects everything in the city. Furthermore, though Boeing did its job magnificently and every year during the war found ways to reduce significantly the time and money it took to build a plane, its cost-plus-fixed-fee arrangement meant it was saving money for its customer and had no way itself to build up any significant amounts of investment capital. The very simplicity of the operation, for all the huge complications involved in altering designs, procuring material, and keeping employees in a tight labor market, gave Boeing little flexibility in its operations. It was not its own boss, and it could do little to help Seattle's economy except provide its huge payroll.

Seattle had found, or inherited, the means whereby it could become a company town, a fate it had apparently been waiting to receive ever since it had dissipated its energies in the years just before and during World War I. Boeing was here because William Boeing had been here and he happened to think he could build better planes than the ones he had seen. It was not a particularly logical place for an airplane company, though by their nature planes are less distant from their markets than cars, shoes, or furniture. The economy it came to dominate was in no real sense ready for it. When Henry Ford made his first assembly line Model T in 1907, almost everything he needed was made in or near Detroit. When Boeing began making assembly line B-17s and B-29s, it and Seattle were providing only the design, the testing expertise, and the place of assembly. Huge aluminum plants had been built along the Columbia River to take advantage of the power provided by the new dams there, but most of that metal had to be shipped elsewhere, often as far away as New England, to be finished before it could be shipped back to Boeing. Puget Sound businesses never provided more than 5 percent of Boeing's subcontracting services.

There the company was, one of the centers of the entire war effort, yet in important ways it was having no impact on its local economy. Boeing itself has always argued that by not encouraging local suppliers it can reduce the impact on the local employment scene whenever there is a fluctuation in its business. This is quite true, but also illustrative of the way in which it tended to be frightened because it had so little flexibility. If the situation is bad, or can only get worse, then Boeing's policies may well be correct. The difficulty is that Seattle, in becoming specialized into a city only for engineers and aerospace mechanics, thereby had little chance to develop ancillary businesses which, as the best possible source of new work, might eventually make the economy less dependent on its major employer.

All this was enough to make people wish that maybe the war would not end. But end it did, and in 1945 another event took place that was also of considerable importance. Philip Johnson died (and was buried, incidentally, on a little plot tucked in behind the large Denny family tombstones in Lakeview Cemetery), and William Allen, Boeing's attorney, became president. He immediately had to make a few major decisions, his first being that Boeing would stay in business. The company tried to pretend that the Stratocruiser, its old transport plane revamped to carry passengers on commercial airlines, was as important as its Superfortress B-29s, but that was far from true. In the first full peacetime year of 1946 Boeing's Seattle employment dropped from over 40,000 to 11,000, and the company worried about what it was going to do even with those remaining. Its sales fell from over 600 million dollars to 14 million dollars. Allen tried to renegotiate the company's contract with the aerospace mechanics union, arguing that even without deeply straitened circumstances the company should hire its workers on merit, not on seniority. The union struck, and Allen allowed Boeing to make a deal with Dave Beck, who crossed the aerospace workers' picket lines and proceeded to try to reorganize the union under Teamster control. Nothing Allen could have done, perhaps nothing Beck could have done, could have made them more hated and feared by other unions and by those parts of the community friendly to labor. But the plan worked to the extent of settling the strike on Allen's and Beck's terms in 1948, even though two years later the aerospace workers did manage to get out from Beck's control.

Allen was a tough man, and his company was in trouble, but he managed to ride out his labor problems until the war in Korea bailed him and Boeing out, or at least gave them a little time. The great Cold War planes, the B-47 and the B-52, were developed, both immensely impressive machines, the result of an alliance between the appetite of the military for more hardware and the ability of Boeing's engineers to transform military dreams into technological fact. But this meant that peacetime Seattle continued to operate successfully only in a wartime economy, and needed wars and threats of wars to keep itself going.

But William Allen knew better than to allow his company to remain strictly a creature of the military or the federal government, since even in the most hawkish of times such business can prove uncertain. In 1952 he decided to move once again into commercial airlines, this time with something new, a jet transport, the 707. With no federal government to foot the bill for research and development, Boeing had to decide to tie up almost all of its potential capital into building the plane, and in effect to hold its breath during most of the fifties until it could put its plan into operation. It was 1959 before the 707 became operational, and Boeing's gamble paid off beyond its wildest dreams. The 707 put Boeing all by itself among airplane companies, and put airplane companies at the heart of American technology. With the money gained from its success with the 707 it developed the 727, a shorter-range airplane, then the 737, then—once again in a move big enough to force the company to tie up most of its capital—the immense 747. All this meant that by 1960 Boeing was depending on the government for less than half its business, and throughout the next decade the proportion showed an overall decline.

When one looks at Boeing from the point of view of the aerospace industry or of the national manufacturing economy, the Allen years are remarkable. The company has consistently recognized that its strengths lay in its unsurpassed engineering excellence and it has, with a combination of daring and determination, worked from its strengths to develop a rightfully proud industrial giant. It has, in effect, moved from Ford's position as the first mass-producer of airplanes into General Motors' position of being the dominant business in the industry. The other major aircraft companies have managed to stay competitive only through mergers, through wrangling increased military contracts, or from direct federal handouts. By comparison Boeing is clean, tough, strong. Its people are almost all extremely low-keyed and hard-working and, among the older major figures in the company, touchingly loyal to William Allen. Except for Allen himself, they are engineers, showing all the technical competence, love of work, and narrow vision for which the profession is famous.

For the vision of Boeing is narrow, though the perspective of the aerospace business or of the national economy does not reveal this. The relations of Boeing to Seattle have always been obscure and uneasy, mainly because Boeing's leaders see themselves as developers and manufacturers of airplanes and as almost nothing else. They are as aware as anyone of the stranglehold they have on the local economy, but they have never done much to alter this or even to have shown signs that they care. Boeing operates plants elsewhere, in Wichita, Philadelphia, Cape Kennedy, and Huntsville, Alabama, but its leaders are Seattle people and do not want to go anywhere else. When each of their new planes has been announced, there has been great scurrying among real estate developers, local governments, and highway people to find out where they are going to build their new plant, since so much depends not just on Boeing's being in Seattle but on its particular locations. Boeing itself, not wanting to be involved in such speculation more than it must, is extremely secretive about its plans. Its efforts, even when apparently well intentioned, almost always end up seeming clumsy, and to its detriment it remains notorious for its aloofness from local politics and its aversion

to being more than a minimal patron of the arts and civic organizations. Most of even the well-informed people in Seattle would not be
able to give the names of Boeing's major executives, or to recognize
them by sight.

Still, most of the local resentment of Boeing's management, except
perhaps for the resentment of its labor policies, is little more than ill-
concealed awe at its hugeness and its success, plus apprehension
over the area's heavy dependence on what happens in the heads of a
few people no one seems to know. It is scary, after all, especially
when Boeing can really only be accused of being an engineering firm
with a boyish absorption in the task of making machines, and that
accusation is one Boeing itself would wear as a badge of pride.

The real question, however, is why Seattle continued for so long to
be so nakedly dependent on its one magnificently successful company. If one does not relish the fact that the postwar years were and
maybe still are the Boeing years, far better not to blame the baby but
to look carefully at the bathwater in which it swam.

POSTWAR ECONOMY

After World War I the Seattle economy reverted to its simplest possible condition, and, especially given Boeing's own slump in the late
forties, it might be expected that a similar slump and reversion
would occur after World War II. It did, and it didn't.

To help gain a sense of what the loss of wartime business can do to
a city's economy, let me quote from Jane Jacobs' description of Los
Angeles:

> Aircraft manufacturing, the city's largest industry, laid off about three-
> quarters of its workers by the end of 1945 and operated at about that
> reduced level, sometimes lower, for the rest of the decade. Shipbuilding,
> the second largest wartime industry in Los Angeles, almost closed down.
> The Hollywood motion picture industry was in the middle of its decline.
> Petroleum, once the city's largest export and still an important one until
> 1946, was thereafter lost to the city's export economy because people in
> Los Angeles itself took to consuming so much gasoline that the city ran a
> deficit and became a petroleum importer. Some of the city's oldest depot
> services were lost, those concerned with nationwide distribution of citrus
> fruits, walnuts, and avocados grown in the city's hinterland. This loss was
> incurred when the groves were uprooted to build suburbs and highways
> and—still further out—to make way for truck farms to feed growing Los
> Angeles.

Almost everything Jacobs says here about Los Angeles was true for
Seattle as well: loss of aircraft employment by about three-quarters,
decline in shipping, decline in lumber exports, relocation of farms.

Jacobs goes on:

In 1949 the Los Angeles export economy was probably at its nadir—perhaps lower than at any time since the Great Depression. At the war's end many people had, in fact, predicted severe economic distress and depression for Los Angeles. They would have been right if the city had nothing to grow on but its export work and the multiplier effect of that work. But as it turned out, work and jobs in Los Angeles did not decline; they grew. In 1949 Los Angeles had more jobs than it had ever had before.

The reason for the growth was that Los Angeles was replacing imports, making for its increasing population many things it hitherto had brought in from outside. We have seen this phenomenon before, in Seattle between 1890 and 1910, and its effects can be startling indeed: "They poured forth furnaces, sliding doors, mechanical saws, shoes, bathing suits, underwear, china, furniture, cameras, hand tools, hospital equipment, scientific instruments, engineering services, and hundreds of other things. One eighth of all the new businesses started in the latter half of the 1940s in the United States were started in Los Angeles." That, it would seem, is the model for the postwar adjustment all American cities wanted. In Seattle it happened, and didn't happen.

In the years right after the war Americans embraced the potential productivity of peacetime with gluttonous energy. Instead of depression there would be boom, and even if the Cold War meant the defense budget would not shrivel, it was not defense that would maintain the boom but houses, cars, highways, refrigerators, television sets, washing machines. Having won their major legal victories in the late 1930s, most industrial labor unions followed some version of Dave Beck's plans for success and sought to extend the possibility of peacetime prosperity to all their workers. The formula was to keep pressing for increased wages, to let management set higher prices, to count on continuing prosperity to allow for everyone to pay for it all. Having woken up to the fact that America was a great industrial state, returning servicemen embraced the G.I. Bill, went to college, joined the vast technological and managerial system. Having been told for years of the pleasures of the suburbs, the country glutted itself on them, on their single-family homes, their station wagons, their "good schools," their newly created place for women as queens of the house, their families of four, five, and six children.

All this happened in Los Angeles, until Los Angeles became the name for everything between the desert and the ocean. Much of it happened in Seattle. In 1939, the last Depression year, Seattle had 24,000 employed in manufacturing adding 75 million dollars in value to the raw materials by that manufacture. In 1947 King County (Seattle figures ceased being available) had 54,000 workers employed in adding 265 million dollars to raw materials by manufacture; in 1954 it had 78,000 workers adding 520 million dollars. In fifteen years the number of workers had tripled, the value added by manufacture had jumped 600 percent.

Whatever had happened to The Boeing Company after the war, it had not led to the kind of depression that hit Seattle after World War I. To be sure, 1939 was such a bad year that by comparison all later years are bound to look good, but it should be noted that the ratio of workers to value added by manufacture was constantly improving. In a truly simple economy it takes many workers to produce what a more complex economy can do better with fewer workers. When the city and county tripled their manufacturing work force but increased their manufacturing value sevenfold we can see a great gain in the complexity of the economy.

The figures don't lie, but don't tell even the whole story figures can tell us. In the following list we have the manufacturing figures broken down by industry, in 1947 and again in 1954.

	1947		1954	
	Number of Workers	Value Added by Manufacture	Number of Workers	Value Added by Manufacture
Food processing	7,980	$44,000,000	7,507	$ 54,000,000
Lumber	5,562	37,000,000	5,021	32,000,000
Furniture	1,065	4,000,000	938	5,000,000
Printing and publishing	3,225	22,000,000	3,632	27,000,000
Chemicals	1,032	7,000,000	975	10,000,000
Primary metals	2,499	13,000,000	2,304	17,000,000
Fabricated metals	3,574	21,000,000	3,884	32,000,000
Machinery	3,248	16,000,000	3,138	23,000,000
Transportation	20,156	67,000,000	40,471	193,000,000

First, in every industry it was taking relatively fewer workers to add more value to the manufactured product, ample testimony to technological advances throughout the economy. Second, transportation was not only much the greatest industry, but in the seven years between 1947 and 1954 was gaining in importance. Third, in 1947 The Boeing Company employed about 10,000 workers, or half the total for the transportation industry, while in 1954 its employment was 35,000 or almost the entire total for the industry. The other industries may have been refining their processes and increasing their efficiency, but most were not growing. The Boeing Company was refining its processes, increasing its efficiency at an even greater rate than were the other industries; it was also growing, becoming *the* transportation industry as transportation was becoming *the* industry in Seattle and King County. In other words, Boeing had managed between 1947 and 1954 to make a successful transition to a peacetime economy, and had secured vast quantities of new business to do this. At the same time, the rest of the local economy was by comparison standing still.

In 1947 Boeing employed about one out of every five of King County's manufacturing workers, in 1957 about every other one. The city had in effect retied its fortunes to Boeing's, and we can begin to say why by exploring what else might have happened. The most obvious opportunities here were exactly what they had been in Los Angeles, in consumer goods to satisfy an expanding and prosperous population. When people came to Los Angeles in the 1940s, just as when people came to Seattle in the 1890s, they created opportunities by their very presence. They became the potential market for goods and services that hitherto had been imported or forgone, and in creating goods for that market, they set the stage for another period of still greater growth: Los Angeles grew more in its second decade after the war than in the first; Seattle doubled its size between 1890 and 1900, and tripled that between 1900 and 1910.

This pattern was not followed in the 1950s in Seattle. The growth remained tied to Boeing's growth, and the city became a kind of colony, supporting manufacture that was to be shipped elsewhere, importing a great deal of what it needed. The argument usually offered to explain this failure to diversify is that Seattle is too far from national markets and too small to induce major national manufacturers to set up shop here. It is a self-fulfilling argument, since those who believe it can also make it come true. The fact that the economy was expanding means more expansion was possible, and every expansion in some new kind of work means the possibility of replacing an import and the possibility of making something that eventually could be marketed regionally or nationally. Every expansion in some old kind of work tends to re-enforce the assumption that the local economy can only go on doing what it has always done.

There were three obvious inhibiting factors at work here. First, Boeing's insistence that it was basically an engineering firm and an assembly plant meant, as we have said, that it never allowed spinoff industries to be located here. Second, Dave Beck's Teamsters

Brotherhood, reaching the peak of their power, worked to "stabilize" industries by discouraging new firms or anything out of the ordinary being done by old firms. This made labor costs high, rewarded existing businesses, but discouraged everyone else. Third, banks, retailers, investment houses, shippers, Port officials, and railroad people all expanded their operations in the most ordinary ways possible, if they expanded them at all. The banks put most of their energies into developing branches, as did the major retailers, and people involved in transportation, whether or not they were tied by the Teamsters, sought no new ways to develop their markets.

One could be back in 1910, when the new rich first retired. Of course Boeing, Beck, the banks, and the retailers had not actually retired, but their whole way of thinking had been developed twenty, thirty, forty years before, and nothing was about to change it. As to the facts in the case, few people have ever disputed them, and those who defend the practices that kept the economy colonized usually say that they are protecting themselves and the local economy against a rainy day. If Boeing does not encourage local spinoff work, if the banks and retailers do not encourage new manufacture in consumer goods, then, so the argument goes, when a layoff or cutback comes the economy is not as badly hit as it would be. The argument for this kind of "stability," of course, insures that rainy days will come, though probably those actually responsible for the stabilizing will be hit least hard. Does not all this seem reminiscent of our description of Tacoma in the 1890s? The only protection against the devastations of shifts in Beoing's business is to create other kinds of business. It was true when Boeing was expanding, and real possibilities were opening up, and it was true later, when Boeing laid off two-thirds of its workers.

The one area of the economy that did boom along with Boeing after the war was real estate and home-building, and the roster of people who came into new wealth in the early postwar years is mostly a roster of these businesses. And here we find a second reason for comparing Seattle and Los Angeles in this period. If Los Angeles was splendidly developing its local consumer economy, it was also making the city people love to hate, for its sprawl, smog, freeways, and indulgence of nonessential consumer "needs." If that is the model for conversion to peacetime economy, most people aren't having any. Unfortunately Seattle was not doing some of the good things Los Angeles was doing, and it was doing a great many of the bad things.

In the first decade and more after the war old Seattle stayed very much as it had been for years. It was not until 1960 that Mark Tobey decided he had had enough, and he might well have continued to find Seattle lovable even then had he lived somewhere other than the University District, which was changing sooner and faster than most of old Seattle. Downtown, indeed, was strikingly as it had been since the late twenties; if there was boom, it was not noticeable in the most obvious places, but on the boundaries of the old city. The major push was first north and then east, across the lake. In 1945 the north city limits were the same as thirty years before, along Northeast 65th and North-Northwest 85th. In 1955 they were at 145th and the expansion spread north from there. Expensive houses were built in Windermere, Inverness, Innis Arden, Blue Ridge, anywhere that commanded views of water and mountains; less expensive ones were built in View Ridge, Wedgwood, Lake City, Olympic Hills; cheap ones were built almost everywhere else.

It was the era of the bulldozer, the ranch-style house, the shopping center, the long runs of commerce on arterials filled with car lots, drive-ins, real estate agencies. No one seemed to care what a house, a street, or a store should be except that they should be like all the others. After the long depression and the war, surely people had earned something. But seldom had growth been as mindless or monotonous, seldom had so many people cared less about value for money.

Up to the old city limits Aurora Avenue is almost a parkway, winding between Woodland Park and Green Lake. North from there it is an enduring symbol of postwar glut. Bothell Way, running northeast out through Lake City, could have become a first-class retail street, since its neighborhoods carry with them considerable pretensions, but it resolutely stuck to selling cars and hamburgers. In between was Northgate, a huge shopping center in the middle of what had been, and what in a different way continues to be, nowhere. Northgate had a hundred stores, a skyroof, a mammoth parking lot, and it offered nothing unique, beautiful, tasteful, or offensive. In recent years it has become *de rigueur* to speak of blights caused by freeways, but the I-5 freeway in Seattle, when it came, did less damage to its surroundings than did Northgate or Aurora Avenue.

Virgil Bogue had offered a list of places for development of parks in the north end, but this was ignored, because parks were only places where people might meet other people. Off the arterials all was houses, and if house-by-house the building was never worse than ordinary, block-by-block the total effect was devastating. Commerce was made ugly so it could be shunned, and all else was given over to private life. It was the fulfillment of what might be thought of as Dave Beck's dream for the average teamster, or the suburban real estate developer's dream for the average office worker. It was thus fitting that after many years of living in an ordinary brick house in old Seattle Dave Beck and his family moved into a complex of houses in Sheridan Beach, just north of the city limits. Robert Kennedy once described Beck's compound as palatial, but, typically for Beck and the north end, all there was had nothing grand about it—big cars, a rumpus room where movies could be shown, expensive, but nothing more.

On one street, and perhaps on only one, was the postwar north end developed as it should have been, as much of it could have been. Just west of the Sand Point Country Club one can turn off Northeast 88th, a street of quiet ordinariness, onto 42nd Northeast, then down to Northeast 92nd, and for a half mile one is in a different world. It is more expensive, but here for once the expense seems worth it. The quiet yields birdsong, the houses are secluded and landscaped, if at all, with simple casualness, the bumpy and winding street offers a sense that it is easy to get pleasantly lost here. It is the postwar equivalent of streets of equal seclusion and retirement in Washington Park or Mount Baker. Thus, houses have one story, there is lots of land between houses, and between houses and the street. And just to prove it is not simply a matter of money, one can swing out of Northeast 92nd onto Northeast Paisley Drive and up to Inverness, where the houses are larger and more expensive, but where money has only bought what money can buy, and the streets are as monotonous as streets that cost half as much.

The one place where people who moved to the north end agreed to take any care other than their homes was in their schools, but the kind of care they took is revealing of the monotony and mindlessness of the surroundings. "Good schools" became a watchword, and people were willing to pay levies and meet in PTA groups to guarantee good schools. But what was meant by the term never became clear. The good schools in prewar Seattle had been good in part because high school was the terminus for most students and they could thus offer an insistent and solid traditional education. After the war it was presumed that most students in "good neighborhoods" would be going on to college, and thus the colleges came to do the effective post–elementary school educating. No real alternative to traditional education was offered, and the traditional education itself gradually declined. Nor could the schools offer to serve as a melting pot, since the students had been pretty well homogenized before they arrived. As a result these new north-end schools—Nathan Hale, Ingraham, Shoreline, Shorecrest—could promise little in and of themselves, only a future somewhere else, in college.

Not, to be sure, that students at these schools were markedly different from those elsewhere. The difference lay more in the expectations of parents than in anything else. When the students failed those expectations, or failed to gain the benefits from their education their parents presumed they should, they tended to become blank as college students. They were "going to college," but often could find no other or clearer reason for being there.

It was perhaps inevitable, when the disaffection of the young became noisy in the 1960s, that it was often those from the north end who were noisiest or most alarmed their parents. Perhaps human life isn't meant to add up very clearly for people at age eighteen, but many, especially from the newer parts of the city, felt they had been told it did, and they minded when it didn't. I remember asking a group of freshmen at the University of Washington to write about their surroundings, working out from their homes and stopping as soon as the landscape became unfamiliar. Well over half were from north-end high schools, and almost all of them had no place they could clearly name as familiar between their homes and the mountains. No sense of street or meeting place, no image of school worth remembering, no sense of Seattle as a city.

This story of disaffection is perhaps familiar enough to need no insisting upon, and it belongs here only because it seems to have hit hardest those new postwar neighborhoods that embraced house and lot and rejected almost everything else. One incident is enough to reveal the results. In 1969 the Seattle Parks Department offered the city council a plan for a series of walking trails in the northeast part of the city, mostly focused on Thornton Creek and its numerous branches. After Hans Thompson showed some slides of land that had been acquired and spoke briefly about the benefits of trails, he was greeted with swarms of protesting citizens. Where Thompson had been vague about precisely what land would be needed, the citizens were precise: that is my property, my creek, my privacy and many had slides to show what he or she had done to make that property into a place that wanted no trails.

The Parks Department was not the only party to be distrusted, however. As more and more people spoke, it became clearer that no one was to be trusted. People spoke against their neighbors, against their neighbors' children, against their own children, against the school system and the highway department and all local, state, and federal governments. What was at stake soon was no longer a matter of public versus private interests, for had it been just that, even someone who believed in public footpaths could believe the citizens had a point. It was these people, themselves united only in their antagonism, against the world, and it was clear they felt they were losing and wanted to claim some triumph somewhere. They loved their creek, they knew the turns it took and the trees it watered like the backs of their hands. But the moment they considered any human intrusion they were frightened and mistrustful, and anything a neighborhood or a city might do was nothing but an invasion of privacy. Whatever image of suburban pastoral they had achieved, it was at the price of peering and blinking out at the rest of the world. It is sad but true that such outcomes are not hard to predict when land is originally developed that way.

But this outcome is not the only possible one. Time does not move in just one direction, and what is most harmful at one point can be transformed later on. One sees this in many areas of old Seattle, especially the commercial streets. If a neighborhood settles down at all well, one thing that can hold it together is good residential commerce, locally owned places, one-of-a-kind places. There need be nothing elegant or outstanding for these businesses to do their bit to glue the neighborhood together, and one finds such streets of commerce on North 45th in Wallingford, on Greenwood, in the University District, on Broadway, in Madison Park. Given time, Bothell Way, or Lake City Way as it is now called, could become such a street, if the area as a whole comes to recognize that it needs such cohesive forces.

On the other hand, there is another kind of commercial street that also, over the years, can develop into something special. Seattle has one of these in Rainier Avenue South between Dearborn Street and Sick's Stadium. There is very little neighborhood here at all, but the businesses are not neighborhood businesses either. The Black Manufacturing Company makes men's and boys' outdoor clothes, and has a retail outlet on the premises. Kusak's Glass Works is owned by a Czech immigrant who can show more good cut glass and crystal, and talk better about it, than anyone in the city. Oberto Sausage Company has its retail outlet on Rainier, and one gets there the best pepperoni made anywhere. Then comes Remo Borracchini's strange and eccentric Italian bakery, followed by Mutual Fish, an excellent Japanese market. It is a most unprepossessing street: each of these excellent businesses seems to have little to do with the others being there, but together they form a fine run, perhaps the best place in Seattle to go to be impressed by the wonderful variety of things a city can toss up in the process of being itself. Aurora Avenue in the north end could be like this, not a neighborhood street at all, but a place where things could be made, and repaired, and sold, with one-of-a-kind quality. Nothing like that can be more than glimpsed there now, but since the real estate people and car lots have moved farther north, and the I-5 freeway has relieved some of the traffic congestion, such changes are possible.

But the success of such commercial streets depends on the willingness of people to care about neighborhoods enough to support residential business and to care about quality enough to support one-of-a-kind stores that may be farther away than a fast-buck place doing the same kind of business. As yet the newer areas of the city show few signs of developing this kind of willingness and caring, but as the lure of suburbs farther out pulls away those who seek only status and privacy, as the houses weather and new people move in, changes are possible, real estate values can become more realistic. There is no present cause for hope in these neighborhoods, but no need for enduring despair either.

NATIVES AND NEWCOMERS

Just as the stagnation of the economy did not tell the whole story about Seattle between the wars, so too The Boeing Company and the mad building rush in the north end do not tell the whole story in the postwar years. The population boom brought many others besides suburbanites, and of course many suburbanites turned out to be interesting people. The stories one hears about why people came during the Boeing years offer too many reasons to be classifiable, but one strain in almost all of them is that Seattle seemed to offer something fresher, newer, less spoiled or jaded than someplace else. The jet airplane and the interstate highway really did shrink the country so that while Seattle for most people continued to seem like a place far away, it became less difficult to imagine coming. The mountains and the water were there, as always, only now such wonders began to seem more valuable, more explorable to more people. "In America," wrote bemused David Brewster in *Seattle Magazine*, "the Irish run governments, Jews write novels, and WASPs camp." No better place to live if one is going to camp than Seattle, and so recreational equipment became an industry, especially since the Irish had never run the government here and the Jews had never written novels.

If to the natives Seattle had begun in the postwar years to seem utterly different from what it had been, to the newcomers it seemed to offer much that had always been magical about it. In addition, many who didn't particularly want to come to a citylike city were content in Seattle because it wasn't busy or crowded or ethnic-oriented or plagued with bad water or smog. Sedate maybe, unexciting maybe, but livable. The very fact that it was far away could begin to seem an attraction if what one wanted was something unlike other cities in the east or midwest. In *A New Life* Bernard Malamud had derided the idea implied in his title; but he had, after all, imagined that new life in Corvallis, Oregon, and it was a good deal easier to imagine a new life, a new lease on possibility, in Seattle.

On the other hand there were the natives, those who had grown up assured in the quiet Seattle between the wars. Nancy Wilson Ross and Constance Green, as seen in quotations in earlier chapters, have judged these people to be complacent, narrow, or provincial. Insofar as such a view represents people settling in prematurely, embracing private life as an alternative to all others, such views seem justified. The first full-fledged Seattle native who came to full-fledged power was Dave Beck, after all, and Beck, as we have seen, represented a strain deep within the heart of Seattle. But Beck never was the whole story, and the postwar years were the first in which a large native population in Seattle could come to its maturity, so we must look carefully at what these people did before making any kind of secure judgment. If Seattle had been a great place in which to grow up, presumably that fact would breed qualities other than narrowness and complacence: care for a city worth keeping, strength and even wisdom in ministering to that care.

In the activities of natives and newcomers in postwar Seattle, especially in those places where the two groups mixed, clashed, and harmoniously created, there is a great story, an indigenous story too. A bourgeois city may well be active, but it is apt to be weak in precisely those areas where other cities are strong: in ethnicity, in politics, in newspapers. As a result, those frames of reference which work well in discussing New York, Pittsburgh, or Detroit may be barely relevant here. On the other hand, other frames may prove useful here that are of no use elsewhere, and in the various minglings, happy and unhappy, of native and newcomers one has something that tells more about the city than other categories do, and as much as the influence of Boeing.

To set the scene, let me quote two outsiders viewing Seattle in what each took to be its native state. First, Earl Pomeroy, professor of history at the University of Oregon: "Only Seattle has seemed so much [as Los Angeles] the product of the twentieth century, of the automobile, the airplane, the assembly line, the advertising agency." Since these pages have offered a good deal of evidence to support Pomeroy's view of Seattle, let it not be scorned as the view of a rural Oregonian. Rather, place alongside it this from Malcolm Cowley, resident of New York, Paris, and the world:

> By contrast I spent the early months of 1950 in Seattle, where everything was modern, including the excellent food in private homes. Everyone seemed to be middle class and literate, no matter what his trade. We lived on a street lined with picture-window houses that were owned, not rented, by business people, skilled mechanics, and college professors. The milkman, the dry cleaner for the neighborhood and the cleaner's wife were college graduates, as were many of the taxi drivers.

Pomeroy's scorn is Oregonian, and is an old view of Seattle shared by many in the northwest, including many who live in Seattle. Especially in its wartime and postwar phases Seattle was like Los Angeles, a plaything of cars, airplanes, assembly lines, and advertising agencies. Almost since it first was a successful city, however, people from other parts of the northwest have liked to see it as a city more intent on growing than on any idea of what it might grow into being.

Yet Malcolm Cowley was neither the first nor the last to come to Seattle and to feel that here was something different, a city of possibility where all was not yet ravaged and the bourgeoisie still strong. His view was newer than Pomeroy's, one that was gaining strength in the postwar years, especially from people coming from farther away than Eugene. People might deplore the complacency of middle-class Seattle, but even the dourest saw possibilities here, because it was a city built well, a city that had been great to grow in. Turn the city one way and its natives would seem healthy and glowing while, from the same view, outsiders would seem gloomy, excessively energetic, and fussy; turn it another way and its natives would seem chauvinists and provincials whose only hope lay in letting newcomers save them. The people in Pomeroy's ad agency and the people in Cowley's taxicab were essentially the same people. The question was how they would respond to change, when that change consisted of so many people suddenly arriving from outside.

METRO

It was not newcomers who first pointed out the direst consequences of postwar growth—the gradual and then sudden pollution of Lake Washington, the gradual and then sudden cry for more and bigger highways, the gradual and sudden proliferation of hundreds of governmental units dotting and crisscrossing the entire area. It was natives, people who had grown up in the prewar quiet and who saw much that was dangerous in the Boeing boom. The key figure here is James Ellis, a graduate of Franklin High School, a resident of suburban Bellevue but essentially a downtown lawyer; almost everyone else behind the formation and then the administration of the Metropolitan Municipality of Seattle—Metro—was old Seattle, a native.

The city had had its sewer system built by R. H. Thomson, who had insisted on carrying his lines away from Lake Washington to West Point, off Magnolia Bluff, and so out into the Sound. But postwar Seattle came suddenly and carelessly, especially in the north end, and one result was the Lake City Sewer District, which blithely began pouring tons of raw and treated sewage into Lake Washington. Almost all the new sewer districts were doing the same, and many private homeowners in these developing areas thought nothing of building a septic tank and hoping a nearby stream would carry away the sewage. The land was plentiful and the labor sloppy, so soon after the war the lake was getting dirtier at an accelerating and alarming rate.

Most people didn't want to pollute Lake Washington, but almost everyone seemed to want each adult to have a car and all governments to build roads. The floating bridge across Lake Washington had been a marvel of modernity when it had opened in 1939, but by the early fifties it was clogged morning and night; so too with Aurora Avenue and Bothell Way to the north, the Marginal Ways and Pacific Highway South to the south. So up went the cry that was always associated with Los Angeles, with either pride or alarm: build freeways, build more bridges across the lake, make it easier to get downtown and to the Boeing plants. Virgil Bogue in 1911 had said that rapid rail transportation was essential in a sprawling and hilly and water-divided city like Seattle, because people had so far to get to work. By the early fifties people were spending longer getting to work than on anything else they did besides work and sleep. But since they now had cars that could go much faster than Bogue had imagined, they also wanted enough roads to allow them to get to work at high speeds in their cars. Since the federal government under Eisenhower was committed to building whatever roads people wanted, plans for an interstate freeway running north-south through Seattle were quickly drawn up, and no sooner was that planned than the need for a second one was envisaged as well as one or more new bridges across the lake and another freeway on the east side.

As an almost perfect expression of the new sprawl, hundreds of governmental units popped up, each with seemingly great enthusiasm for its job and each with bland disregard for all the others. Before the war, the cities around the lake were Seattle, Renton to the south, Kirkland to the east, Bothell to the north; shortly after the war Seattle had suddenly expanded five miles farther north, and there were Mercer Island, Bryn Mawr, Newport, Bellevue, Clyde Hill, Hunt's Point, Medina, Juanita, Kenmore, Lake Forest Park, Lake Hills. Some of these had their own sewers, or police, or fire departments, or schools; those who did not either banded together or else relied on King County. Thus boundary lines went everywhere, through and across other boundary lines for other governments, all of which had the right to ask for taxes and to acquire public land. They were all jerry-built very quickly, and with an almost shocking confidence.

Jim Ellis was part of a campaign as early as the beginning of the fifties, when he was barely thirty, to get a new charter for King County that might start to straighten out the developing mess. The only people taking any interest were those who felt that somehow Seattle was out to control its hinterlands, and the idea was turned away in a 1952 election. Ellis came right back. At a meeting of the Municipal League to which had been invited lots of city and county officials, he proposed a new metropolitan government, along the lines of one recently formed in Toronto, which would be designed to solve the problems that the small cities and governmental units could not handle. In 1956 Ellis was made chairman of a committee appointed by Mayor Gordon Clinton and the county commissioners, consisting of forty-eight members, almost all the important ones being Seattle natives struggling to make sense out of a world they thought they were about to lose. The committee drafted and lobbied legislation, which was passed by the 1957 legislature and placed on the local ballot in March 1958. It provided for a Metro council of fifteen members, eight from Seattle, seven from the suburbs, to supervise the building of sewers, the development of a rapid transit system, and the establishment of area-wide planning.

As one might imagine, the biggest outcry against the proposed Metro came from those areas that seemed least to benefit, and, in response, it was agreed that areas between Seattle and Tacoma that originally had been included could get out if they wished. As also might be imagined, if the postwar "development" or "suburban" mentality is understood, the next to protest were people from those areas most responsible for the conditions requiring Metro's creation in the first place: the eastside communities from Renton to Bothell, and the north end of Seattle. These people were afraid, and while they outwardly expressed fear of Seattle and of higher taxes, their fear can really be identified as the fear of anything that lay outside the small circles they had drawn around themselves. Planning was anathema; rapid transit wasn't needed, and there would be far fewer traffic problems if people in Seattle would approve the construction of a second bridge across the lake; the existing sewers were good and the pollution danger exaggerated. When scientists at the university and doctors verified the pollution problem, it was replied that of course the downtowners who had dreamed up Metro could get the university and the Medical Association to front for them.

The irony was that none of the people in city government, none of the people on the Metropolitan Problems Committee, could possibly be described as carpetbaggers, and very few could conceivably stand to gain in power or money from Metro's success. They were hardly the obvious heirs to the new wealthy of the turn of the century, either, but rather people who had grown up in Seattle between the two world wars and were appalled at what the wartime and postwar growth had produced. Since the aim of Metro was not to perform jobs normally given to local governments, but to perform jobs that clearly had gotten too big for those governments, the fear of super-government really was unwarranted. Ellis, unfortunately, was a partner in one of the two Seattle law firms recognized as able to sell local government bonds, but that could not begin to account for his tirelessness in conceiving and selling the idea of Metro. If he made mistakes, they were political mistakes, mistakes in calculation. Since he had grown up in a quiet and unthreatening Seattle, he apparently underestimated the extent to which the new postwar people could look upon Seattle as a big bad wolf. In the March vote, where a separate majority was required in both the city and the suburbs, there was a majority in Seattle, but Metro lost elsewhere, by about 7,000 votes out of 47,000 cast.

The campaign had sufficiently exposed Metro's weaknesses that Ellis and the others revised it, aided by a report by the engineering firm of Brown and Caldwell that for the first time offered some sense of what the cost would be: 83 million dollars before 1970, 80 million dollars after 1970, which meant something between two and four dollars per month per household. Since that was for sewers only, it was clear that in order to get the sewers, the rapid transit and planning functions of Metro would have to go. There was clearly only one way to clean up the lake, which was getting noticeably dirtier, while people kept feeling that transit problems could be solved with roads and bridges, and that planning was only a sign of Big Brother watching everyone. The size of the Metro area was reduced, furthermore, on its southern border, to exclude places that could not be expected to be excited about a clean Lake Washington or Puget Sound. This time there was no stopping the proposal. Not one official was against it, and opponents were forced to become awfully strident in their cries of socialism; in September of 1958 Metro got an even larger majority in the suburbs than in Seattle, most likely because all the campaigning had been done there since the March defeat.

To reduce Metro to an agency that built sewers and treatment plants did not sit well with everyone, especially Ellis. But, given the difficulty of getting regional cooperation of any kind in those years, given the speed with which lakes and rivers all over the country were becoming blithely polluted in those years, getting Metro at all was really a major triumph. It was a triumph of an R. H. Thomson sort, where the right thing to do gets done, in this case by local Seattle people, mostly natives, alarmed at postwar sloppy expansion. It would be almost a decade before the sewers would be in, the Renton and West Point treatment plants built, and the lake would become visibly cleaner and the Sound beaches swimmable. In the meantime the pollution kept getting worse, a splendid confirmation of the disaster that had been averted.

Every year since Metro went into operation it has become clearer what a jewel Lake Washington is, a mountain lake at sea level, incapable of resisting the effluent of the Lake City Sewer District but large and active enough to handle the scum and noise of powerboats. It is rich in beaches, richer still in private waterfront property, offering magnificent views of Mount Rainier, Mount Baker, and the Cascades, sullen and even wild in winter, placid and relaxing in summer, of all Seattle's natural gifts perhaps the most beautiful. By 1970 the sockeye salmon were running again. The city of millions that Virgil Bogue saw surrounding the lake had almost been built, and if it did not have Mercer Island for a park it did have Lake Washington getting cleaner and clearer every year. It is a fine legacy of the people raised in an older Seattle to their children and to those who had just arrived.

Metro had been allowed to exist only as a sewer system, and when it went back to the voters in 1962 in another attempt to get permission to go into public transportation, it was once again rebuffed. The cry still was for more roads. After the first public transportation defeat in 1957 the city reluctantly approved long-pending plans for a second bridge over Lake Washington, and even before that the federal government was pressing for a freeway through Seattle.

There was considerable debate about the best route for a freeway, and it was finally the influence of downtown business people that secured the route running closest to downtown, coming down through the north end, over Lake Union on a bridge, then skirting the western side of Capitol Hill, the eastern edge of the downtown area, and so south to the industrial tidelands. It was one of the first energetic things people downtown had done since deciding they could live with Dave Beck back in the thirties.

Given the economic and population booms of the war and postwar years, downtown had changed very little since the twenties. The older blocks and stores had in appearance weathered well and gained charm, but it looked as though downtown was succumbing to the trend to build at the edges of the city and to let the center die slowly. Prohibition had taken away downtown night life and its best restaurants, and there was little hurry to get any of that back; it was illegal to buy liquor by the drink in the state until after World War II. City government was still a caretaker affair, mostly looking after the least interesting aspects of the downtown business establishment: status quo when the status of the quo was moribund.

When downtown people woke up to the fact that the center of the city was dying, they tended to react clumsily. The first new buildings of the late fifties—the Norton Building, the municipal library, the Logan Building—were ugly glass affairs. The route chosen for the freeway involved brutal cuts in Capitol and First hills, and some severe and very expensive engineering problems. When it was suggested that some of the damage could be repaired by putting a lid on the road, downtown people and the federal government scorned it as frill (though twenty years later a freeway park is being built, with their blessing, at much greater cost). When all that was settled, the downtown people wanted to go on and develop a ring road system around downtown that would compound the bad effects of the freeway and the Alaskan Way viaduct. But more was needed. Metro was fine, and downtown gladly supported Jim Ellis and his cohort, and the freeway would certainly help; but the sense of sluggishness remained. Try a world's fair.

In *Century 21* Murray Morgan gives a full account of the 1962 Seattle fair, and while many details are fascinating, the outline is sufficiently familiar that it can be passed over lightly here: civic energy, hard-working people, ups and downs in making plans, delays, getting money, getting sued, the show going on. There were also some unfamiliar aspects: the fair was well managed, it made money, and its principal attraction was a science center. The real point about it, though, is that land and labor once again became the precedent conditions in downtown Seattle. The fair itself took place outside downtown, at the far end of David Denny's original claim near the foot of Queen Anne Hill, but it was a downtown project, and in an important way downtown people did in 1962 what their counterparts had failed to do in 1911 when they had rejected Virgil Bogue's plan for a civic center. Everyone important in making the fair was a downtown person and a Seattle native or long-time resident: Edward Carlson of Western Hotels; Ewen Dingwall of the Washington State Research Council; Jim Faber of the *P-I*; Joseph Gandy of Smith-Gandy Ford; Ray Olsen, the fair's broker in the state legislature; Senator Warren Magnuson, the major force behind the creation of the Pacific Science Center and the fair's sponsor in Washington, D.C. The Seattle Center, the Space Needle, the Science Center, the rebuilt Opera House, the monorail—none of these is above reproach and some are not even above ridicule, but they worked to make the fair a success and they remained to provide a genuine new focus for activity, the first that old Seattle had had in years.

The Seattle Center was put together with great limits on both time and money, and so it ended up seeming something of a messy jumble. But it has good halls for hearing music, for watching plays and sports events; it has landmarks in the Space Needle and the Science Center that look better a decade later, it has amusement parks and cheap eats and some lovely fountains and an art pavilion. There is nothing elegant and little beautiful about it, but it worked during the fair and it has continued to work since. People go there, and on weekends and during the summer lots of people go there. It is a watering place for the Employed and the home of the symphony and the opera company. High school football and professional basketball and soccer are played there. It mixes and sorts and mixes people, over and over. Barely ten years after the fair a good deal of the jerry-built and ramshackle were beginning to show and the city, which owns the land and most of the buildings, had to go back and ask for 20 million dollars in bonds to make it cleaner and do it better. But it is a bargain, one of those odd and not really well-planned successes that can make city life so valuable.

After the success of the fair, downtown people really began to think better of themselves and their prospects. They decided that what they wanted was to become, to use the term then popular, big league. The manufacturing base of the economy was someone else's business, really—downtown people have always regarded The Boeing Company with a kind of holy dread—but going big league suddenly became their business, meaning, of course, big league sports, convention business, downtown skyscrapers. As long as the Boeing payroll continued to rise—and in the middle 1960s it got close to one hundred thousand—growth could mean not just more suburban projects but an affluent, confident, and proud downtown. One could be amused at the number of times sentences offered both in public and private would begin "We have" or "We've got," because, of course, to be big league in Seattle was to be imitative, to catch up, to belong or take one's place. Seattle would become like all the other cities in America that were at the same time, and perhaps a little earlier, finding ways to belong: Minneapolis, Atlanta, Houston, San Diego, Phoenix, Portland.

The most obvious and visible sign of this new confidence was the skyscraper. For fifty years Smith Tower had been the tallest building in Seattle, though it had long since ceased being the tallest west of the Mississippi. But beginning in 1964 that suddenly changed. Seattle-First National Bank, having established itself throughout the state through a long series of purchases of smaller banks, wanted to be able to say that no one need any longer automatically go to New York or San Francisco to get financing for a major project, and they planned and built an enormous, even monstrous, fifty-story office building to prove it. Soon to follow were the Bank of California Building, the Financial Center, the new Federal Office Building, the Washington Plaza and Hilton hotels, and, as this is being written, the Rainier Bank and the new Pacific Northwest Bell buildings. The end of this spate of building is probably now in sight, and its results are far from being all good. All have created a deadening effect on the street life near them. Their huge value also has tended to drive the price of downtown property so high that many older and charming and serviceable buildings will become uneconomical. Temples of Mammon, citadels of power, they necessarily allow for little compromise with their surroundings, little possibility for ameliorating amenity or activity.

Yet, one is inclined to say, so be it. If the power they assert is brutal and clumsy, these buildings show nonetheless the vitality that such power can have. Though they have multiplied the available downtown office space a number of times over, they have not yet lacked for clients. They have increased the number of people coming downtown and thereby have created problems that are very much worth solving. Above all, they have produced the feeling that downtown Seattle could be an extraordinarily exciting place, even though the buildings themselves convey very little of that excitement. Action has created reaction, and unquestionably more people both know and care more about downtown than ten or twenty years ago. There was pride and confidence in evidence in the first decade of the century when the last major building boom took place downtown, and those excellent buildings were followed by complacency and withdrawal. That seems much less likely this time.

GROUP HEALTH

Metro, the I-5 freeway, the World's Fair and Seattle Center, the new skyscrapers were all home-grown projects, and when newcomers got into any of these acts they tended to be against them. But what Malcolm Cowley came and enjoyed in 1950—Seattle as a city in which bourgeois life could thrive—others before and many others after him came and found. These newcomers tended to be professional or upper-middle-class people of some sort, those who in effect felt themselves driven out of older American cities: engineers, teachers, lawyers, doctors.

What some wanted when they came was just a jumping-off place for recreation on the water or in the mountains. What some wanted was just a place to live, where they could settle and feel in the harmonies of a quiet city what they had been unable to find in the jumbles and jungles of noisier ones. What many others still wanted was a place where some kind of urban activity in which they were engaged or interested could thrive. In the story of Group Health Co-operative of Puget Sound is one of the finest instances of that thriving, for in this case we find a mixture of energetic newcomers and some of what was most vital in old, native Seattle.

Group Health has a number of different components and points of origin: a farmer's grange, no less, on the east side of Lake Washington; the aerospace and longshoremens' unions; a health service for the indigent, the King County Medical Service Clinic, begun in the thirties. The first two of these had been interested for a long time in some health care plan for their members. The third had been some-

Japanese Americans from Bainbridge Island, being shepherded to a relocation camp in California, in front of hundreds of their fellow citizens (courtesy of the Seattle *Post-Intelligencer*)

Boeing Plant #2 on the Duwamish River during World War II, the roof mocked up to resemble a residential district to camouflage it from Japanese planes that never could have flown far enough to see it (courtesy of the Seattle *Post-Intelligencer*)

B-29s being assembled during the war (courtesy of The Boeing Company)

James Ellis (courtesy of the Seattle
Post-Intelligencer)

Metro's way of dramatizing the pollution of Lake Washington (courtesy of the Municipality of Metropolitan Seattle)

One of those lovely instances where it is the parking lot that is taken away. Above is Occidental Street in 1970; below is the park that replaced it, in the summer of 1972 (courtesy of the Seattle *Post-Intelligencer*)

Harbor Island in the foreground, with the Port of Seattle's container cargo cranes loading ships. The new downtown skyscrapers to the north are in the background, Lake Union on the upper left, Lake Washington on the upper right, and the Kingdome stadium is going up on the right (photo by Harry Gilmour, courtesy of the Port of Seattle)

The Port of Seattle's giant grain elevators at Pier 86, with Kinnear Park and Queen Anne Hill in the background (photo by Harry Gilmour, courtesy of the Port of Seattle)

The Pike Place Market at dawn above, open for business below (courtesy of the Seattle *Post-Intelligencer*)

Forward Thrust's Waterfront Park just before it opened, October 1974; the wall of the Alaskan Way viaduct in the immediate background shuts it off from downtown (courtesy of the Seattle *Post-Intelligencer*)

The University of Washington campus, spring 1970, during the Kent State–Cambodia crisis (courtesy of the Seattle *Post-Intelligencer*)

The south end of Union Bay, near the Arboretum, in the summer of 1975 (see pages 251–52) (courtesy of the Seattle Post-Intelligencer)

thing of a naughty stepchild of the King County Medical Association which inherently mistrusted co-operatives and free or prepaid medical services. In 1945 the Medical Service Clinic bought Saint Luke's hospital on 16th Avenue on Capitol Hill; at the same time the grange and union people were meeting in Renton with some doctors to explore the possibilities for establishing a co-operative.

Since at that point a great deal happened quite quickly, let me choose as a symbol of the co-op's origins and of the kind of institution it was to become a meeting that took place in suburban Kirkland during the fall of 1945 at a panel discussion concerning health care co-ops. Present were a member of the King County Medical Association who busily went into all the reasons co-ops were wrong; Jack Cluck, a Seattle attorney who was representing the grange and union people; and William A. MacColl, a doctor from the Medical Service Clinic. After the panel was over, Cluck and MacColl quickly realized they had much in common and went out to see what could be done. Cluck was a native, a liberal, not a union person but a friend of labor, not a New Deal politician but interested in what the New Deal at its best had been interested in. MacColl was a Bostonian, a graduate of Tufts and Harvard, a pediatrician who had come to Seattle during the war and joined the Medical Service Clinic.

The result, not just of that meeting but of many others like it, was Group Health Co-operative, which opened its doors for business at Saint Luke's on January 1, 1947. Although at the time most of its members were from the grange and the unions, its intention was not to provide services for groups but to establish a membership of individuals, each of whom in effect would own part of the co-op, each of whom could vote on its policies. By means of a prepayment plan each member was entitled to all the services of the co-op, which included the hospital, the staff of doctors, and a pharmacy. The board elected by the members would set the rates, the salaries, the policies as to management of funds, extent of coverage, means of recruiting new members.

As might be expected, the established medical profession was not going to let this happen without a fight, and Group Health's doctors soon found themselves effectively blacklisted from using the services of other hospitals and new doctors coming into Group Health from elsewhere often found it difficult to obtain a license from the local medical association. This was Cluck's finest hour. He sued the medical association and Swedish Hospital (as a representative of the medical establishment) in the name of Group Health's doctors and of one of its members (so as to prevent any attempt to argue the matter was strictly an internal matter among physicians). There was a trial in 1948, and Group Health lost; there was an appeal to the state Supreme Court, and Group Health was upheld. After 1950 Group Health's right to exist was never questioned, though it is not clear even now that it has been fully accepted by the local medical profession.

What Cluck in effect represented was a residue of a feeling—it is hard to know better how to define it. It was certainly not the feeling embodied in Jim Ellis' drive to establish Metro, or that expressed by downtown business people when they organized the World's Fair, though it may share with such people the desire to make active and credible various kinds of local action. Cluck's feeling was perhaps closer to Jesse Epstein's when he built Yesler Terrace, but while Epstein was pulling the strings of government to create an image of local possibility, Cluck was translating into reality the desire of ordinary middle- and working-class people to do collectively what they could not do singly. People who did not know each other, people who might have nothing else in common, people who represented nothing other than themselves and their families—it is an almost perfect expression of Seattle, confident, bourgeois, hopeful, and suddenly very able.

After the lawsuit was settled, it soon became apparent that the suit had held together people and postponed problems, which emerged the moment the common enemy disappeared. The major problem concerned relations between the board and the staff, and while it would oversimplify to say that the board simply represented native Seattle and the staff newcomers, that was the case more often than not. Perhaps the sorest point was the question of who was responsible for the personnel. From the beginning the board had had a hand in hiring doctors and so it saw no reason why it should not also have a hand in firing them. The doctors, on the other hand, felt they knew best not only who was most competent but who fitted in best to group practice. This was perhaps Doctor MacColl's finest hour. In 1952 he agreed to become the first doctor to take on the job of director for a year. He stayed for three, and by the end of his tenure Group Health really was fully established, growing in its membership almost in quantum leaps, expanding its staff, facilities, and services at an accelerating rate. In a book he wrote some years later, *Group Practice and Prepayment of Medical Care,* MacColl set out as in textbook form the theories and experiences of Group Health. Perhaps its key point here is the way MacColl shows among the doctors the same kind of spirit that animated the members: a desire to do collectively that which cannot be done singly, a meeting of specialist, general practitioner, and general public that provides each what simple private practice could not.

It is probably no accident that Group Health's staff has been recruited from all over the country. It has made its staff better by not being local, just as it has offered its staff undoubtedly something they could find elsewhere only rarely and, even then, in different form. The remarkable fact is the most obvious one, that Group Health doctors become citizens of the community just by joining the staff. Like most essentially conservative institutions at their best, Group Health can seem almost radical to a doctor trapped in the rigamaroles of hospitals and private practice. Yet what it in effect does, both for members and staff, is that which bourgeois life is always trying to do, create hope by giving satisfaction.

In less than thirty years Group Health has grown from a membership of a few thousand to one of two hundred thousand; the facilities at the central clinic have never once not been in the process of being expanded, and clinics are now open in Renton, Northgate, Redmond, Lynnwood, Burien, Federal Way, and Olympia. The one policy it has not been able to maintain is that of trying to achieve a membership of individuals and families; since groups seeking health care abound, the co-op has never been able to count more than half its patients as individual member-owners. On the other hand, it has surprised even itself by its ability to do its own financing. As late as the early 1960s Group Health was unable to get a loan from local banks for expansion of its hospital, and so it turned around and floated a fully successful bond issue among its members.

It is difficult to say just what has made Group Health so successful—it is now the largest member-owned health care center in existence. One reason, surely, is that in this case the needs of the native members (though by now it has plenty of newcomers in its membership) and those of the outsider medical staff were, while not being exactly the same, harmonious. The impulses—on the one hand to claim the best of a native heritage, and on the other to find in Seattle a new life through a new way of working—meshed, and, for all its present size, are still there.

UNIVERSITY OF WASHINGTON

The University of Washington has always been bringing in newcomers. With each step it took, from high school to college to university, it managed its shift and its growth by means of hiring someone with prestige or clout from farther east. Vernon Parrington's university, however, had the look and air of a home-grown place. The students, of course, were almost all natives of the Seattle area, and a great many members of the faculty traditionally were recruited from the ranks of former students. Its character was predominantly populist and liberal as each new generation of students discovered that such strains were the best in their heritage. Before the war one of the best-known and best-remembered features of the campus was its luncheons or informal afternoon seminars involving undergraduates, graduate students, and faculty; one recently retired teacher recalls that one of the significant days of his life was when he was asked as a sophomore to join these gatherings.

The war changed much of that, and it all went smash in a vicious episode in the years immediately after. State Senator Albert Canwell from Spokane chaired a legislative committee that conducted the kind of investigation we now associate with the name of Joseph McCarthy. Six members of the faculty, most of whom had been students of Parrington's, were raked over the coals for having been or for continuing to be members of the Communist party, and the university administration was at best indecisive and not altogether honest. The best account of the happenings is Melvin Rader's *False Witness,* and in the early part of his book Rader conveys very well the kind of populist–liberal–New Deal–leftist place the university had been before and during the war. Three of the six accused faculty were dismissed, the other three "put on probation," and the result was a bitterness that lasted until the whole generation of faculty involved had retired.

Even had none of this taken place, however, the university was destined to become a very different place from what it had been. It was growing steadily, it was relying more heavily on increasingly available federal funds to expand its research facilities and faculty, it was beginning to formulate an unwritten rule that all new faculty would be recruited from outside, usually from no nearer than California. Charles Odegaard became president in 1958 and moved quickly to make all these processes deliberate and self-conscious and, if he could, triumphant. Odegaard insisted that the experience of universities in California, Illinois, Minnesota, and the Michigan he had himself come from showed there was no incompatibility between the dreams of scholars for a great research center and the requirements of the state for the public education of its citizenry. His entire effort was to take the university away from whatever had been local and traditional in its moorings and to pull it into what he took to be the mainstreams of higher education in America.

In an institution of sixteen thousand students, the university's size when Odegaard arrived, to say nothing of a school of twice that number, which the university was when he retired fifteen years later, it is not easy to see what effect a president can have on the day-to-day life of faculty and students. In a standardly arranged university, colleges and departments are shaped into something like fiefdoms and duchies that create the curriculum, hire and fire the faculty, and it would seem the president has little power to change this. The president deals with the Board of Regents, the legislature, and the public more than with the faculty or students.

Yet a strong presence like Odegaard's made itself very much felt, if not day-to-day then year-to-year and decade-by-decade. For instance, when college enrollments exploded during the sixties, Odegaard pressed for the creation of a large system of two-year community colleges, and opposed any significant expansion of the four-year colleges and universities other than the University of Washington itself. This meant the university would accept an increasing number of community college transfers, students coming in as juniors and ready to declare a major; that, in turn, downgraded the university's own freshmen and sophomores and re-enforced the tendency of individual departments to concentrate on their majors and graduate students. If a "great university," which is always what Odegaard wanted Washington to be, is oriented toward research and graduate work, then a strong community college system relieves the university of most of its burdens in general public education. Furthermore, Odegaard promoted all potential ties between the university and the federal government until, when he retired, the university ranked second to M.I.T. in the size of its federal grants. This too, of course, tended to push the school away from general education and toward an increasing emphasis on research, especially in engineering, science, and medicine.

All this had a curious but predictable effect on the Seattle community at large. On the one hand people have become increasingly respectful and proud of the university's achievements as a research center, and on the other it has become more and more suspicious of the university's size, autonomy, and what is often taken to be indifference to its undergraduate students. As a result, Odegaard's relations with the public and with the legislature were always more respectful than cordial. This was something Odegaard could afford and perhaps even court, since the university had funds available to it that were not derived from the state, both from the federal government and from the income derived from the Metropolitan tract downtown on the acres originally given to the university by Arthur Denny.

Yet in important ways the university has thrived not because it has become aloof, isolated, or autonomous, but because it has also been very much a part of its surroundings. It is true that Mark Tobey no longer wanted to live in the University District shortly after Odegaard came because it was becoming less a neighborhood commercial area and more an appendage of the university, but that was because the university had not walled itself off. The University District changed a great deal as the university went from under ten thousand to over thirty thousand students in two decades, but it managed to remain one of the most exciting and pleasant areas of the city because it could keep striking perilous balances between the pull of the university, of the Safeco Insurance Company, which established national headquarters there, and of its old moorings as a residential shopping district.

President Odegaard himself did one small thing that may turn out to have been of crucial significance in achieving this balance. In the mid-1960s relations between the young and the police came under a great strain, mostly because of a greater and more open use of drugs by the young. During the summer of 1967 one could walk through the District and feel sure something was about to explode or tear apart as the kids and the cops both became more pugnacious. Along 15th Avenue Northeast is a stretch of the campus adjoining the University District that became known as Hippie Hill as the young adopted it as a sanctuary where they could use whatever drugs they had available. Odegaard could have done nothing, or he could have invited the police onto the campus. Instead he announced that the university would continue to make every effort to police itself, which meant that Hippie Hill remained a sanctuary. Since a large number of the young involved were not university students but drop-outs and high school students, it would have been easy for Odegaard to have used that fact to do the opposite of what he did. The natural gap between the young and the Olympian Odegaard was wide enough so the kids did not take his announcement as an invitation to run wild but, rather, as a signal to proceed, with discretion. Everything calmed down noticeably. Soon a lot of the hippies had turned capitalist and opened small businesses in the District, so that when the emphasis shifted from drugs to the Vietnam war in 1968–70, co-existence had been practiced long enough that the disasters occurring on campuses and in communities elsewhere did not happen here.

There were other ways that Odegaard and the university have managed not to lose touch. In remaining largely a commuter school, the university has diminished its ability to withdraw as a community in itself and has maintained thereby its ability to be part of the larger and more amorphous community. It is a school for greater Seattle, and in its continuing education, its lectures and concerts, its museums and its arboretum it has done a good deal to make it part of the ongoing life of the city. Its employees can walk or bicycle to work. All this means that neither faculty nor students are ever isolated, so that "going to the U" or "teaching at the U" are not in most parts of Seattle considered strange things for people to do.

There is, however, as I have implied already, one great drawback to Odegaard's ideal university, and it may well become felt most in years to come. The university had to expand to just under thirty-five thousand students to gain the financial base it needed to build a major research establishment. It is almost preposterous to imagine that any school that large, especially one that had no tradition of high pretension, could actually hire a faculty good enough to justify the claims suddenly being made for it. The emphasis on research forced many faculty and students into work for which they were unsuited. Worse, it allowed for the development of the quite unwarranted assumption that published research is the necessary mark of an excellent scholar. Were the university smaller, or wealthier, it might have managed to justify more of its pretensions; but it isn't, can't be, probably shouldn't be.

In our present context we can say that the difficulty is that the relation of newcomer to native is potentially wrong at the university. If the faculty person coming from the outside feels that he or she is trailing clouds of glory from the other "great university" from whence he or she received a Ph.D., then it is easy to feel that the average student at the university is pretty average indeed, not worth much of one's time. If that faculty member is then encouraged to believe that job security is strictly a matter of what is published, even then the time that is given the student is spent with less than full or best attention. Since most students know when they are being treated this way, they develop suspicions and resentments even as they recognize there is little they can do about it.

If the relation of newcomer faculty to native student is disturbing, then the relation between newcomer faculty and native community is quite a bit better. As Malcolm Cowley pointed out, in Seattle the natural tendency of faculty people to draw into and to isolate themselves has been blunted, and the college professor often lives on the same street as the business person and the skilled mechanic or the city employee. Responsible in part are the university's seamless relation with its immediate surroundings, the wide dispersal of "good" neighborhoods of differing atmospheres so that there are no faculty enclaves, and the presence of large numbers of people in Seattle who have gone to the university and thus are able to modify the traditional mutual distrust of academic people and "the real world." Seattle is precisely the kind of city that is best for university people, and both it and they are better off for it.

Finally, there is that which is for many the essential connection between the university and Seattle: Husky Stadium, the football team, the six or seven Saturday afternoons in the fall when the team is home. Since the demise of minor league baseball in Seattle, the two "native" spectator sports are hydroplane racing and Husky football, neither of which is very interesting to anyone not close to fully converted. In their worst years the Huskies have drawn only slightly fewer spectators than in their best. Interest in the football team is seldom very great on campus, but elsewhere in the city it is staggering in size and solemnity. Is there any other city where, for over a mile in various directions from the football stadium, there are signs that are totally irrelevant 359 days a year, saying "No Parking 10 AM–6PM Day of Football Game"?

SEATTLE MAGAZINE

With *Seattle Magazine* we come to our first open clash between native and newcomer, one that is in itself exciting and telltale, one that is perhaps indicative of the clashes that may come later. What worked harmoniously at Group Health, what has thus far worked well enough at the university became nakedly feisty and acrimonious with *Seattle Magazine*.

Though the magazine was aggressively run by newcomers, it was the brainchild of a long-established native, Stimson Bullitt, then head of KING television and radio, bred with prominent family connections and established Seattle wealth. Bullitt had run unsuccessfully for Congress as a liberal Democrat in the early 1950s, and later wrote a book called *To Be a Politician* as a reflection on this experience. What is most striking about the book is not just that it isn't a personal memoir but that it says so little about Seattle. Bullitt is both intelligent and compassionate, yet his book expresses a striking aloofness, even disdain, for the people of Seattle when considered in the mass or as political groups. He was educated at Yale, as many of his era and station in Seattle were, and while he has always been a

Seattle person strongly dedicated to its well-being, he seems never to have lost his conviction that he knew better than anyone else what should be. With KING and then with *Seattle Magazine* he displayed a strong desire to bring in people from the outside who might be counted on to shake up the locals. To edit *Seattle Magazine* he hired Peter Bunzel, an extremely intelligent and competent easterner steeped in the traditions of other cities and their leading publications.

The magazine began in 1964. At that time Boeing and the university were entering their last great phases of expansion, suburbs east of the lake were booming, and the cry for more freeways and floating bridges was very loud. In 1963 Seattle had turned back an open-housing ordinance, an experience that revealed to the city the fact that it had a black ghetto as well as its desire to wish that it didn't. Metro was working on its treatment plants, SeaFirst was laying its first plans for the first of the new downtown skyscrapers. The mayor and the city council looked and acted like holdovers from a previous generation. Changes were taking place, clearly, that to a man like Bullitt seemed less than healthy. To a newcomer like Peter Bunzel, here was a city that had not undergone the worst experiences of other cities but that seemed determined to head in that direction.

Seattle Magazine lasted a few issues longer than six years, and it not only monitored these years of impending crisis but seemed to preside over them, perhaps occasionally even to cause them. On the surface the magazine's manners were impeccable, its pages glossy, its writers professional, competent, and cool. Underneath it was all missionary, determined to tell the city what was wrong, determined to speak as though only its people knew what was really or potentially right. Within a few issues it had lost its advertisement from Frederick and Nelson, the city's foremost department store and a leader in bestowing or withholding ads. As a result, it never got a number of other large accounts, and, as a result of that, it had to hope quite unrealistically to be able to support itself with subscriptions and sales. Bullitt apparently was, if not completely delighted, quite willing to underwrite all losses, but Bunzel insisted it should try to find a way to pay for itself.

The way was to press ahead with its own idea of what it meant to be a big league city—though it would never have used the word. If downtown people looked to see what Minneapolis or Atlanta or San Diego were doing, *Seattle Magazine* looked to New York and San Francisco. Its demeanor was sophisticated, its tone activist. Ten years later one can read through issue after issue and be surprised at how well it reads, how aptly its subjects were chosen, how balanced most individual stories could be. Yet one sees, too, that it was all wrong: stubborn, arrogant, aggressive.

Bunzel developed in his head a reader or a target that he wanted not so much to attack as to ridicule. This reader was local, a booster, a complacent provincial who liked the World's Fair and the new downtown buildings, who was a hearty or a frightened know-nothing about blacks, who loved Husky football and freeways and hydroplane races and who believed in everything most destructive about progress. Bunzel treated this reader or target like a hick. He was always looking for a way to get an edge, to imply that even the best in Seattle wasn't very good, or good enough. *Seattle Magazine* covered the racial situation better than anyone else in town, yet in a way that managed to patronize blacks as well as whites. It attacked the public and private schools with intelligence, yet in ways almost unblinkingly liberal and obtuse. It introduced a reasonably good issue on the university with a pointedly nostalgic Ivy League cover and the caption: "Your Son: Should He Go to the U," as though the university had no women and people in Seattle no daughters. It seemed never to get beyond the fatal flaw of the national weekly news magazines in mistaking balanced views where "all sides were heard" with full and careful views. Throughout its run it made the characteristic 1960s mistake of believing that no one under twenty-one who gave a sign of thoughtfulness could ever be mistaken.

Withal, there was much its sophistication and aggressiveness could bring that could indeed make local people take a better and more careful look around them. The writer known as Edward Harvey did an excellent job reviewing restaurants; the *Esquire*-like charts of the Establishment and of the tastes of the young were impeccable; the lists of Places to Bring Back, Places to Get Rid of, and Places to Retain were and still are intriguing. At their best these newcomers did what so often only newcomers can do, really look at what exists in a place. Though its own pretensions were enormous, they were always of a sort that derived from a clear sense of what was or could be best in Seattle, so that if they carried on like carpetbaggers they were also carpetbaggers who would stay if they could be made welcome.

Yet the magazine's immediate aim of gaining one hundred thousand subscribers was patently unreal, and it was doing well to get half that many. Since it demanded an audience that was, with or without formal degrees, educated, it needed to make a subscriber out of almost every educated person in Seattle at the same time as its stance and tone were guaranteeing that would never happen. If there was no necessary conflict between native and newcomer, between "big league" as defined by skyscrapers and "big league" as defined by good restaurants, there was certainly a potential antagonism. The suspicions of natives could be easily aroused and the snobbery of the cool and stylish could be itself suspicious. *Seattle Magazine* failed because it decided the antagonism had to exist, and thus locked itself into an adversary position. Letters to the editor became either cheers or boos, my side or their side. Had it moved more slowly and flexibly, it might have found ways to express a truly intelligent and critical love of Seattle. Because it did not, in its latter days it began to trap itself as Mayor George Cotterill had in the earlier impending crisis in the city. In that instance it wasn't really Colonel Blethen who had trapped Cotterill but Cotterill's inability to see where he was. In this case it wasn't even the worst provincial native that trapped *Seattle Magazine* but its own determination to go down fighting.

There are many possible conclusions one might draw from these various stories of the way the old and the new met and clashed in the Boeing years, and perhaps no single good conclusion is possible. It is obvious, however, that we can see here something essential about the city Seattle had become and was becoming in the postwar era. Its population had, in effect, been all immigrant for a long time and, except in the case of its Asians, those immigrants were people who had already lost much of their original ethnic or traditional basis by having lived in one or more places in homogenizing America before they came. Those immigrants who created the city of a quarter of a million by 1910 then settled into and became the native population of 1920 and after. The impetus of the war, of The Boeing Company, of postwar mobility and despair of city life elsewhere brought to Seattle a new wave of immigrants, marked not by ethnic origin but by their professional status; we have looked at doctors, teachers, engineers, and magazine editors here, but many other professionals were coming, too. Here they met the descendants of the earlier immigrants who were seeking ways to respond to the changes wrought by The Boeing Company as well as to the newcomers.

The outcome is still mostly in doubt, though individual triumphs and failures are already clear. In the next, and concluding chapter, we must keep an eye out for ways in which these groups went on being the important major forces as the city went into what seemed to be a climactic phase at least as important as the earlier one during World War I.

VII

The New City

In the summer of 1968 The Boeing Company employed more than 104,000 workers, an all-time high for any northwest company. The years 1965–66 had seen a stimulation of the economy throughout the Puget Sound region because Boeing's demands for labor, in exceeding local supply, brought new people in and caused a boom in homebuilding and led to estimates of future growth which gave downtown people the confidence they needed to begin the almost wholesale production of skyscrapers. The economy was strained in a dizzying way. There was a sharp increase in imports, especially in consumer goods, to accommodate the new population. By 1968 Boeing was readying the giant 747 for production and beginning extensive work on its SST.

During the summer of 1968 police helicopters circled over the Central Area night after night and huge squadrons of police cars were parked outside the fire station at 23rd and Yesler. Groups of Black Panthers drilled in the Madrona playfield, and white and Asian business people throughout the Central Area fled or built large protective screens around their stores. Hard-as-nails Police Chief Frank Ramon promised order would be maintained, and entrenched County Prosecutor Charles O. Carroll insisted dissidents represented a minority of the black community, a statement approximately as true as it was irrelevant. The "long hot summer" that black and white civil rights leaders had warned of came, as "civil rights" itself was replaced by "Black Power" as the rallying cry.

The situations at Boeing and in the Central Area were both alarming, and both were signs of impending crisis. Boeing had become so big Seattle was taking on signs of being a full-scale colony, and the

Central Area was claiming it was no longer willing to be a colony within the larger one. Seattle, Boeing, and the black population had all grown enormously in the previous two decades, and quite obviously Seattle had not ever really learned how to live well with the other two. Since Boeing was still hiring, and still seeming to promise a future of unlimited growth, little alarm was felt about it, except perhaps among the few who realized how precarious the giant's future was. The situation in the Central Area, though, was front page news, and many people throughout the city began reacting as if to catastrophe, often without any clear sense of what the catastrophe was, what had caused it, what they could do about it. Even the least informed or most frightened citizen may well have sensed, and this time rightly, that a different city would emerge from the crisis. It was not just the racial situation that was changing, but it was the crisis in black and white that signaled the beginning of a new and different Seattle.

BLACKS

A few details of the story of Seattle's black community can be offered here as backdrop. Back in my survey of Seattle in 1897 I made no mention of blacks, but they were here, although in small numbers. There was a downtown hotel known as Our House that is still spoken of affectionately by elderly black pioneers. There was the First A.M.E. Church, already built on its present site at 14th near Pine on the south end of Capitol Hill, and the first recognizable black community was beginning to form at 23rd and Madison, on land Henry Yesler had sold to a black named William Grose. In its earliest days the city and the territory were strongly antislave and antiblack—Free Soil meant, out here, freedom from both slave and slave-owner—so blacks as a group had never been welcome on the northwest frontier. Many of the blacks who came in the nineteenth century were imported as strikebreakers during labor disputes we have here associated with the Knights of Labor and the anti-Chinese movement. The number of blacks remained small, however, until World War II. There were skirmishes before then, within the Garfield High School area especially, about blacks on athletic teams, or at dances or parties, but the number of blacks was small enough that they had to take what they were given and the whites could feel generous in giving it to them.

After the war all this changed, though a 71 percent increase in black population between 1950 and 1960, as opposed to a 3 percent white increase, still gave the blacks only 5 percent of the city's population. A ghetto was formed, recognized as such by both blacks and real estate agents. Three-fourths of the blacks in 1960 lived in nine of the city's 121 census tracts, half within four of these, and most of the elementary schools within what was called the Central Area were more than 90 percent black. This was one of the oldest residential areas in the city, and it consisted of streets of houses ranging from the plain and bulky to the plain and shacklike. Almost surrounding the ghetto, and effectively walling it off, were some of the best neighborhoods of earlier days. To the west lay First Hill, which no longer had many houses at all and was the main hospital district. To the north was Capitol Hill, which changed from solid bourgeois Catholic to elegant and lavish as one went north on it. To the east lay the prime heritage of old Seattle on the ridges above and going down to Lake Washington, Washington Park, Denny Blaine, Madrona, Leschi, Mount Baker. Only to the south, toward Rainier Valley and Beacon Hill, could the ghetto easily expand without running into full-scale opposition.

In the late fifties and sixties along the edges of the ghetto one found bourgeois blacks and newcomer whites, the latter usually of the university or Group Health variety, each taking advantage of suddenly reduced real estate prices to attempt to work out terms for integrated living. These people made up the bulk of the active civil rights groups, and their early achievements were both impressive and too little. There was a preschool project that became a national model for Headstart, and an early Great Society community action project called the Central Area Motivation Program, or CAMP. But at the same time Seattle as a whole was massively rejecting an open-housing ordinance by a margin of more than two to one, and this election, furthermore, gave a number of older, entrenched city council people another term in office. In the mid-sixties increasing amounts of federal money became available for poverty neighborhoods and schools, but the nature of Seattle's ghetto always seemed to defeat any full sense of dedication or crisis. On the one hand, people in Seattle had gone on feeling theirs was a quality school system, when in fact almost nothing new had happened in a generation to adjust to any changes in education or society. In turn, it was easy to place the fault on the poor and the blacks, not on the schools themselves. On the other hand, the fact that there weren't ten blocks in the ghetto that looked and acted like a slum seemed to blind all but the most committed whites to the pockets of deterioration, blight, and neglect that were everywhere. That one could find, on a street of abandoned or overcrowded houses, one that its brave and determined owner kept bright with paint or garden fostered the notion that all "those people" needed was a little more will and self-respect. Finally, the fact that blacks were last hired and first fired, that black unemployment was twice as high as white unemployment, could be shrugged off because, after all, Boeing was hiring.

That Seattle was not Detroit or Newark or Watts thus hurt at least as much as it may in other ways have helped or diminished ills and evils. The relatively low total number of blacks and poor meant they did not have and could not gain the kind of city or state political base that blacks in other cities had. Help could come only from the federal government and activist whites, and both were more willing than able. Civil rights legislation had little impact because state law already covered voting rights, protection against flagrant discrimination, and public accommodations. Federal poverty projects were usually administered either by whites or by blacks brought in from outside, neither of whom were fully in touch. Since most blacks were new to Seattle, the ghetto had not had time enough to create a genuine community, and communication and trust among blacks could be easily strained, especially between older and younger people.

As the sixties went on, token efforts in housing, employment, and the schools, tokens which had often been gained by sustained hard work, became increasingly insulting. Those who had worked hard to gain them were among those most vehemently denounced. The older and traditional sources of ghetto power and action—the churches, the Urban League, the NAACP—seemed to the younger and angrier only pawns used by whites, as much in need of change or obliteration as the most nakedly racist group. In the spring of 1968 the Black Panthers began marching, fire bombs began to be thrown, and Frank Ramon's police were responding in kind.

What the blacks were saying and showing, in effect, was that Seattle was not immune. That was taken to mean at the time simply that Seattle was participating in a distinctly racist American habit of feeling and institutional prejudice. In a deeper sense, it perhaps meant that Seattle was a *city*, subject to precisely the pressures, changes, and disasters of other cities, and therefore in need of a fundamental reason to exist without which most pressures and changes would quickly turn into disasters. It had had such a reason during its years of first major growth, it had had a different reason in its years of quietude, but by the sixties the quiet was gone and growth had been simply a joy ride of highways and new housing created out of a desire not to be a city at all. For all its Boeing boom, for all its Metro and Group Health and university, a good deal of Seattle had become stagnant, had lost its reason for being, and the blacks were the first or the loudest to proclaim this. Yesler Terrace could not renovate the ghetto, Headstart could not educate the black children of the city, Boeing was ill-equipped by temperament and experience to become flexible in hiring and training programs, and, above all, city government was essentially as it had been since the demise of populism into middle-class progressivism.

For good and for ill, the major energies of the racial crisis moved to the University of Washington campus. For good because in his response to the blacks President Charles Odegaard had perhaps his finest moment; for ill because the university was not really able to do what it most needed to do; for ill because after the bursts of crisis energy had abated, a good deal was left unchanged in the ghetto.

When the federal government asked the university to begin an Upward Bound program on its campus in the winter of 1966, I was asked to become its first director. Traditionally the university had been as indifferent as any major Seattle institution to the problems of blacks, minorities, and the poor. It did as everyone did: took qualified applicants. Upward Bound was designed to take high school poverty students of some ability but little achievement and to help them get ready to go to college. It was, in effect, one of the safer of Great Society programs; but the university, at least as I saw it then, was puzzled. Why us? Why this? Since the average entering student at the university had better than a B average in high school, what would the university do with students with mostly under a C average? Still, they agreed to have the project, and to admit those who applied. The twenty-two who entered in the fall of 1967, though a third were white, added significantly to the black and Indian enrollment of the entire university. I was told by various older and wiser people that the university, because it was clearly unready for them, would inflict its unreadiness on the students. This turned out to be true in many cases, and some of the students began to drift away before the first quarter was over.

But the winds of change were blowing. The student Afro-American Society and the student branch of the Student Non-Violent Coordinating Committee combined in 1968 to form the Black Student Union, which began immediately to kick up a storm. A small group of students, including many of the Upward Bounders who had barely arrived, confronted deans and department chairmen, telling them they had better start doing something right then. In the spring of 1968 members of the BSU effectively held captive a meeting of the Executive Committee of the Faculty Senate and presented it with a series of demands. In alarm, concern, sympathy, and panic, the faculty, administration, and white students saw the BSU become the focus of the entire campus.

President Odegaard had the previous summer made his decisive move to keep the police and narcotics agents off the campus, and he knew, as every college president knew at the time, that the success of his presidential tenure was dependent on his continuing to deal well with increasingly loud and ominous cries from the students. If at first it had been the hippies and fringies, if at present it was the blacks, soon it would be all manner of student protesting the American presence in Vietnam and the complicity of colleges and universities in accommodating the government and the military-industrial complex. Ever since the Free Speech Movement at Berkeley in 1964, Odegaard could have known it was only a matter of time before he would have to deal with the problem.

It is most interesting that Odegaard's response to pressure from the blacks was not so much a campus response as a city response, and that as a direct result it was successful. Rather than do as at least some other presidents were doing at the time, and treat the matter as one strictly between students and administration, Odegaard made the university involved as it had never been before in seeing its obligation to the black, minority, and poor communities. He told the students, in effect, to go out into the community and recruit anyone who would come. He told the legislature and faculty, in effect, to pay for whatever it cost. He established the Special Education Program out of an Office of Minority Affairs with a university vice-president to run it. At the same time, then, that the Panthers were marching and the police helicopters were circling, recruiters were out doing their best to convince the disaffected that the university was open to them, as they were.

It was morally right, and politically right, and one because of the other. Odegaard could turn to the faculty and say, "Here is your problem." He could say to the students, "Vietnam is beyond the university's power, but minority education is not." In putting the matter this way, he moved around or through any question of whether the students had behaved themselves; if what they said was true, and he agreed it was, then the university must act. His gesture was especially useful during the peak of the antiwar protests in 1969–70 when, messy and cantankerous though the campus became, it never got out of hand. However aloof Odegaard personally could be, however crusty, he had earned the trust of his adversaries.

His gesture to the faculty did have, to be sure, more of an air of hopeful bravado about it. He had sought to create a "great university" oriented toward research, and thereby he had helped make a place that was ill equipped to respond well to the sudden arrival of large numbers of less-than-well-educated minority students. Odegaard had done nothing to encourage faculty to think they were there to educate the citizenry, and so they could hardly be expected suddenly to know what to do. They neither wanted nor knew how to recruit a minority faculty, they neither wanted nor knew how to become good at compensatory education. As a result, Odegaard's gesture in the years since it was first made has remained a gesture and little more. The moment the furor died down, the university discovered it really need do little to alter the way it thought of itself.

At the time, however, Odegaard's gesture was crucial. The summer of 1968 was tense, and the public schools experienced an onslaught of angry blacks in the fall of 1969 from which they still have not yet recovered. But since many of the young black leaders were students or became students, the university rather than the ghetto itself became the focus of activity, and what passed for law and order returned to the Central Area. There has been no year since then without its ugly incident involving blacks and police, but the ghetto has remained intact, unhappy but not ravaged.

Those who claimed that militancy was all that would work were right in that once the militancy declined, many began to think the problems had been solved or had gone away. Bourgeois life constantly offers its palliatives, and many of all races were willing to accept them. As too often happens with militant movements, those who gained most in the long run were middle-class people who knew how to take advantage of new opportunities open to them within the previously established system. Those who had suffered most before were helped least. Schools, large companies, and branches of government took on many new blacks, and often placed them higher than ever before. But the plight of the poor remained, and the ghetto itself is little different in 1975 than it was in 1965. Blacks unquestionably have individually and as a group increased their power as consumers, but they remain a small group in an alien society, ill-equipped as producers, as genuinely independent people. The largest black-owned business in Seattle is not large at all. The biggest agent for help is still the federal government. The ghetto is still a bad place to own property, and the banks and real estate people still continue to avoid it when possible. There is still no effective black political base, no real structure of power to serve as broker for black interests. It will, apparently, take another large influx of blacks to create any significant change.

All this is ironic, because elsewhere in the city changes were taking place aplenty, almost all of which benefited from the increased awareness of city problems that the blacks helped to create. As Seattle discovered what it meant to be a late-twentieth-century city, as Seattle did a great deal to respond with great vigor to that discovery, it was the blacks, who always had been city dwellers par excellence, who stood in line the longest as the benefits of these changes were being passed out.

CITY ACTIVISM

During the late 1960s *Seattle Magazine* was seeking to become the conscience of the city, and the plight of black people was only the first item on its long laundry list of causes for concern and alarm. Others were deteriorating schools, the stranglehold of Boeing, the disaffected young, freeways and suburbs, a staid and uninteresting Establishment, a moribund city government. Of all these it was city government that was most obviously in need of change, and, perhaps for that very reason, it turned out to be the easiest to change.

Politics had been a business-as-usual affair for so long that by the time changes began blowing in the wind the mayor and city council and major city agencies looked ludicrous. The strong council–weak mayor system had worked at least to the satisfaction of the citizens as long as they demanded little of it. Seattle City Light, once the great symbol of progress, had grown powerful and autonomous and indistinguishable from a private power company. The park system had not changed in fifty years. The planning agency came up with fewer ideas in ten years than Virgil Bogue had in one. The police were more responsive to the county prosecutor than to anyone in the city. As late as 1967 the city council consisted of nine people, all over fifty-five and most much older, who collectively continued to understand their task as keeping City Light happy, keeping downtown people happy, and keeping the books in balance.

All around the city council things were happening. The mayor, Dorm Braman, who once had in effect run the city as city council finance chairman, began advocating a strong mayor system, seeing a reason for rapid transit, seeing that blacks had legitimate complaints. The downtown people had their World's Fair and were doing their clumsy best to keep downtown from becoming just a brokerage house for suburban development. The founder of Metro, James Ellis, was putting together a new citizen effort called Forward Thrust that was looking at the city's needs precisely in ways the city council was not. The Port of Seattle, which as late as the 1950s had been operating with equipment and management techniques derived from the railroad era, had begun to modernize itself. But the city council remained a relic of another era, the worst and narrowest expression of the native population that had grown used to a static Seattle between the wars.

In the municipal election of 1967 Phyllis Lamphere, Tim Hill, and Sam Smith were elected to the council, and change was underway. These three had little in common besides being native or long-time residents and being unlike the holdovers still on the council. Lamphere was an extremely intelligent and articulate woman who probably knew more about city government than anyone else, and who was responsible for the quick passage of a charter amendment to create a strong mayor system. Hill was a brooding young maverick concerned primarily about the many ways in which the city government had grown away from the people. Smith had been the only black in the state legislature for years and he had become successful by being openly and happily a politician in a city where such a style is traditionally mistrusted. He was so obviously a man seeking public office that many blacks were unsure how much they could trust him.

Along with these three came a group called CHECC (Choose an Effective City Council), which expressed something new in the mixing of natives and newcomers. Most of the original CHECC people were natives, almost all of whom had gone south or east to college and had been caught up in the activist style of the Kennedy and early Johnson years. They had come back to Seattle, as convinced as Mark Tobey or James Ellis that Seattle was a great place to live, but convinced, too, that it needed a new way to see and to govern itself. A few years earlier such a group, lawyers who were under thirty-five and smacked of Harvard or Yale, could easily have been dismissed as young puppies. But in 1967 they not only seemed square compared to some other groups but also to be talking about something important and aiming at a very vulnerable target. Though CHECC had little money and not many members, it gained publicity and force far in excess of any actual power it might pretend to wield.

CHECC supported Lamphere and Hill in 1967, George Cooley in 1969, John Miller and Bruce Chapman in 1971, and in perhaps their most significant victory, Chris Bayley in his triumph over County Prosecutor Charles O. Carroll in 1970. Bayley, Miller, and Chapman were themselves CHECC members, and the last two of these were newcomers who had come to Seattle expressly to be activist. Furthermore, CHECC was partly responsible for the election of Wes Uhlman as mayor in 1970, and even the new council people they did not support, Smith, Wayne Larkin, Jeanette Williams, were people who never would have been part of the old city council. Thus, by 1971 the entire city government, with the exception of City Light, was new, filled with people committed to change, and each year seemed to bring more such people onto the staffs of the elected people and into various branches of the executive.

All this signified a new sense of possibility at least as much as any large or immediate changes in the way the city was run. Most of the CHECC people and the other new activists, for instance, were people who chose to live in old neighborhoods in old Seattle and to proclaim the advantages of living as close to downtown as possible. Most were interested in the arts, in the development or renewal of neighborhoods, in historic preservation, in stopping the construction of new big highways, in placing city offices in various old downtown buildings and not in new ones. In effect the basis of new possibility was old Seattle, the city that had been built by 1915. The style was professional only in the sense that most of the new activists were members of a profession, and the activism itself was oriented toward citizen participation and organization. In a city without partisan elections, either groups of citizens or coagulations of money will make whatever politics there is, and for the first time in fifty years it was citizens who were gaining power. These weren't University of Washington or Group Health people but downtown people, lawyers and government officials, who therefore saw in the conduct of downtown's affairs the key to Seattle. Though many were themselves natives, they seemed to the old downtown establishment like newcomers, because they were young and what they wanted was a different kind of city, a Seattle more urban and more urbane.

Perhaps the high-water mark of the whole movement came in 1971 in a vote on an initiative to establish the Pike Place Market area as a historical district. In this case the force of activism was shown to be so strong that the citizens began to outstrip their own elected officials in imagining that the best could happen. The buildings which housed the Market had never been the best in the world, and most were sixty years old; the surrounding areas, never more than marginal as business or as residential places, likewise showed many signs of wear and decay. In the early 1960s Urban Renewal got its eye on the Market, and many downtown people interested in making

Seattle big league supported measures designed to renovate the whole area.

But Urban Renewal and downtown people who wanted to make the city big league were precisely what the new activists were committed to opposing, while the Market was precisely the kind of old Seattle place and institution they were committed to keeping. Gradually they chipped away at the plans for renovation until, by 1970, the city was prepared to "keep" the Market and to concentrate its efforts on facelifting its buildings and on improving the surrounding areas. This had the full support of the Desimone family that owned the Market buildings and land, as well as the support of many of the newly elected people on the city council. Mayor Uhlman was committed to it. In a 1968 editorial Peter Bunzel of *Seattle Magazine* declared himself satisfied with the city's plan, and warned those who weren't not to get too choosy.

Choosy, however, was exactly what those who wanted to make the area a historical district felt they had to be. The sponsors of the initiative were called the Friends of the Market and the symbol of their leadership was architect Victor Steinbrueck. Steinbrueck was as native to Seattle as anyone, the author of two books of line drawings depicting what was best in old Seattle, and he had been fighting as long as anyone could remember every effort of governments and money to change it. He insisted, as Mark Tobey had before him, that the Market was not just fruit and vegetable stands and not something just pleasantly quaint and tacky, but a way of life, especially for people who had no other other—messy, anachronistic, individualistic. As far as he and the Friends of the Market were concerned, one couldn't "keep" the Market except by making the whole area safe from planners and investors. To those who approved of the city's plan such arguments were sentimental and nostalgic, and they continued to point to many who worked at the Market and supported them. As a result, the Market looked to be an issue that might divide the activists into friends and foes and might therefore dissipate the whole movement in a battle that seemed to many as though it never should have been fought.

Had the city won and had the initiative failed, such a prediction might well have been right. But in the November 1971 election, when the Market issue dominated the ballot, the initiative passed by a considerable margin. This fulfilled something close to an impossible dream, and, far from splintering the activists, it gave them new strength. What in effect the election said was that the Market did not belong to its owners, or to the city government, but to the people. It was the perfect expression of the new feeling, which was of course the old populist feeling, because it made clear that on the edge of the new frontier was the past. CHECC could dwindle in importance, as it did, and some of the new activists could begin to seem like establishment people, which they did, but the essential statement had been made that the future of the city depended on keeping a vital relation to what had been.

Given their success with the Market initiative, it is not surprising that in a subsequent election the new city activists mopped up by defeating a proposed new freeway link from I-5 to the Seattle Center. They also kept the pressure on the city to resist all the blandishments of the federal government, the state highway people, and the suburbs to allow construction of a third bridge across Lake Washington that might sweep eight, ten, or twelve lanes of highway into downtown.

At the heart of the new politics, thus, was old Seattle, the Seattle that had been built during an earlier time of downtown building and populist ferment. The new activism was much less ideological than the old, though no less given to seeing villains in established power. Perhaps one major sign of its vitality was that one of its villains was the federal government, that potential handmaiden of the people that kept threatening by the force of its vast funds and bureaucracy to make every American city into a version of every other American city, its green and white interstate highway signs the banner of its supremacy. In turning back the feds on every significant point, Seattle was insisting on its identity and was thereby achieving it.

FOWARD THRUST

From the time Metro was created without a mandate to plan or to build area-wide transit systems, James Ellis was looking for the best time to come back with a new version of his dream. He chose 1965, the first of a sequence of boom years at Boeing, and he called his plan Forward Thrust. He told a meeting of the Rotary Club that the population of Seattle and King County would grow by 750,000 in the next twenty years, and that it was time to put together a major capital improvement drive that would prepare adequately for the Pugetopolis that was coming. The demon was Los Angeles, the victim of endless postwar sprawl; the possibility, as Ellis envisaged it, was not so much a new or different Seattle but one which by planning found ways to hold on to the best it already had. Forward Thrust's brochure photograph was hill and water at sunset.

Ellis knew what he wanted most, and that was a rapid transit system; but he also knew that the success of the venture depended on planning, and that meant going to the citizens and finding out from them what they most wanted in the way of things that money could buy. He and his people emerged from their forays into the community with a large, impressive, and apparently expensive package of more than half a billion dollars, a good deal of which would be used to secure federal funds of an even greater amount. There was the 385-million-dollar rail transit proposal, plus 121 million dollars for parks, 78 million dollars for arterial highways of less than freeway size, 68 million dollars for flood control in the county and 70 million dollars for a storm sewer separation in the city, and, perhaps as the leading come-on for the entire package, 40 million dollars for a domed stadium for major league sports.

The proposed rail transit system wouldn't be as comprehensive as New York's or London's, but it would be much more of an interurban system than San Francisco's BART. Away from downtown it moved northeast past the university and out to Lake City, northwest to Ballard, south through the industrial district to Renton, and east across the lake to Mercer Island and Bellevue. It could boast that it would be the best new city rail system in the country in this century, and that it would be adequate to serve the city and county well into the next century. It was for Ellis the crucial item, the most farsighted and most necessary; perhaps for that reason, it never stood a very good chance of being approved.

The stadium, on the other hand, was much more clearly an idea whose time had already come. The sixties had seen a boom in major league sports, and cities that a generation earlier had assumed the big leagues were all in the east and midwest had been begging for and getting major league expansion franchises, until Seattle was the largest city in the country without a big league team. The first breakthrough came in 1967, when a Los Angeles carpetbagger, Sam Schulman, bought an expansion franchise in the National Basketball Association and settled it in Seattle. The team was a box office success almost immediately, but basketball did not at the time have either the traditional value of baseball or the new glamour of pro football. All the success of the Sonics had shown was that Seattle was "ready" to be big league. As a result, though there would be grumblings, though twice before the voters had rejected stadium bond issues, this looked like the most attractive part of the Forward Thrust package.

The other parts were apparently less important, because people felt they could vote for or against them without much fuss. Although people at Forward Thrust knew how important community centers, parks, highways, flood control, sewer separation and the like could be, they knew there was nothing very innovative or interesting here. The task was to capitalize on the growing enthusiasm for a stadium and to use the whole group as a means of saying the citizens had to plan for growth, which included an adequate rail rapid transit system. If such a strategy could work, the Forward Thrust people would make it work. They crisscrossed city and county, speaking here and offering slide shows there, quite outdoing the opposition in energy and in numbers of people reached. The arguments against Forward Thrust were never worth attention; the question was simply whether the voters could be made willing to vote themselves over half a billion dollars in increased taxes.

They didn't. In a special election in February 1968, the bond issues for parks, highways, sewer separation, and the stadium were approved, but the others, including the rapid transit bonds, were turned down. Depending on where one lived, that meant voting for between 250 million and 300 million dollars, but the heart of the dream was left unfulfilled. There were two obvious reasons besides the great amount of money involved. First, the second bridge over the lake had been opened in 1963, the I-5 freeway in 1965, and by 1968 even the boom in population had not been enough to make rush-hour congestion very bad. Finding no present cause for alarm, people were not about to begin divorce proceedings between themselves and their cars. Second, almost all the areas that had voted against the original Metro proposal—the newer neighborhoods within the city, almost all the suburbs except those most convenienced by the proposed train system—still were given over to seeing the city and the area as a simple extension of their own pocketbooks. People who had moved into the postwar neighborhoods remained inward-looking people. Not for them the new activism, the new interest in downtown or in old Seattle. Theirs was a suburban, not an urban sense of the world, and until stop-and-go traffic clogged the freeways every night, rapid transit was a bubble, and perhaps a socialistic bubble at that.

But Ellis had encountered all this before—the Metro proposal had taken two votes to pass—and, nothing daunted, he mounted an even greater public relations effort and resubmitted Forward Thrust's proposals for transit, flood control, and community centers for a special May 1970 election. But before the election could be held Boeing's boom began to bust, and the prospects for the future held not overcrowding but depression and out-migration. Against that threat Ellis and his cohort stood little chance, and all the resubmitted issues were again defeated, rapid transit by an even larger margin than before.

The votes that brought in a new city council, that passed the Market initiative, that rejected the new freeways did not cost anyone a dime. They were not therefore unimportant, but their importance did not directly affect the taxpayer, especially those who did not live in the old Seattle, where the new city was being formed. Major sections of old Seattle could vote for rapid transit as much out of fear of new freeways as from any benefit they might derive from the new trains. But that feeling, that way of feeling, simply had not extended out into the new parts of the city and county, where the marriage of cars and people was strongest, where the Boeing layoffs hurt most. The feeling there was still negative: it costs too much; it belongs only in overcrowded cities; it wouldn't help me directly; it's just a plan to help downtown people. The vote against rapid transit was essentially an anticity vote. Saul Bellow has said that in a city you use what other people use, and one has the feeling of doing that much more on trains than in cars.

The stadium had been approved, however, and stadiums generate ways of using what other people use as much as do trains. After a prolonged fight about where to put it, and the usual struggles with contractors and unions, the stadium opened in the spring of 1976 and the Seattle Seahawk NFL team will begin playing there in 1976. In 1969, however, Seattle had a fling with major league sports that could serve as a warning: the abject desire of newer cities to become big league is often seen by those in older cities as the needs of rubes. Immediately after the vote on the stadium the American League awarded a baseball franchise to Seattle. The city agreed to cannibalize Sick's Stadium by expanding its seating capacity for interim use. The franchise itself was backed by an unlikely combination of a Cleveland businessman and the local Soriano brothers, who had proven themselves good sports people but who were woefully underfinanced. The general manager, Marvin Milkes, was one of those perennial losers who keeps getting jobs by learning how to get along with people with money or influence. Milkes went for faded "established" players to lure fans, and set his admission and concession prices out of sight. The team did all right for a third of the season, and the total attendance for the year was not bad considering, but it was an operation in which no one trusted anyone else very much (the details can be glimpsed in Jim Bouton's classic, *Ball Four*) and, rather than try to do anything about the situation, the league decided after one season to move the franchise to Milwaukee. The caveats that could be made to aspiring cities like Seattle on the basis of this one experience are enough to indicate that in the big leagues established money and power play rough and can seldom be trusted.

Nor is there full recognition yet that the lesson of the debacle with the baseball team has been learned. The new football franchise seems on solid footing, to be sure, with a consortium of wealthy local people in control. But the National Hockey League has played fast, hard, and loose, first by destroying the local minor league hockey franchise that had always shown remarkable signs of strength, then by refusing to do any more than dally with local people trying to join the big league on its terms. The name of that game has been greedy money all along. Big league baseball did little better for a long time. The city, county, and state sued the American League for breaches of contract and promises and, when settlement was reached in 1976 after a lengthy trial, finally got a new expansion team seven years after the first one had left. For the past ten years, almost, the sports pages of the city's two major papers have committed themselves to reporting any rumor, no matter how vile or fanciful, about major league sports coming to Seattle. One is reminded of Jim Hill's endless postponing of his decision about his terminal for the Great Northern, and in the present case Seattle has acted as badly as it did in that one, and for the same reason: it refuses to think well enough of itself, it is willing to make itself the plaything of other people's power and wealth.

All this may seem to take us far from the central issues of Forward Thrust, but in fact it does not. What one sees from whatever angle one looks is the precariousness of the situation, its tippiness or fragility. The city had been changing for a generation, and seemingly at an accelerating rate. For those committed to it, energetic activism and a new relation with old Seattle could seem close to ends in themselves. For those uncertain of it, especially for those who lived directly in the shadow of Boeing, change more likely carried with it loss rather than gain, and it was not just blacks who could feel excluded. A stadium and big league sports, at least to a majority, felt much more like their dream, whereas rapid transit persisted in seeming more like someone else's dream. Along with any such dreaming is a questioning that keeps asking if Seattle feels like a place for oneself or a place for other people. Put one thing in front of people and, during this period, they would answer the question one way, but put something different in front of them and the answer would be different. Forward Thrust succeeded under these conditions when the money it sought could be spent quickly and the benefits quickly realized, and it failed when the money would be spent over a long period of time and the benefits were as likely to be realized by one's children as oneself.

If, finally, one tries to put the new activism together with the Forward Thrust votes, one sees the way the nature of Seattle's arena was changing. For twenty-five years in postwar Seattle the distinction between natives and newcomers was felt by many people and played a vital role in giving shape to the city's most interesting events and changes. But the years after the end of the sixties seemed to herald a change, and the important distinction became as much a matter of where one lived as of when one had come to the city. Old Seattle, especially the parts built before World War I, seemed to come alive, and seemed also to become pitted against the newer areas of the city, the post World War II and more suburban areas. It is worth noting that the activists fared much better at the polls when the election was confined to the city, and to do less well when it included the whole county. Since comparing these elections is also comparing issues with and issues without money, however, such conclusions may well be premature.

THE BOEING RECESSION

There were two major causes of Boeing's recession in 1970–71, and either by itself could have been enough to cause major damage. First, both the airlines and the airplane builders mistakenly projected that the increase in air passenger travel between 1955 and 1965 would continue into the 1970s; when it did not, the demand for the widely heralded 747 fell way short of expectations. Second, the United States Congress decided in 1971 to terminate its commitment to build an SST, and the project on which Boeing had been working for almost a decade came to a halt. The first cause laid off the aerospace workers, the second more workers and also a large number of engineers. Between January 1970 and December 1971, Boeing cut its work force by sixty-five thousand people, or almost two-thirds. Within a space of a few months it became clear that the Boeing era was over.

The most widely held presumption was that Seattle itself was over as well. Unemployment went from under the national average to double the national average, 12 percent and up, the highest in the country and the worst in any major city since the Depression. One hundred thousand people were out of work, and by late 1971 many of those who had been first laid off had exhausted their benefits and were not finding work elsewhere. Seattle made the national news on a larger scale than at any time since the World's Fair, and the tale most often told outside of the bleak unemployment figures was of the billboards and bumper stickers that asked the last person leaving Seattle please to turn out the lights.

In June 1971 one of the area's most widely respected economists, Miner H. Baker of Seattle-First National Bank, tried to be as candid as possible about the situation:

> It is quite true that there are a number of indicators on the Seattle scene which do not reflect the full measure of our distress. It is also true that the situation has been overstated by the *Wall Street Journal*, the *London Economist*, and other outside observers. The overwhelming fact remains that we are losing buckets of blood and it is not within our power to staunch the flow. It is time—and past time—that the other Washington recognize this unique state of emergency and marshall the full resources of the Federal government toward our recovery.

Such a recogniton was never made. The Congressional delegation did a great deal to keep having unemployment benefits extended another thirteen or twenty-six weeks or indefinitely, but responding well to local economic disaster areas has never been the strong point of Republican presidents, especially since Washington State had voted for Hubert Humphrey in 1968.

But nonetheless the lights did not go out in Seattle. The last person did not leave, and for a while it looked as though not even the first person was going to leave: out-migration from the area during the early seventies was never more than 15 percent of those laid off. The unemployment rate stayed high for a long time for precisely that reason. People did not want to leave. Though the local economy was losing buckets of blood, it was not losing what it needed most, people, people with talents and ideas. Soon after Boeing held its employment level at around forty thousand, it became clear that, for all the hardship that had been endured by those most affected, Seattle had a chance, its first in a generation, to do something about changing its relation to Boeing. If the city had not taken advantage of boom to begin manufacture of consumer goods, it perhaps could take advantage of bust to begin to look for other things to do.

There were a number of bellwethers during the worst of the storm, some of short-term benefit, others of potentially long-lasting value. First, although the housing industry simply stopped, downtown construction that had been committed or begun during the boom went on, and, as noted before, the new skyscraper office buildings have been consistently successful in filling up. Second, and much more important, the Port of Seattle was in the midst of its most successful period ever.

The Port had had its own crisis a full decade earlier. It had gotten along for a generation as the plaything of the railroads, but by the 1950s its facilities were outmoded, its management clumsy and inefficient, and its business was falling compared to that of other west coast ports. A League of Women Voters study in 1958 showed that ports governed as was Seattle's almost always lacked strong leadership, and a KING documentary, *Lost Cargo*, dramatized the consequences. In 1960 it began to change itself by expanding its commission from three to five members, including two elected at large so that people who knew the waterfront had a better chance for election. In that year it also began a modernization of its facilities, starting with a 10-million-dollar bond issue and continuing through the sixties. By 1970 the Port, which included Sea-Tac International Airport, had spent almost a quarter of a billion dollars in expansion and modernization. The money was most visibly spent in the huge cranes that began to dot the waterfront to handle containerized cargo, a huge grain terminal at the foot of Queen Anne Hill, and a huge new parking garage and terminal complex at the airport. Beginning in 1963 the Port had a string of years, still unbroken, in which it expanded its business, both in tons and in dollars—it leaped 23 percent during the first recession year of 1970.

The ancient dream of the port as the northwest gateway to the orient began to be realized. Ships from Japan had earlier begun to go the long way, to San Francisco or Los Angeles, or, when their goods were headed farther east, through the Panama Canal to the gulf ports. By modernizing both equipment and management the Port turned all that around, and Seattle went from last to first between 1960 and 1970 among west coast ports in shipping to the Overland Common Points farther east. Traditionally Portland had enjoyed an advantage over Seattle in shipping eastern Washington and Oregon wheat, but the new grain terminal cut sharply into that advantage. Finally, the planning and the building of the Alaska pipeline provided a huge increase in what had always been the bread and butter of the Port's business.

There were setbacks. To the public the worst was the Port's unwillingness to do anything to ameliorate the ugliness of the grain terminal, which was not hidden from view down near the other Port facilities on Harbor Island, but placed starkly at the foot of residential Queen Anne Hill and near the Seattle Center. To the Port the worst setback has been the endlessly tangled city-state-federal battles about funding for a high bridge over the Duwamish to West Seattle. The only feasible place for the Port to extend its waterfront facilities is down the Duwamish, but that is cut off by the low Spokane Street span.

But perhaps what the Port of Seattle needs most now is not something that would have any great bearing on its own future growth or operation but which could seriously alter the way Seattle sees its waterfront. One reason that the Port's great success in the 1960s could go ignored so easily is that Seattle as a whole, and especially Seattle downtown, is effectively turned away from the water. This turning away began when Railroad Avenue was constructed in the 1890s, and was accentuated when the Alaskan Way viaduct was built in the 1950s to connect Aurora Avenue, the major arterial north, with the industrial area to the south. That both Railroad Avenue and Alaskan Way have lost their former importance only aggravates the problem. Between First Avenue and the water, which would be prime land in any city that clearly understood itself as a port, there is nothing but blight.

The dream of Nancy Wilson Ross—and many others—of Seattle as a great Pacific Rim city has been made possible in recent years by the huge success of the Port of Seattle. But since this is not just a matter of doing business, but of feeling part of an ocean rim that contains more than a billion people, getting the right relation of this city to its own water is essential. Seattle has a superb harbor, and its one great geographical (as opposed to topographical or climatic) advantage is its closeness to Alaska and Japan. Yet as long as the viaduct remains, as long as the downtown area is turned away from the water, this situation will remain more understood than felt. There are Forward Thrust park funds presently being spent in planning a waterfront park, but nothing can be realized as well as it should be until the viaduct comes down and the land is opened up both for restoration and new development. This is not, strictly speaking, the Port of Seattle's business, but it is of such importance to the way the Port and the city finally see themselves that repairing the current situation is perhaps their major capital expenditure task of the coming years.

Nonetheless, even should the whole downtown waterfront area be changed and developed superbly, the problem of the city's relation to Boeing would only be lessened, not overcome. Undoubtedly the port is going to play a larger and larger role in the city's economy as time goes on, and the economy can do well just by serving as a depot. But export manufacture and import replacement manufacture remain essential ingredients in any kind of full or healthy economy. The moment the Boeing slump came, the cry went up that Seattle needed a more diversified economy, but it almost always went up without any but the most minimal recognition of what that might mean or entail. "It is not within our power to staunch the flow," said Miner Baker, acknowledging as he said it that in important ways Seattle had in 1971 achieved the fate of Tacoma in 1893. As far as the leading economic expert of the leading bank could see, though he himself had long advocated moves to diversify the city's economy, Seattle manufactured airplanes.

Of course, Seattle has always looked and acted less like a manufacturing city than most—it is not a warren of smokestacks surrounded by a clutter of brick houses—but that fact made the truth harder to see. Baker, and perhaps many others in similar positions of knowledge and power, failed to understand, however, that diverse manufacturing is something achieved only when people gain opportunities. The fact that the people did not leave Seattle when they left Boeing gave the city a great advantage. But unquestionably it was going to be harder to capitalize on that advantage in a depressed economy rather than during Boeing's boom years, when money was more available and risks potentially more profitable.

Still, the essential holding actions have been made. The population of the city between 1970 and 1975 fell only slightly, and that of King County even rose slightly. The health of the Port and the continuation of downtown building helped. But holding actions are holding only so long, and it is not clear yet that the economic situation has changed fundamentally. Many were elated when, in 1973, Boeing began rehiring workers; had the nature of the situation been fully understood, they might well have read such elation as a danger sign that the city was willing to lull itself to sleep again. Much more hopeful potentially was the formation of a Seattle–King County Economic Development Council designed expressly to explore the ways and means of diversification. The council immediately identified a whole host of areas in which such diversifying seemed both possible and desirable: oceanography, health technology, special chemicals, electronics, environmental protection equipment, nuclear power plant manufacturing, recreation equipment and services, metal fabrication, general aviation services, factory-fabricated buildings, food processing. Boeing itself began to recognize the perils of its situation and put research and development money into land reclamation, a computerized inner-city transit car, and desalinization of water.

Looking around the city in 1976, one sees mostly mixed signs of anything new happening. Physio-Control, a firm specializing in health technology, has sprung up and done well. Senator Magnuson has done enormously well in locating federal funds to help oceanographic and meteorological development. Dynamote, a Ballard firm making electrical generators, has expanded its business greatly in the last five years, as have Olympic Stain and Western Photographics, both of which now do full nationwide business. Custom-Bilt Products, specializing in draperies, has increased its business 25 percent in the last two years. A number of small plastics firms have begun and caught on well since 1970.

All this is healthy; the problem is how much of a difference such and similar small firms make. The smallness itself is not the least disturbing, since one of the habits that needs to be overcome is that of thinking a business must do over 100 million dollars in sales a year before it counts. But it is as yet unclear just how much that is potentially expansive in a significant way is happening. It is simply too early to read the signs of diversifying recovery with any assurance.

One reason to believe that major diversifying may be a long way off is the nature of the business establishment which, for various reasons, is not just conservative but staid. "There has been a great reluctance to commit dollars to new industries here," said Gerald Weinstein of Electro Development Corporation. "What people here call venture capital would be a bankable loan anywhere else," interpreted a corporate investment lawyer friend of mine. Of course, a reluctance to release major amounts of money into new industries is understandable in times of recession, but the habit of thinking small goes deeper than that, and is much older. One hears it said that the trouble is a kind of geographical provinciality among bankers, retailers, and marketers, a habit which thinks of all Seattle industrial markets extending only to the Cascades and the Columbia River. Even Chamber of Commerce people will admit that this habit of thinking has existed in the past. The point to remember here, perhaps, is that those presently in command of the business establishment all grew up in prewar Seattle. Just as that fact led to the formation of Metro and Forward Thrust, it also led to a fundamental lack of interest in growth, a fundamental lack of curiosity about how economic growth takes place. This is one reason why growth, when it has come, has often been as essentially colonial as it has been, and since colonial growth is hard to trust, it self-fulfills the mistrust of all growth. When the expansion or contraction of the economy offers no fundamental change in the nature of that economy, then it is perhaps natural to be gloomy, staid, wary in periods of expansion, warier still in periods of contraction.

But with changes of other kinds taking place in Seattle and in the rest of the world, this habit of mind in the business community may be in for change eventually too. If a whole new kind of person could begin to move into city government, a whole new kind of person could begin to move into business management. It is interesting to note that when, in the summer of 1975, a group of business people known as Civic Builders was formed with the announced intention of removing from the city council some of the new breed that had been elected since 1967, they looked to many to be a vestigial, almost nostalgic organization, not even truly representative of the current establishment.

At present Boeing's employment stands at around 55,000; for the last two years industry in the Seattle area has done better than the national average; the Port of Seattle continues to grow; none of the dire predictions of 1970–71 has come true; without any massive help from the federal government the flow of the buckets of blood has been stanched. It is not clear, however, that anything significant has changed, and in its economic habits Seattle seems more wedded to old ways than in any other part of its existence. Those ways caused the original withdrawal in the years before the first war, had a whole generation between the wars to become habitual, and another generation under the Boeing umbrella to feel protected and secure. They will not be changed overnight.

NEW PRODUCING, NEW CONSUMING

Here we come at last to the new city in its most visible and perhaps most important modes of expression. One sees it in Pioneer Square, and at the Pike Place Market, all around Seattle Center, on Capitol Hill, in the University District, or, more precisely, one sees in these places what one can feel almost everywhere in old Seattle. Put in its crudest terms, Seattle in the last ten years, and especially in the last five years, has become a great place in which to buy things, but it is clear right away why those terms are too crude.

To try to tell the story of the rise of the new consumer, one would have to go back a little, and a good place to begin would be with architect Ralph Anderson's opening of his office on South Main and Richard White's opening of his gallery on Occidental Avenue South, both in renovated buildings south of Pioneer Square. The area had become mostly derelict, and a home for derelicts, in the postwar years, but the buildings that had been built right after the fire of 1889 were still there, and still much more adaptable to various uses than any built later. Work had to be done on the interiors, but at much less total expense than building something new and not as good elsewhere. Other new-old businesses came in slowly, and then, when François and Julia Kissel opened the Brasserie Pittsbourg restaurant in the basement of the Pioneer Building in 1969, everything began to change very rapidly. Within a year or so there came a flood of other restaurants, galleries, boutiques. What had been a quiet area for lost souls suddenly became extremely fashionable and, given the fashionableness, surprisingly good. CHECC lawyers and activist government people flooded the area at lunchtime, a new city ordinance made it possible for sidewalk cafes to open, Pioneer Square was designated a historical district like the Market, street vendors appeared in the spring and summer, and suddenly Seattle had something close to an honest-to-God tourist trap where, five years before, all had been silent.

Like the Market initiative, the revival of Pioneer Square–Skid Road had its roots in an appreciation of something old. In the Market the old had never died, and in Pioneer Square it could be quickly made over into something new. A whole generation of Americans, after all, had been traveling, especially in Europe, and they had seen some of the ways great cities live in their retail business and crowded streets and good places to meet and eat. The moment a few business people showed them this was all quite possible in Seattle they responded in force, and, because it was all done by private individuals, it was done according to individual enthusiasms and talents rather than according to plan. Though anything but an old city, Seattle was old enough to have a past that could be used and re-used. Just as a sense of other places can create an awareness of possibility, so too could a sense of other times; the moment the past isn't dead, it can open up new things indefinitely.

When the site of the Forward Thrust stadium was finally settled just south of Jim Hill's King Street Station, a splendid tableau resulted. The stadium was the essence of what might be thought of as the older generation's desire to make Seattle into a big league city, but the decision to put it near the "new" Pioneer Square historical district alarmed all those for whom the stadium just meant new parking lots and parking problems. In the name of something as old, then, as 1890, and as new as 1970, people began scurrying around to diminish the impact of the stadium, and in the confrontation itself whole different generations of the city became visible and important, blurring in their overlapping and in their antagonism. It was a post-Boeing Seattle struggling against an older Seattle in the name of a still older Seattle.

But if the historically preserved Market and Pioneer Square were focal points for a newly cosmopolitan consumer, they were only that, and throughout old Seattle in the last five years similar changes have been taking place on commercial streets. New consumers need new things to consume, no matter how aged the premises, and new producers seemed to crop up everywhere. Cottage industries appeared with such profusion that it began to seem that everyone laid off at Boeing had been nursing a secret desire to throw a pot, turn a lathe, cast in metal, or make an omelette. Hippie capitalists took over the north end of the Market, parts of the Fremont district, and a good deal of University Way. Cheeses, wines, and coffees Seattle had never heard of became available as young entrepreneurs learned about importers hitherto unknown to the city. Quality and nostalgia movie houses in old buildings began to outdraw newer first-run theaters. Street fairs followed one after another all spring and summer. New theater and dance groups found their way into disused buildings in odd corners of downtown and Capitol Hill. Restaurants that a few years earlier might have claimed to be one of the best in the city opened by the half dozen, and most thrived.

The restaurant situation is perhaps the most visibly successful of all these new conditions. Until 1947 it was not legal to sell liquor by the drink in the state, and so restaurants had no way to offer more than staple fare before then. Perhaps the best restaurant in Seattle between 1947 and 1969 was Rosellini's 410, an elegant expense-account restaurant in the White-Henry-Stuart Building in the heart of downtown. The 410, recently closed because the building is being torn down to make way for a new skyscraper, had great decor, great service, a great bar, mediocre food at high prices. The Kissels' Brasserie Pittsbourg, the first of the new wave of restaurants, could at times be imperiously noisy, feature slow service and an ordinary bar, but almost always offered excellent food. Following the opening of the Brasserie, lots of new places have opened all over the city, and some have managed to get by using Victor Rosellini's formula, but the ones that have kept on doing good business have had to rely on good-to-excellent food of some kind.

Perhaps the most telltale sign of the change is the existence of *A Gourmet's Notebook*, a monthly commentary on food and eating places put out by David Brewster, former managing editor of *Argus*. When it began publication late in 1972, one would have said there just weren't enough places to write about to keep a magazine like that going; but the restaurant business has boomed so much, and has in general improved so much, that the *Notebook* has not once been forced to review admittedly mediocre places or to try to distinguish among fast food franchises for the prize of the least bad hamburgers. By being both reasonably demanding and reasonably flexible, Brewster has been able to come up with lots of restaurants to write about, almost all of which have opened in the last five years. The existence of the magazine, and of Brewster's book, *The Best Places: A Gourmet's Notebook Guide to the Pacific Northwest,* which made its first appearance in the fall of 1975, is testimony to precisely the kinds of spinoff work that become possible when new work is being made in a healthy city economy.

Perhaps in the overall economic picture this new producing and consuming does not in total dollars of business generated amount to much more than a holding action, but in every other way it is of major importance. It signifies a new awareness of the importance of downtown land and downtown buildings. It signifies a new awareness that the culture of a city is not just to be measured by its symphony or opera company but in the number, variety, and vitality of its theater groups, music groups, dance companies, and in the way these things, like restaurants and all other manner of small business, can make all public places more engaging and alive. It forces people out of the simple traffic patterns of their lives that are formed by home and place of business, takes them to places in the city they haven't been to before, or not in years. It does wonders for the tourist business. It says as nothing else can that there is a potential profusion of activity in a city of half a million that must be unknown in smaller cities and towns, and this becomes in itself a new statement of justification for existence. To see the crowds at the Sonics' basketball games, at Longacres, at the spectacularly successful Seattle Sounders' North American Soccer League games, is not just to see Seattle becoming big league, but to see Seattle being excited about itself. It practically guarantees at least for a generation that Seattle will be keeping its visible past alive in its finding of new uses for old buildings. Land and labor have become the conditions precedent in ways that can be seen and understood by anyone. Sheepish comparisons between Seattle and Portland, or Seattle and San Francisco or Los Angeles, simply have become less relevant because plenty is happening here.

Beneath all this new activity, giving it both present vitality and hope for the future, is the fact that so much of it is being done by young people, and of both sexes. As recently as a decade ago someone starting out in life who was "going into business" was joining the corporate establishment, climbing some long ladder. That in effect meant that business success was possible only for a certain kind of man, and for almost no women. The new producing and consuming has circumvented all that, because it is being done with sufficiently little capital to keep one from being beholden to banks, in different places from those frequented or coveted by the business establishment, and by people who generally could not work well in a large corporate structure. People under thirty are doing well. Women who a generation ago were consigned, like it or not, to home and housewifery, now run taverns and restaurants, make and sell things at the Market and at street fairs, manage photography studios, open law firms, become consultants, find work—and occasionally excellent-paying work—pretty much outside the confines of big businesses and bureaucracies. When it is obvious that the talents of many more people than a few years ago are being put to work, it matters less how absolutely talented or financially successful each one is, and matters more that a sense of possibility is being created.

Five or ten years do not a city make, but the new producing and consuming show no signs at present of leveling off, and they do touch many important qualities in Seattle, do create future possibilities. The new awareness of the past is so marked and strong that it can afford to have large strains of nostalgia and sentimentality in it and still have much that is useful, reviving, instructive. The making of things, especially the making of things with care and skill, inevitably leads to a sense of beauty and culture that is much more broadly and healthily based than the awkward sense of all culture as high culture that seemed to mark the city a decade or more ago. Diversity creates instinctive tolerance as nothing else can, and cities are always in need of more instinctive tolerance. Finally, a sense of the possible is always the necessary first step in the creation of a sense of the excellent. If it would be rash to predict that Seattle can move from its current activeness into an era of greatness, it would be folly to ignore the obvious fact that it has a better chance to do this now than at any time in the last sixty years, perhaps a better chance than at any time in its history.

BOGS AND MARSHES

In the midst of all the new activism, new producing and consuming, there remain four bogs or marshes of major consequence in Seattle. I have mentioned them all at one time or another in the last two chapters, but as I come closer to attempting some final assessment, another brief look at each is necessary. They are the public schools, the manufacturing economy, the ghetto, and the neighborhoods built mostly in the Boeing years. All are related, to each other and to all the new good things that have happened despite them.

The nature of the population of Seattle has shifted. Between 1960 and 1975 the total number of people has declined, from 550,000 to 500,000; since the population of the county has risen about as much as Seattle has declined, layoffs at Boeing are not the reason. John R. Walker of the Population Studies Division of the Washington Office of Program Planning notes that young couples without children and mature couples with grown children have been moving into the city from the suburbs at the same time as young couples with children continue to move from Seattle to the suburbs. As a result, the number of households in Seattle has increased, but the size of the households has shrunk: "Since 1970 the decline in household size had accelerated, reflecting the general decline in births, young adults leaving home to form their own households, postponement of first births for young married couples, and the elderly family members no longer remaining with their grown children." Though Walker's figures are not so refined as to indicate which areas within Seattle reflect most strongly which of these changes, it is safe to say that old Seattle is the new home for childless couples moving from the suburbs and is the area where the number of households has increased most sharply. At the same time it is from the newer, postwar neighborhoods that the exodus has continued to the suburbs. To Walker's figures we can add the fact that in recent years real estate values in most of old Seattle have risen, sometimes strikingly, whereas they have held steady in most of the north end.

Some reasons for these shifts in population and real estate values are manifest in everything we have been looking at in Seattle's recent experience and need no restating here, but to them we can add another. In responding to the crisis in the ghetto in the late 1960s the public schools began a program of mandatory busing in 1972 that included the Central Area black students and white students from the near north end in the Roosevelt and Lincoln High School areas. It was a decently motivated effort, but it was clumsily done and the results have not been good. There was a sharp decrease in the total public school enrollment from Roosevelt and Lincoln areas as people moved out or sent their children to private schools. In an attempt to ameliorate the effects of the busing program, the school district tied it to a shift to middle schools comprising grades five through eight.

That, however, couldn't be done properly because the school district didn't have the right buildings and didn't have the money to build them. There was a continued floundering in the Central Area schools as they tried simultaneously to push programs of integrated education and programs designed to promote black awareness and compensatory education. Pulled in a host of different directions, the schools tried to do everything a little bit and ended up doing nothing well.

The trouble with the busing program really only reflected an increasing uncertainty throughout the school system. It has always been the argument that Seattle's schools were "quality schools," "better than" those in comparable cities, but no one was sure what this quality or superiority consisted of, and probably had not been sure for a long time. The old schools had been sternly traditional, but all that had eroded without any clear sense of what should or even what was taking its place. Some of the problems it shared with other school systems: sharp rises and sharp drops in enrollment caused by shifts in the birth rate, racial troubles, general disaffection of students as the result of being expected to go to school for sixteen or twenty years without much indication of what the experience could yield. At least one problem it shared only with other schools in the state, where an arcane and archaic tax structure forces the school district to ask for "special" levies every year, which are not for anything special at all but for ordinary maintenance. The public schools, like the University of Washington, tried to remedy this by using federal funds; inevitably, no matter what good this money did, it led to an increase in administrative costs and staff which in turn became a sore point with the voters, who were already disaffected because of the Boeing slump, rises in property taxes (though in fact they were extremely low compared to most states), and clear signs that the schools were not all they were touted as being.

For a number of years the Seattle school district had to submit its levy twice annually to gain approval, and then, finally, in 1975, it failed both times. Every element within the system—the school board, the administration, the teachers, the students, the voters— seemed to have lost faith with every other element, and no one knew what it would take to remedy the situation. The newer neighborhoods with the newer schools, which had been the bulwark of the system, seemed the worst off, or at least the most resistant. By 1975 many of the postwar children from these neighborhoods had grown, a lot of younger couples had moved out, and the impetus to go on supporting the schools even in an operational way was diminishing.

In much of old Seattle the problem was less in evidence, though not necessarily any less severe, because the population there, younger and more apt to include many single people and childless couples, was making less emotional investment in the schools.

The situation almost certainly will get worse before it gets better. Perhaps the best first step is for the schools to admit they are in serious trouble, and not just in financial ways. A sense of crisis that does not simply induce an increased sense of I-Me-Mine is important. One obvious fact is that after the third or fourth grade, when most students have learned the rudiments of reading, writing, and mathematics, most schools run out of good or interesting things to do. Boredom becomes a major problem, first for exceptional students, then for those who haven't learned the rudiments well, then gradually for everyone else. Teachers become worn down not just by the great demands placed on their energies but by their frustration with themselves, the students, the administration, the curriculum. If this is a national problem, then there is no better place to begin facing it than in an otherwise healthy bourgeois city. Two Catholic schools in the city are trying to solve it by joining forces and making high school and college six years rather than eight. Almost certainly shorter school days would help, especially if that could lead to a fuller commitment to really doing something while school is in session. But whatever is needed, it will take not only money but a really different sense of what schools are all about.

The ills of the public schools most immediately and urgently affect the newer neighborhoods on the one hand and the poverty neighborhoods, especially the ghetto, on the other. In the north end, as previously indicated, the passing of time by itself can help create the necessary changes. The fact that real estate values are in relative decline there means some adjustments are already being made. The original impetus to move into the north end probably has pretty well disappeared a generation after the simple good house–good school impulse took over. The residents there are getting older at the moment, but in time the north end should become a good place for the average young couple to settle, especially if changes are made in the habits which led to great masses of houses and few runs of commercial streets. The existing north end schools may not have deserved the attention fixed on them when the area was first built, but they probably are no worse than any of the others. At present the north end is the bulwark of taxpayer revolts—against Forward Thrust, against the county assessor, against the schools, against the legislature when it tried to raise its salaries—but a lot of that should pass with time. In the meantime it would perhaps be most helpful if elected officials from this area—on the school board, on the city council, in the state legislature, in the United States Congress— would confront the citizens with the facts of their plight.

In the ghetto, however, time is not an ally and not many people there need to be told the facts of their plight. Of all the areas of old Seattle the ghetto has been able to respond least to the new activism, the new producing and consuming. Much more than whites, blacks who have been successful in the last ten years have had to use the existing corporate and institutional system, to become government and school officials, to take advantage of whatever affirmative action produced in the way of management training. On the whole those who W. E. B. Dubois once called the Talented Tenth have done well enough, and maybe that tenth is now a fifth or a quarter, but far too many of those left over have had little happen to change the conditions of their lives. These people, unfortunately, are more dependent than most others on those institutions that have been the least revitalized in recent years: the middle-sized and large manufacturers, the schools, the real estate and lending institutions, the labor unions. There needs to be a considerable increase in the number of blacks in Seattle before any of them can wield the political power they need, and that increase can only come from an increase in the manufacturing economy and from a total change in the attitude of unions. There needs to be a much greater clarity and a much greater dedication in the schools concerning those traditionally left semi-educated. There needs to be a major effort by local lending institutions to make cheap money available to people in the ghetto for housing and businesses. At the same time that real estate values in many places surrounding the ghetto are rising, at the same time as commercial streets in downtown and in Madison Park and on Capitol Hill and on lower Queen Anne and in the University District are thriving, the houses and commercial streets of the ghetto are at best getting no worse.

During the first prolonged civil rights struggles in the early 1960s many southern blacks kept saying that racial problems would be settled sooner in the south than in the north. Fifteen years later it seems clear they were right. The deepest of our racial sins is ignorance. In the south, where whites and blacks have lived, however badly, for generations, that ignorance turned out to be shallower than in many parts of the north; in Seattle the ignorance runs deep. People here were uninterested in the Chinese in the 1880s, in the Japanese in the 1940s, in the blacks in the 1960s. When thus uninterested, they become victims of sleazy myths. When enabled by bourgeois comforts and possibilities to remain ignorant, they practically embrace it. On this matter the city does not seem to have begun to grow up.

We are led back, directly by some routes and indirectly by others, to the business and labor establishment that is the legacy of the early retirement of the affluent, of the generation of quiet, of Dave Beck, of Boeing. It is our clearest reminder that if cities can create new possibilities, if Seattle has indeed created many such in recent years, cities also must live with what their past has created for them, and Seattle must live with the fact that entrenched business and entrenched labor tend to see little need for anything new. It must do this, furthermore, without looking for villains. The forces that created Seattle-First National bank, the Bon Marche, University Properties Inc., the Teamsters, Western International Hotels, and all the rest were distinctively Seattle forces. Institutions by their very nature place self-perpetuation above all else, and Seattle's institutions have been aided in this by much that everyone knows and loves about the city. Its pleasures and wonders tend to dull the edge of reforming zeal, of cries of pain, of needs for change, and so its established institutions will necessarily tend to be dull and complacent, not villainous, not noted for rapacity. In business management, so we are told, changes may well be coming; if they do, they will probably result in making Seattle more oriented still toward its port, its waterfront. In the labor unions it would take a sharp eye indeed to see anything resembling change, though it is notable that the public service unions—the police, the fire fighters, the teachers—have not been able to wield the power here that they have in other large cities. But obviously the new city will have to be built alongside the establishment, defiant of it only in issue-oriented politics, otherwise hopeful that there can be enough new created that the lion and the lamb can lie down together in some kind of decent, if not good, relation.

CONCLUSION

At the end of *Northwest Gateway* Archie Binns sounds the uneasy note that is also played at the end of almost every other good piece of writing about Seattle:

> The city offers great opportunity for the enjoyment of life, with its lovely summers and mild winters, its surrounding mountains and forests, and its infinite variety of salt water and fresh, and water and land interpenetrating. Seattle people enjoy life as much as they can, and more than most people, but some ingredient is missing, or there is too much of too many

things, and life falls short of its possibilities. There is so much loveliness, and so little peace and security for enjoyment.

Murray Morgan says much the same thing, as do Nancy Wilson Ross and Constance McL. Green. I know no one, native or newcomer, who has been touched deeply by Seattle who has not felt this sense of life falling short of its possibilities even as there is so much that is enjoyed.

Bourgeois from its first breath, Seattle has had to struggle with finding out what that means. For a long time it has meant rich possibilities for private life: homes, gardens, recreation, feasts for the eyes and the fingertips, all enhanced by those lovely summers and mild winters. Only slightly more recently it has meant ways of letting business and labor live in relative harmony with each other. More recently still it has meant possibilities for the shared urban experience of good commercial streets and centers, crowds, places where the sights are people as well as forests, mountains, and water. If the sixties and early seventies of this century were a crisis like the years of World War I, it can be said that now there is less mistrust and more sense of possibility than there was then. In yesterday's Seattle *Times,* on a single page, were stories of François Kissel's newly opened City Loan Pavilion restaurant, of turnaway crowds every night at Shelley's Leg discotheque and gay bar, of Shorey's antiquarian book store getting a new lease on life as it moves to larger quarters at First and Union. One simply cannot overlook these things, or underrate their potential importance.

The one major virtue of a city like Seattle that is apt to go unstated or be played down in the usual summing up is the energy created by its other virtues. One reason for this, surely, is the prolonged reaction against the city boosters who once lauded the Seattle Spirit as though it were something that could be bottled and sold as insurance against any future: just remember the Mercer Girls, the May Day picnic of 1874 that laid the first Seattle and Walla Walla track, just remember the fire or the Alaska Gold Rush. But all that sense of spirit has gone either into faint nostalgia or into the less interesting or laudable desire to become a big league city. More enduring and interesting is what one feels in the making of the Cornish School, or Yesler Terrace, or the Metro plants, Group Health, the Market initiative, the revitalized Pioneer Square. One can go back before any of these and point to the original founding of the university, to the creation of the still lovely park and boulevard system, to R. H. Thomson's regrades. All these are public actions of private citizens either ignoring government or making it suit their immediate needs. All these seem the result of people working from a sense of possibility, or occasionally alarm, generated by their sense of satisfaction with what they already have. Hope seems liveliest in Seattle when based on people feeling, first individually and then collectively, the riches and content of their past.

But these all are spurts of energy, and so they tend to die rather quickly. As a result, most of what has been done best in Seattle has been that which could be done rather quickly, in a year or a few years rather than over a long period of time. When energies lapse, often little is left to take their place until they rise again. Seattle is not a place that builds enduring structures. It has very little hierarchical sense of its society or of its land. It has consistently refused to organize itself into political parties, and has as a result saddled itself with a ridiculous tax structure and a generally weak government. Its response to ethnic diversity has been to seek homogeneity rather than structures of diverse groups. Its sense of neighborhood is fluid rather than organized, and its neighborhood organizations, like most of its public commitments and achievements, tend to be ad hoc rather than permanent. It has large public rituals, like hydroplane races and Husky football and summertime in Seattle Center, where strangers meet, but it has very little in the way of street or neighborhood rituals where acquaintances and friends renew their common experience.

All this would be more alarming but for the persistence of the fact of the energies, spurting here and lapsing there, throughout the city's history. If there are insufficient structures to create solutions to nagging problems, like the public schools and the ghetto, there have been enough created by one spurt or another that have endured to make the city demonstrably a fuller place as time goes on. It would take only one such spurt, for instance, to bring down the Alaskan Way viaduct and re-create the land between First Avenue and the waterfront, and once it was done it would be done, as Metro's cleanup of the lake was done, as the parks and boulevards were done. All, or almost all, that was best in Seattle's past is still here, and can remain indefinitely. Its very lack of structures means that while it can lapse into quiet fairly easily, it probably will remain resistant to demagogues or other violent forces capable of really doing permanent harm. "Seattle is a success," wrote Murray Morgan twenty-five years ago at the end of *Skid Road*, "but the city has yet to achieve the assurance of success." That may still be true, but it is much less so than it was in 1950, and this is a process which will continue, if only in the fits, starts, and fallings off that are Seattle's characteristic way of getting things done.

One example can show at least how the process has worked. Victor Rosellini opened his 410 restaurant about the time Morgan wrote *Skid Road.* As noted earlier, it was an elegant sort of place, perfect for the downtown people of the last generation who wanted Seattle to be, or at least appear to be, big league. It was deficient only in the quality of its food. In 1974 Rosellini was the major backer for a new restaurant, Rosellini's Other Place, run by his son Robert, a young man who had gone to Europe to learn precisely the one thing about restaurants his father could not tell him: simple classic French cooking. One need not agree with David Brewster and *A Gourmet's Notebook* that The Other Place is the northwest's first restaurant of national consequence in order to acknowledge, first, that it is a major improvement on the 410 and, second, that the sequence whereby it came into existence is a classic instance of new energy, in this case strictly native energy, rising up, building on something that was already here, making it better. In this case for obvious reasons it took a generation for the new energies to find ways to create from the old. In others, such as the revitalized Pioneer Square, it may take as long as two or even three generations for this to happen. In others, such as the Seattle Center that stayed lively in the wake of the closing of the World's Fair, the sequence may be almost continuous.

The key to the future lies not just in the past but in a fuller understanding of that past. When Seattle has given itself over to progress, as progress has usually been defined in this country, it has done some pretty horrendous things, most of which have included a destruction of something old and the replacement with something merely new. In such cases it was only when the old wasn't much to begin with that the changes have been for the better. For Seattle, since most of the old was built well, such improvements have been few and far between. But almost without fail, whenever someone or some group has understood the old, they have found ways ranging from good to excellent to make it new. Sometimes it has been the native who has understood the past best, sometimes a newcomer arriving with a fresh burst of energy and curiosity; in each case it seems that the sense of what was important or unique about Seattle was acquired through comparison with other places, the native having gone away for a time, the newcomer having come from someplace quite different. The natives who have done worst are those who never let their horizons expand beyond what they have always known, and the newcomers who have done worst have simply tried to impose their sense of someplace else on Seattle, wishing it were San Francisco or Chicago and so not seeing how Seattle is the rhododendron it is and not a maple or an oak.

Given the nature of much of Seattle's growth in the Boeing years, people in the 1970s have reason to be shy of future growth, to hope it will not have to face any major influx of new people, to fear the response of the local business and labor establishments to any significant changes in the economy. But that feeling, though understandable, is based not on an understanding of the past but nostalgia concerning its present. Nothing has created new energies and new possibilities in Seattle so much as a sense of itself growing, and without its two major periods of expansion, 1890–1910 and 1945–70, there would be little here worth bothering about one way or the other. Perhaps it would be best if Seattle did not have to face another such period right away, for there is still much it can do within itself, and much it needs to find out about itself. But it must come, not only as one means of solving existing problems but as the necessary means for creating new work in areas where Seattle is still dependent, still a stepchild of other cities and of the federal government. Nor is there any reason to fear any growth, however large, if the city in which it happens has kept its past alive. The way forward and the way back are the same way.

In 1917, when the Hiram Chittenden Locks were opened to connect Lake Union and Puget Sound, all the freshwater lakes and bays were lowered by as much as twenty feet. Union Bay, which extended west from Lake Washington, became partly a marsh, near the university arboretum on its south end and to the east of the university campus on its north end. Within a few years the marsh had developed its own ecological system of cattails, blackbirds, beavers, and ducks. Someone coming new to Seattle in the mid-1920s might imagine the marsh had always been there, the creation of nature only.

Later the city and the university, which owned the land on the north end of the bay, worked out an agreement whereby the city could use that part of the marsh as a dump. When the land was full, the university would regain possession. At the extreme north end of the marsh a viaduct was built down Northeast 45th Street and, on land once owned by a Japanese truck farmer, a shopping center was built (rumor has it the land was confiscated when the truck farmer was incarcerated during the war). Then, in the late 1950s, a second bridge was built across Lake Washington and its road was extended westward across Foster's Island and the south end of the Union Bay marsh, through a tip of Montlake, on across Portage Bay and up to

Capitol Hill, where it joined the I-5 freeway. Unfinished extensions south from that bridge were to connect with another expressway, the R. H. Thomson, which was planned to come down from the north end and go either over or under Union Bay. Shortly thereafter the Army Corps of Engineers and the Seattle Garden Club built a trail extending through the marsh from Foster's Island to the Montlake Cut just across from Husky Stadium. Meanwhile the university began building on its filled-in land: new tennis courts, an enormous parking lot, a series of athletic fields, a golf driving range, a group of buildings in which the Art Department could teach ceramics.

It may seem that here, as with so many other places where people got busy in the 1950s and early 1960s, that God had proposed well and man had disposed badly. But no. However it acquired its land, University Village became the finest shopping center in the city. The new courts, driving range, and playing fields became part of an admirable renewed awareness that one doesn't have to be on an intercollegiate team to play hard or stay in shape. The University Canal House, on the edge of Union Bay, rents canoes, and from there one can take trips, often in astonishing quiet, to both ends of the marsh. The marsh walk itself is a wonder. Many of its clients are joggers and cyclists going past signs saying "No Jogging or Cycling." They and the others get a chance to see what no one on foot could know about before, the endless subtle shifts in the marsh life as the seasons and weather change. Finally, though the R. H. Thomson expressway was scrapped during the antifreeway activity of the early seventies, the unfinished extensions remain, and from them kids dive into the water at the north end of the arboretum. Part of the deliciousness of this irony is that the kids are a scruffy lot indeed, youth with a vengeance, given to drink to make them rowdy, drugs to make them unresponsive, and to wearing no clothes.

Top to bottom, this sequence is one of the finest things in Seattle, and one of the city's most characteristic expressions of itself. Nature created, to be intruded upon and then to change and endure, needing both itself and the intruders to mix into a landscape of wonderful and incongruous variety. It is good enough as it is, but, like almost everything else vital in a city, it becomes more absorbing and more poignant as its history is known and understood. The sight of cliff swallows nesting underneath the freeway is enough by itself to convince one of the inscrutable fascinations of time passing, tempting the curiosity, rebuking the doctrinaire conclusion, yielding an enduring sense that the urban creations of land and labor are among the most wonderful things we can know.

Notes on Sources,
and a Bibliography

AT THE outset I said I hoped my readers could see this book as a kind of partnership, in which my sense of Seattle's past and present could be used by others to concur, deny, add, and subtract. Given this, it seems appropriate to end with some account of my own collaborators, the many sources I have drawn on in writing this book. There is no bibliography of all the published material on Seattle, as there should be, and I cannot pretend to offer one here, since my way of working has not led me to try to be comprehensive in my coverage. But I can say where I have been, so if anyone wishes to trace my footsteps or to begin to sample the great variety of material available, I can be of some help.

It has taken six years to write this book, a fairly long time but nothing like long enough. When I declared to myself that I was willing to look at any aspect of Seattle's experience, I opened myself up to more than I could handle, in six years or a lifetime. There have been leads I never traced adequately, projects I began and abandoned when they seemed to lead me too far afield, people I was told to see with whom I never spoke, or never got back to, or couldn't find. As I look over the notes and notebooks and scraps of paper and earlier drafts, I see an awful lot I have not done. I did too little with churches, with the courts; I know too little about Portland, or Alaska. My readers will be able to add to that list, I am sure. But sooner or later one must bear one's witness and try to stop worrying about all that might have been done.

In 1916, when Clarence Bagley published his *History of Seattle*, he and his readers may have thought he had written *the* history of the city when in fact he had only collected materials about a small percentage of the people and the events that had happened. Nor could he claim to have written an official history, because a city is not like a company, or the estate of a famous person, able to authorize a body of materials and say "This is all ye need to know." What he had done, however, was to begin the long job of collecting, and people who thus collect, even if they don't really know what to make of what they have, begin to make available the facts and lore without which people coming along later cannot make much sense of what happened.

There are perhaps four other different kinds of materials that I have drawn on extensively in writing this book. The first is the work of scholars, and of this kind Seattle has a considerable amount. Much of it, however, is accessible only locally, in the form of graduate theses and dissertations at the University of Washington, done mostly under the guidance of Robert Burke of the university's Department of History and based on the vast storehouse of original sources being assembled by Richard Berner, director of the university's manuscript collection and archives. Very little of this is lively reading, because graduate theses are hardly meant to be that and because the work assiduously isolates its subject from the context of the city as a whole. But I have been grateful many times over to these writers, for the time they saved me, for the information they offered, for the sources they uncovered.

Second is the work that, by comparison with the university's scholars, would be called informal, journalistic. The emphasis tends to be on legend and lore, so here it is the early periods that get the most attention. The best books of this kind, which I take to be Murray Morgan's *Skid Road* and Archie Binns's *Northwest Gateway*, are very good, and Morgan in his way is as good a scholar as anyone. But there is a lot more here that is admittedly of only local interest, and the two major local newspapers have been good about printing as much of this as they think the public can stand, bits and pieces, about the great trees that used to be in Ravenna Park, or the earliest black settlers, or some astonishingly thin houses, or the origin of street names. Take this stuff away, take away the people who are fascinated by such matters, and the city would soon have no past left out of which to make a history.

Third are the memoirs, the biographies, the autobiographical novels, and the political journalism that often are dotted with telling glimpses of the way things were. The testimony is most ample among two groups, the pioneers of the first generation and the radicals of the early twentieth century, and for that reason a later writer ends up feeling most confident about these two periods. When people feel they are part of important events, they tend to write their memoirs, or to inspire others to write about them. This kind of writing seems to be done less now than formerly, which is a shame, because on the face of it Doc Maynard or Anna Louise Strong are not more interesting or important than William Allen or James Ellis, though they are more colorful. I note, for instance, that a project begun by E. J. Brisker to do a documentary of the Black Student Union of the University of Washington has not gotten off the ground, from lack of funds or perhaps lack of interest. It is regrettable, because if something like this isn't done soon, a little piece will disappear, and eventually there will be many such pieces lost.

The fourth kind of available material is the most voluminous, usually the least articulate, sometimes the most helpful: newspaper stories, official documents, the conversations of older people, the boxes and boxes in the University of Washington's archives, the United States Census. With these come the most fun and the most frustration. It took a month, working mostly with the Seattle City Directory, to make my residential survey of the city in 1897; it was fascinating and dull, as plodding work often is. I felt I was learning about Seattle in ways I could not have learned otherwise, and yet all I had was names and addresses when what I wanted was people and places. I was left free to imagine but unable to verify. With the correspondence of George Cotterill, or the Olmsteds' outlines for their boulevards, or the conversation of people of former prominence, or the official publications of The Boeing Company, one is always seeing and not seeing, because the evidence is scanty or what seems most important is being screened out.

I hope this makes clear why I don't think I have written "the" book on Seattle, and why I don't think such a book could be written. There is just too much, and it takes too many people to know what to make of it all. More evidence keeps coming to light, but the past recedes. Had I finished this book in the year in which I began, it would be one chapter shorter; had I written it ten years from now, it probably would be very different, especially concerning more recent events. One writes something definitive only about a part of the past that is dead.

CHAPTER I, "GRAY AND GREEN"

No need to mention sources here, but this is as good a place as any to lament the absence of a good guidebook to Seattle. A census of historical buildings is presently being compiled by the city in conjunction with various citizens' groups, and this will help fill the gap. Many issues of *Sunset Magazine* have notes of interest about Seattle, but they are not easily put into a collection; Jim Faber's *Irreverent Guide to the State of Washington* (Garden City, N.Y.: Doubleday and Company, 1974) only begins to offer a newcomer a sense of places to see. David Brewster's *The Best Places: A Gourmet Notebook's Guide to the Pacific Northwest* (Seattle: Madrona Press, 1975) is altogether more helpful, but it is restricted to restaurants and shops for the most part.

CHAPTER II, "THE FOUNDING"

There are, besides Clarence Bagley's, two other similar works which assemble data about the early years: Thomas Prosch, "A Chronological History of Seattle from 1850 to 1897" (typescript, dated 1900–1901, Northwest Collection, University of Washington library); and Welford Beaton, *The City That Made Itself* (Seattle: Terminal Publishing Company, 1914). Bagley's work is *History of Seattle from the Earliest Settlement to the Present Time*, 3 vols. (Chicago: The S. J. Clarke Publishing Company, 1916). A later book, more simply restricted still to facts and statistics, many quite interesting, is J. Willis Sayre, *This City of Ours* (Seattle: n.p., 1936).

On the migration to the northwest there is immense material. For me the most useful or stimulating were Bernard DeVoto, *The Year of Decision: 1846* (Boston: Little, Brown and Company, 1943); Hubert Howe Bancroft, *History of Washington, Idaho, and Montana, 1845–1889* (San Francisco: The History Company, 1890); Donald W. Meinig, *The Great Columbia Plain: A Historical Geography, 1805–1910* (Seattle: University of Washington Press, 1968); Ezra Meeker, *Pioneer Reminiscences of Puget Sound* (Seattle: Lowman and Hanford, 1905); James G. McCurdy, *By Juan de Fuca's Strait: Pioneering along the Northwestern Edge of the Continent* (Portland: Metropolitan Press, 1937).

On the pioneers, first, is Margaret Collins Dixon, *Denny Genealogy*, 3 vols. (New York: National Historical Society, 1944–51); and then Arthur Denny's own work, *Pioneer Days on Puget Sound*, ed. Alice Harriman (Seattle: A. Harriman Company, 1908), and an autobiographical sketch and a brief narrative of the founding of Washington Territory in *Washington Historian* 1, no. 1 (1899): 1–12, 13–15. Two generations later come the rather full accounts of three of Denny's descendants: Roberta Frye Watt, *Four Wagons West: The Story of Seattle* (Portland: Metropolitan Press, 1931); Emily Inez Denny, *Blazing the Way* (Seattle: Rainier Printing Company, 1909); and Sophie Frye Bass, *Pig-Tail Days in Old Seattle* (Portland: Metropolitan Press, 1937), and *When Seattle Was a Village* (Seattle: Lowman and Hanford, 1947). A major source for Murray Morgan's sketch of Doc Maynard is Thomas W. Prosch, *David S. Maynard and Catherine T. Maynard* (Seattle: n.p., 1906); but Morgan brings in more and makes it much more interesting.

Along with *Skid Road: An Informal Portrait of Seattle*, rev. ed. (New York: The Viking Press, 1960), the best book on the early period is Archie Binns, *Northwest Gateway* (Portland: Binsford and Mort, 1941), which carries down to the Alaska Gold Rush. Often quite useful in spite of itself is Bill Speidel's *The Sons of the Profits* (Seattle: Nettle Creek Publishing Company, 1967), and Nard Jones, *Seattle* (Garden City, N.Y.: Doubleday and Company, 1973), does a pleasant job of rendering familiar material.

On the founding of the university, see Charles Marvin Gates, *The First Century at the University of Washington: 1861–1961* (Seattle: University of Washington Press, 1961). President Graves's eulogy of Arthur Denny and some other details are in Charles Odegaard, "The University of Washington Pioneering in Its First and Second Century" (Newcomen Society of North America, 1964).

Helpful background on the anti-Chinese incidents can be found in Foster Rhea Dulles, *China and America: The Story of Their Relations since 1784* (Princeton, N.J.: Princeton University Press, 1946); Stanford Lyman, *The Asians in the West* (Reno: University of Nevada Press, 1970); Stuart Creighton Miller, *The Unwelcome Immigrant: The American Image of the Chinese, 1785–1882* (Berkeley: University of California Press, 1969); and Robert Wynne, "Reaction to the Chinese in the Pacific Northwest and British Columbia, 1850–1910," Ph.D. dissertation, University of Washington, 1964. The best source for the events in and around Seattle in 1885–86 is the *Post-Intelligencer*, and also Doug and Art Chin, "Up Hill: The Settlement and Diffusion of the Chinese in Seattle" (n.p., 1973); George Kinnear's memoir in the *Post-Intelligencer*, January 1, 1911; Eugene Semple, "Martial Law at Seattle, Washington Territory: An Inquiry into the Necessity Therefor" (Vancouver, Wash. Terr., 1886), a campaign document, but carefully done. On Semple, see Alan Hynding, *The Public Life of Eugene Semple: Promoter and Politician of the Pacific Northwest* (Seattle: University of Washington Press, 1973).

CHAPTER III, "PREMIER CITY OF THE NORTHWEST, 1890–1910"

During the first thirty or so years of its history, one can make out the economy of Seattle pretty much by tracing individual citizens. After that it all gets more complicated, and, unfortunately, no economic historian has taken the kind of interest in Seattle's economic history that Robert Burke has in its political history. The United States Census for Manufacturing is invaluable, and helpful for this period is Alexander Norbert Macdonald, "Seattle's Economic Development, 1880–1910," Ph.D. dissertation, University of Washington, 1959.

The appalling official biography of James J. Hill is Joseph Gilpin Pyle, *The Life of James J. Hill*, 2 vols. (Garden City, N.Y.: Doubleday Page and Company, 1917); much shorter and more useful is a brief biography by Stewart Holbrook, *James J. Hill* (New York: Alfred A. Knopf, 1956). On Judge Burke and Daniel Gilman, see Robert C. Nesbit, *"He Built Seattle": A Biography of Judge Thomas Burke* (Seattle: University of Washington Press, 1961). Thomson's memoir is *That Man Thomson*, ed. Grant H. Redford (Seattle: University of Washington Press, 1950); see also V. V. Tarbill, "Mountain Moving in Seattle," *Harvard Business Review* (July 1930). George Cotterill's papers are in the University of Washington library manuscript collection, and his book is *Climax of a World Quest* (Seattle: Olympic Publishing Company, 1928).

On some of the larger real estate dealings that helped create the neighborhoods of retirement, see Edwin T. Coman, Jr., and Helen M. Gibbs, *Time, Tide, and Timber: A Century of Pope and Talbot* (Stanford University Press, 1949). *The Highlands* (Seattle: Lowman and Hanford, 1925) offers a historical sketch and some pictures. Almost perfect for setting scene, mood, and visual prospect is *Homes and Gardens of the Pacific Coast,* vol. 1: *Seattle,* a 1913 book republished by Christopher Laughlin and the Beaux Arts Society Publishers. The Olmsted papers, and the often illuminating papers of Judge J. J. McGilvra concerning the Park Board, are in the University of Washington library manuscript collection.

For local color in this period there is nothing as good as the various books by Henry Broderick, such as *Timepiece* (Seattle; Dogwood Press, 1953); *Early Seattle Profiles* (Seattle: Dogwood Press, 1959); *The "HB" Story* (Seattle: Frank McCaffrey, 1969); *Yesterday and the Day After* (Seattle: Dogwood Press, 1958). Broderick is hardly an attractive writer, but in almost every piece of his there is a detail or two that one should not be without. Nard Jones has a good chapter in *Seattle* on growing up in the Denny Regrade area in this period.

There is lots of material on populism and progressivism. Some interesting documents can be found in W. Storrs Lee, ed., *Washington State: A Literary Chronicle* (New York: Funk and Wagnalls, 1969). For a comparable volume, which includes the remarks of the New York judge and the Kansas City park commissioner quoted in the text, see Charles Glaab, ed., *The American City: A Documentary History* (Homewood, Ill.: The Dorsey Press, 1963). On the local scene the papers of Robert Bridges and Joe Smith in the University of Washington library manuscript collection are lengthy and illuminating. See also Robert Donald Saltvig, "The Progressive Movement in Washington," Ph.D. dissertation, University of Washington, 1966, and Wesley Dick, "The Genesis of Seattle City Light," M.A. dissertation, University of Washington, 1965. J. Allen Smith's *The Spirit of American Government* has been edited by Cushing Strout (Cambridge, Mass.: Harvard University Press, 1965); on Smith see Thomas C. McClintock, "J. Allen Smith and the Progressive Movement," Ph.D. dissertation, University of Washington, 1959.

For other miscellaneous views of the period, H. A. Chadwick's *Argus* is excellent. Chadwick is not as good as Henry Broderick at vivid visual details, but in every other respect he is a more sustaining writer, and this period was his heyday. This is as good a place as any to mention Shelby Scates, *Firstbank: The Story of Seattle First National Bank* (Seattle: n.p., 1970), an official history but filled with helpful details of this and other periods. The Erastus Brainerd scrapbooks, 1886–98, in the Manuscript Collection of the Library of Congress, are good on the Alaska Gold Rush, which Brainerd helped promote. The quotation from Nancy Wilson Ross is in *Farthest Reach: Oregon and Washington* (New York: Alfred A. Knopf, 1941), which is generally much better on the region than on the city. An enterprising graduate student could do a nice piece of work on the dislike and distrust of Seattle by people elsewhere in the northwest, of which Ross's book is an interesting example.

CHAPTER IV, "THE FIRST CLIMAX"

Virgil Bogue's *Plan of Seattle,* 2 vols. (Seattle: Lowman and Hanford, 1911) is one of the basic documents in the history of the city, and the text, at least, should be put back in print. I have relied on newspapers in my account of the failure of Bogue's plan at the polls. On the retirement of the wealthy generally, I wish the case could be documented in a more scholarly way, but everything in the works mentioned above concerning the building of their neighborhoods, to say nothing of everything in the subsequent history of this group of people, is really evidence enough.

On moral reform and the changing alignments of the middle class, *Session Laws of the State of Washington: Eleventh Session* (Olympia: E. L. Boardman, Public Printer, 1910) is fascinating for what it reveals as much as for what it says. Norman Clark's forthcoming bicentennial history of Washington outlines the situation in the state very clearly, especially when supplemented with Clark's *The Dry Years: Prohibition and Social Change in Washington* (Seattle: University of Washington Press, 1965). See also Lee Pendergrass, "Urban Reform and Voluntary Association: A Case Study of the Seattle Municipal League, 1910–1929," Ph.D. dissertation, University of Washington, 1972, and Saltvig's dissertation on the progressive movement, mentioned above.

For the internal movement of citizens within Seattle that indicates shifts in status or aspiration, a comparison of the City Directory of 1910 with that of 1915 suggests that most people either (1) went on living in the same place, (2) moved out of Seattle entirely, or (3) moved out of downtown into a newly built middle-class neighborhood. For example, Arthur Gardiner lived at 501½ Main in 1910, at 3638 Meridian in 1915; Rawson Hunt at 916 Stewart in 1910, at 124½ West Garfield in 1915; William A. Hunt at 1300 Weller in 1910, at 1426 South Norman in 1915; Anna Gardner at 916 Stewart in 1910, at 4235 Kenny in 1915; Elden Gardiner at 419 5th North in 1910, at 522 Aloha in 1915. This is just picking Gardners and Hunts, but the pattern is too marked to be misleading.

The memoirs and biographies of middle-class people who took a different route, to the radical left, are Anna Louise Strong, *I Change Worlds* (New York: Henry Holt and Company, 1935); Harvey O'Connor, *Revolution in Seattle* (New York: Monthly Review Press, 1965); Lowell Hawley and Ralph Potts, *Counsel for the Damned: A Biography of George Vanderveer* (Philadelphia: J. B. Lippincott, 1953); Hulet Wells, "I Wanted to Work," University of Washington library manuscript collection; Harry Ault papers, University of Washington library manuscript collection. On the Wobblies, see Patrick Renshaw, *The Wobblies: The Story of Syndicalism in the United States* (Garden City, N.Y.: Doubleday and Company, 1967), and other sources mentioned therein; and Ralph Chaplin, *Wobbly* (Chicago: The University of Chicago Press, 1948). The passage from John Dos Passos' *Nineteen Nineteen* (New York: The Modern Library, 1930), the middle volume of his *U.S.A.* trilogy, need not be verifiable as fact in order to stand well as a convincing symbol. On the Everett Massacre see Norman Clark, *Mill Town* (Seattle: University of Washington Press, 1970); the standard work on the General Strike is *The Seattle General Strike* by Robert L. Friedheim (Seattle: University of Washington Press, 1964).

For the 1913 Potlatch and the United States' entry into the war, it is instructive to go through all the Seattle newspapers day by day, including, for the later event, Harry Ault's *Union-Record*. On the war more generally, Arthur S. Link, *Wilson*, 5 vols. (Princeton, N.J.: Princeton University Press, 1947–65), especially vols. 4 and 5; and Lawrence Levine, *Defender of the Faith: William Jennings Bryan: The Last Decade, 1915–1925* (New York: Oxford University Press, 1965), are useful.

CHAPTER V, "SEATTLE BETWEEN THE WARS"

Beginning with this chapter I have been able to rely heavily on conversations and interviews with people, many of whom are acknowledged in the acknowledgments section for their help and insights.

Though some of its chapters deal with earlier periods, the main interest of Ralph Potts's *Seattle Heritage* (Seattle: Superior Publishing Company, 1955) lies in its details about this period, especially the lists of facts and figures at the end of each chapter.

Potts has a chapter on Dave Beck, and also a novel, *Sir Boss* (Faversham House, 1959), whose two main characters resemble Beck and George Vanderveer. Though a good book on Beck has not yet been written, all that has been done, both pro- and anti-Beck, is in clear agreement on the nature of the man: Murray Morgan's last chapter in *Skid Road*; Richard Neuberger, *Our Promised Land* (New York: Macmillan, 1938); Donald Garnel, *The Rise of Teamster Power in the West* (Berkeley: University of California Press, 1972); Nathan Shefferman's personal account of Beck's downfall, *The Man in the Middle* (Garden City, N.Y.: Doubleday and Company, 1961); Herbert Clay Prouty, "Seattle's A.F. of L.-C.I.O. War of the Warehousemen," Ph.D. dissertation, University of Washington, 1938. The passage from Constance McL. Green is in *American Cities* (London: The Athlone Press, 1957).

For those interested in Seattle, and the state, during the Depression, the following are helpful: Donald Francis Roy, "Hooverville: A Study of a Community of Homeless Men," Ph.D. dissertation, University of Washington, 1935; Wesley Dick, "Visions of Abundance: The Public Power Crusade in the Pacific Northwest in the Era of J. D. Ross and the New Deal," Ph.D. dissertation, University of Washington, 1973; Murray Morgan, *The Dam* (New York: The Viking Press, 1956); Albert Acene, "The Washington Commonwealth Federation," Ph.D. dissertation, University of Washington, 1975.

Parrington's great book is *Main Currents in American Thought* (New York: Harcourt Brace and Company, 1930); on Parrington, see Joseph Barlow Harrison, *Vernon Louis Parrington, American Scholar* (Seattle: University of Washington Book Store, 1929); Richard Hofstadter, *The Progressive Historians* (New York: Alfred A. Knopf, 1938); Lionel Trilling, "Parrington, Mr. Smith and Reality," *Partisan Review* 7 (1940); Robert Skotheim, *American Intellectual Histories and Historians* (Princeton, N.J.: Princeton University Press, 1966). The one book on Nellie Cornish is her autobiography, *Miss Aunt Nellie* (Seattle: University of Washington Press, 1964); those who knew her and The Cornish School in its golden years will, I hope, add to this before it is too late. The best accessible sketch of Richard Fuller is Charles Michener, "Dr. Fuller, We Presume?" *Seattle Magazine* (November 1969); a biography of him would be most welcome. *Tobey's 80: A Retrospective* (Seattle and London: Seattle Art Museum and the University of Washington Press, 1970) has a good collection of reproductions and an excellent introduction by Betty Bowen. There is, also, Tobey's *The World of a Market* (Seattle: University of Washington Press, 1964). The Seattle Municipal Reference Library has a scrapbook of clippings and information on Yesler Terrace and Jesse Epstein.

CHAPTER VI, "THE BOEING YEARS"

As background to the Japanese evacuation, see Audrie Girdner and Anne Loftis, *The Great Betrayal: The Evacuation of the Japanese-Americans during World War Two* (New York: Macmillan, 1971); Kazuo Ito, *Issei* (Seattle: Japanese Community Service, 1973); Bill Hosokawa, *Nisei: The Quiet Americans* (New York: William Morrow and Company, 1969). Calvin Schmid, *Growth and Distribution of Minority Races in Seattle* (Seattle: Seattle Public Schools, 1964), lays out the evidence of the United States Census in maps and graphs. The Emery L. Andrews papers in the University of Washington library manuscript collection contain heartbreaking letters about the evacuation and relocation. The three main texts for my section are Monica Sone, *Nisei Daughter* (Boston: Little, Brown and Company, 1953); for

Gordon Hirabayashi, the Frank L. Walters papers in the University of Washington library manuscript collection; John Okada, *No-No Boy* (Rutland, Vt.: C. E. Tuttle, 1957; paperback ed., Seattle: Combined Asian American Resources Project, distributed by the University of Washington Press, 1978).

Kenneth Munson and George Frederick Swanborough, *Boeing* (New York: Arco Publishing Company, 1972), has full pictures of all past and present Boeing planes. Harold Mansfield, *Vision: A Saga of the Sky* (New York: Duell, Sloan and Pearce, 1956), is the fullest history of the company. Perhaps best, however, is Philip Herrera, "Megalopolis Comes to the Northwest," *Fortune* 76 (December 1967); but see also John M. Mecklin, "Why Boeing Is Missing the Bus," *Fortune* 78 (June 1968).

My sketch of the postwar building boom in the north end is recognizably the product of personal observation and experience; the boom east of the lake, which was similar, is the subject of the April 26, 1963, issue of *Argus,* which has a good article by Fred Bassetti on housing development there.

The Metro library has an excellent scrapbook compiled by the League of Women Voters that includes clippings and other material covering the drive for enabling legislation and the first two elections. The Metro library also has a full collection of its own publications, which give complete information on the financing and the engineering of the sewage projects.

On the University of Washington Gates's official history carries down to 1961; on the Canwell hearings and the atmosphere of the campus from the mid-thirties to the mid-fifties, see Melvin Rader, *False Witness* (Seattle: University of Washington Press, 1969). The February 1967 *Seattle Magazine* is entirely on the university; on Odegaard, see also Shelby Scates, "The Odegaard Regime," *Argus,* February 5, 1965; his stand on the hippies and the police can be found in the *Post-Intelligencer,* September 10, 1967.

Murray Morgan, *Century 21: The Story of the Seattle World's Fair* (Seattle: University of Washington Press, 1962), has all one might want on the World's Fair of 1962. There is no history of Group Health as yet. On its formation there is useful information in John Philip Holden, "Group Health Co-operative of Puget Sound: An Institutional Study of a Unique Medical Service Organization," Ph.D. dissertation, University of Washington, 1951, and Kenneth Fleming, "A Quiet Man Retires," *View* (May 1974). William A. MacColl, *Group Practice and Prepayment of Medical Care* (Washington, D.C.: Public Affairs Press, 1966), lays out his model of Group Health's experience.

Seattle Magazine is much its own best witness. Stimson Bullitt's book is *To Be a Politician* (Garden City, N.Y.: Doubleday and Company, 1959). The quotations earlier in the chapter are from Earl Pomeroy, *The Pacific Slope: A History of California, Oregon, Washington, Idaho, Utah, and Nevada* (New York: Alfred A. Knopf, 1965;

paperback ed., Seattle and London: University of Washington Press, 1973); and Malcolm Cowley, *The Literary Situation* (New York: The Viking Press, 1954).

CHAPTER VII, "THE NEW CITY"

On the Boeing layoffs and the economic situation generally, the quarterly and annual reviews, "Summary of Pacific Northwest Industries," prepared by the Department of Economic Research of Seattle-First National Bank, give all the essential facts and statistics. See also Patrick Douglas, "The Big Squeeze," *Seattle Magazine* (May 1970).

Graphs and statistics on the black population up to 1964 are in Schmid's *Growth and Distribution*, referred to above. There is no good treatment of blacks in Seattle before World War II, but see Horace R. Cayton, *Long Old Road: An Autobiography* (New York: Trident Press, 1965; paperback ed., Seattle and London: University of Washington Press, 1970), for the memoir of a rather special man in an untypical position. See also *Race and Violence in Washington State: Report of the Commission on the Causes and Prevention of Civil Disorder* (Olympia, Wash.: Secretary of State, 1969), and Howard Droker, "The Seattle Civic Unity Committee and the Civil Rights Movement, 1944–1964," Ph.D. dissertation, University of Washington, 1974. *Seattle Magazine* has an almost monthly commentary on blacks in the Central Area from 1968 on.

Victor Steinbrueck's two books are *Seattle Cityscape* and *Seattle Cityscape #2* (Seattle: University of Washington Press, 1962, 1973). These are perhaps not ideal as guidebooks for the tourist, but they are excellent for the newcomer recently moved to Seattle and for the natives whose eyes have become overfamiliar with what they see. The first volume, especially, is good for getting acquainted with Seattle's major architects.

On the Port of Seattle, the League of Women Voters paper on Port government is in the University of Washington Library Northwest Collection. Sadly, KING's print of its documentary, *Lost Cargo*, has itself been lost. The Port's Planning Department has a number of helpful bulletins, especially "Comparative Analysis of the Waterborne Trade of the Seattle and Portland Harbors: 1940–1962" (1964); "Seattle: Container Gateway Port of the North Pacific Range" (1967); "Seattle's Maritime Commerce and Its Impact on the Economy of King County" (1971).

In trying to learn about the present, one longs for so many sources of information that it is best, first, to note that most notably lacking is a genuinely independent commentary on the economy and, second, to be thankful for the best that we do have. For a decade now Shelby Scates has written good political journalism in the *Post-Intelligencer* and *Argus*. David Brewster was managing editor of *Argus* from 1971

SEATTLE, PAST TO PRESENT

to 1975 and during that time turned out thoughtful essays almost once a week; his *A Gourmet's Notebook* can be reread with pleasure even if one has no intention of ever eating in the restaurants described. The new Seattle *Sun* has caught on well, much better than did the short-lived but engaging Seattle *Flag*, perhaps by understanding that it works best if it tries to include most of old Seattle in its coverage.

Finally, since so much of my way of thinking about cities was originally her way, let me offer full references for Jane Jacobs, *The Death and Life of Great American Cities* and *The Economy of Cities* (New York: Random House, 1961, 1969). So many people are now on record as having "read Jane Jacobs" that it seems a shame to feel obliged to report that most who have done so have concentrated on her first book, and not always thoughtfully, and have generally ignored or failed to see the point of her second. At present she is at work on a book that attempts to describe the proper role of government in relation to cities, especially in gaining and maintaining the special differences among cities.

Index